# From War Hero to Peace Promoter

# From War Hero to Peace Promoter

## The True Story of Siegfried Sassoon

Duncan Marlor

Pen & Sword
MILITARY

First published in Great Britain in 2024 by
Pen & Sword Military
An imprint of Pen & Sword Books Limited
Yorkshire – Philadelphia



ISBN 978 1 39905 127 9



A CIP catalogue record for this book is
available from the British Library



Typeset by Mac Style
Printed in the UK by CPI Group (UK) Ltd, Croydon, CR0 4YY.

MIX
Paper | Supporting responsible forestry
FSC® C013604

Pen & Sword Books Limited incorporates the imprints of After
the Battle, Atlas, Archaeology, Aviation, Discovery, Family History,
Fiction, History, Maritime, Military, Military Classics, Politics,
Select, Transport, True Crime, Air World, Frontline Publishing, Leo
Cooper, Remember When, Seaforth Publishing, The Praetorian Press,
Wharncliffe Local History, Wharncliffe Transport, Wharncliffe True
Crime and White Owl.

For a complete list of Pen & Sword titles please contact

PEN & SWORD BOOKS LIMITED
47 Church Street, Barnsley, South Yorkshire, S70 2AS, England
E-mail: enquiries@pen-and-sword.co.uk
Website: www.pen-and-sword.co.uk
or
PEN AND SWORD BOOKS
1950 Lawrence Road, Havertown, PA 19083, USA
E-mail: uspen-and-sword@casematepublishers.com
Website: www.penandswordbooks.com

This book is dedicated to two great-uncles who served on the Western Front with Siegfried Sassoon. Arthur Sandars, a worker on his family's Derbyshire farm, looked after Army mules. Duncan Marlor, a Manchester railway clerk, was a machine-gunner. Wounded and perhaps shell-shocked, he was arrested for overstaying his recuperation leave. He survived the war but with life-changing emotional damage. He died in his 40s.

# Contents


| | | |
|---|---|---|
| *Introduction* | | vi |
| **Chapter 1** | The Poem in the Paper | 1 |
| **Chapter 2** | 'Brother Lead and Sister Steel' | 10 |
| **Chapter 3** | Ottoline | 23 |
| **Chapter 4** | All Over? | 35 |
| **Chapter 5** | 'A Stupendous Blow' | 49 |
| **Chapter 6** | Hospital Reading | 62 |
| **Chapter 7** | The Brasseys | 73 |
| **Chapter 8** | Speckled Eggs | 80 |
| **Chapter 9** | 'Wilful Defiance of Military Authority' | 87 |
| **Chapter 10** | Facing the Music | 119 |
| **Chapter 11** | The Fusilier and the Green Benches | 136 |
| **Chapter 12** | 'Murder' | 154 |
| **Chapter 13** | Mill Town Electioneer | 170 |
| **Chapter 14** | The Peace That Got Away? | 191 |
| *Abbreviations* | | 195 |
| *Acknowledgements* | | 196 |
| *Notes* | | 197 |
| *Index* | | 211 |

# Introduction

How is Siegfried Sassoon known today? Obviously mainly as an author. That was his occupation and in it he was successful, especially with his 1928 *Memoirs of a Fox-Hunting Man*. That title is off-putting now. Attitudes have changed. Sassoon was obsessed with fox-hunting. It is an awkward detail for many (including this writer). He was a product of his class and his times. In other ways he was not. His next book was his 1930 *Memoirs of an Infantry Officer*. Familiar class stuff? That might be the reaction to the title. But Siegfried is a man of surprises. The narrative of this study of him will include a look-in at his campaigning in the 1918 General Election in the industrial north of England, wearing his captain's uniform and speaking for Blackburn's Labour candidate, Philip Snowden, who had taken sustained abuse during the war for campaigning in the House of Commons for a negotiated peace settlement.

Sassoon turned out half a dozen volumes of memoirs between the wars and during the Second World War, but the English examination syllabus has ensured that he is known to generations of ex-school pupils as a poet. His most celebrated work is that which he produced as one of the 'War Poets'. It was controversial in its day. Winston Churchill told him that he had come within a whisker of being banned by the censor. In recent years Sassoon has been touched by controversy again, with claims by some historians that preoccupation with the War Poets has distorted the history of the First World War to the disfavour of the Allies and their cause.

Memoirs, poetry, that is Siegfried Sassoon, not forgetting the love interest and his long search for personal fulfilment. But there is something else, very specific. In 1917, in a public demonstration, he tried to stop the war. This has been downplayed in biographical and other coverage – as a (curious) passing episode. This book will examine an event which just might have changed the course of history.

## Chapter 1

# The Poem in the Paper

There was no shortage of poetry in the Great War. As the conflict between the two monster alliances, with its mountain of casualties, entered its third year, there was no let-up in the martial versification. The home-front Homers and Virgils, are generally best forgotten but on the front lines were some bards of serious quality, pre-war poets now in uniform, adapting their talents. One of their productions caught the eye of a titled lady who moved in artistic circles. Lady Ottoline Morrell lived at Garsington Manor deep in the Oxfordshire countryside. The poem appeared in *The Times* on 15 January 1916.[1]

Maybe Ottoline expected a jingoistic effusion. This poem was no such thing. It was about colours: those in which the poet rejoiced: blue, silver, green. Dull shades of grey and brown wearied this soldier. These were war's hues in a landscape of angry guns, whose flashes were the wrong sort of bright. They yielded no aesthetic delight. He yearned for the colours of peace. 'Return to me', he directly addressed them. This was not an anti-war poem. After all its title was To Victory' But if the theme was winning the war, it was only in the sense that this would return the beloved colours of peace.[2]

The paper was packed, as ever, with reports of the state of the war, embroidered with maps and optimism. The author of the poem that Lady Ottoline noticed was seemingly bashful, simply being called 'a Private Soldier at the Front'. But beneath were his initials: S.S. The verses sat directly beneath the 'leaders' giving the paper's views on the issues of the day. The big news was that the monarchy of Montenegro, allied with the Triple Entente, had fallen to the forces of Austria-Hungary. It was a serious Allied setback, added to the difficulties of Tsarist Russia, the Triple Entente's mighty power in the east. There were the regular 'Roll of Honour' lists ('Killed'; 'Died of Wounds'; 'Wounded'). The names were all of officers, war being as class-conscious as peace.[3]

Lady Ottoline was captivated by the colour theme poem that she lighted on amid all the war news. She loved colour. Ottoline's style was flamboyant bohemian. Sister of the Duke of Portland (and first cousin of Elizabeth Bowes-Lyon, a future Queen and Queen Mother), she and her Liberal MP husband Philip had migrated the previous year from London's Bedford Square to Oxfordshire's rural tranquillity. Here descended Bloomsbury Groupers like

Lytton Strachey, Vanessa and Clive Bell, Duncan Grant and Katherine Mansfield. Ottoline wanted to know about the author of 'To Victory'. She wrote to *The Times*'s editor. This brought a letter from Edmund Gosse, poet, literary critic and patron of the arts, who had sent in the poem:

> ...The author is a very charming, simple and enthusiastic young man, whose name is Lieut. Siegfried Sassoon, 1st Battalion Royal Welsh [sic] Fusiliers, British Expeditionary Force, France. I am sure he will very much appreciate a letter from you. *The Times* romanticised about calling him "a Private Soldier". He enlisted as a P.S. but has since got a commission. His verses have interested me a good deal. He is extremely modest and a little *sauvage* – with a woodland wildness.[4]

Gosse was Sassoon's literary patron. Ottoline wrote to his protégé. Back came a reply:

> Your letter gave me great pleasure... I will send you a little book of my verses when I am in England on leave. I often stayed at Oxford, though I didn't "go" there. I love the Oxfordshire landscape, and the Gloucestershire borders, as I associate them with early summer weather and orchards in blossom.[5]

Ottoline kept a diary. Her sighting of the Sassoon poem is not in it. But Siegfried is mentioned on 26 February:

> I wrote to Siegfried Sassoon whose poem appeared in the Times and today I received a little book of poems from him.[6]

Siegfried Sassoon, 29 years old, had been on the Western Front for just a couple of months, not yet having been involved in the fighting. He had been a poet for much longer, with several small private publications to his name before the war. What of 'To Victory'? There is plenty of poetic interest in it. Commentators have discerned conceits: a priapic theme in the green shoots. Patrick Campbell, author of *Siegfried Sassoon: A Study of the War Poetry*, finds 'an exercise in tone poetry...a painterly effort'. The motif around colours is imaginative and skilful, and rather unusual. Whatever the composition is about it is not the familiar theme of beating the Germans. Nor (despite 'the woeful crimson of men slain') is it a war lament. 'To Victory' is not a 'War Poets' composition.[7]

Were there any signs of anything special in this poet other than a presentable versifier, gathered in by the war? One has to say not yet, but Gosse had hopes.

Siegfried was of the Kent upper-middle classes, reared at Marlborough, and Clare College, Cambridge, where he read history (going down without taking a degree). He was a sportsman: cricket, golf and fox-hunting. A (modest) allowance meant that he did not have to work. He was a gentleman.

The Sassoons were Anglicised Baghdadi Jewish financiers. Sassoon was a byword for wealth, but SS's immediate family was no more than keeping-up-appearances. Siegfried's cousin Sir Philip Sassoon was the MP (Conservative) for Hythe. They did not at this time know each other. Philip's pre-war life bespoke luxury and extravagance. Now he was on the Western Front as a staff officer. The 'red tabs', as his biographer points out, were the focus of some resentment among the fighting soldiers. The *Blackadder* characterisation of 'Captain Darling' is memorable: big ego, effete; and Joan Littlewood's 1963 musical *Oh! What a Lovely War* has secure-from-peril staff officers playing leapfrog (competing for rank). Philip does not seem to have been a skiver. His perfect command of French made him ideal for his role.

Siegfried's father, Alfred Ezra Sassoon, had left the family early and was long dead. His mother was an Anglo-Catholic. In the family she was called Ash, the in-joke being Theresa: Treesa: Ash. Within the family, as the correspondence shows, there was warmth and cohesion. Siegfried loved his sports. He took his cricket seriously enough to dwell on averages and to dream of being a county level player. And there was the fox-hunting. In his early-life memoir *The Weald of Youth*, SS tells of riding his cherished horse Cockbird in point-to-point races. Edwardian life for him was carefree, with occasional debt troubles not being serious. The pattern was: hunting in winter; cricket in summer; poetry in all seasons. Sig hoped that his expensively produced private publications could lead on to something. His *The Daffodil Murderer* parodied John Masefield but slipped into appreciative imitation. It was this that drew the attention of Edmund Gosse. Sassoon was introduced to Edward Marsh, arts patron and civil servant and private secretary to First Lord of the Admiralty Winston Churchill.[8]

During the fateful final days of July 1914, Sassoon was following, via the *Times*, the rippling of the dominos, kicked off by the Austrian ultimatum to Serbia on 24 July. An article on 31 July informed him – in large type – that Britain would 'have to go to war in aid of France', Britain's Entente Cordiale partner within the Triple Entente. In those days, as Siegfried recalled, he was naïve about 'European politics and commercial ambitions and such-like causes of the conflict'. When Britain was pulled into the war, he did not have a frantic urge to get to the battle before it was over, as many of his class did, but he did think that he ought to join up. He had displayed no special interest in war and soldiering previously. Now, he was motivated by the impulse to do his bit for his country. On Saturday, 1 August, as Europe mobilised and H.H. Asquith's Liberal cabinet agonised over Britain's gentleman's agreement with France, Sassoon was being medically examined by the Army as a cavalryman recruit. On Bank Holiday Monday, 3 August, as the Foreign Secretary, Sir Edward Grey, made his famous speech to the House of Commons, informing MPs (in effect) that Britain would be going in, Siegfried was waiting for delivery of his khaki. This celebrated parliamentary occasion has been considerably distorted by subsequent patriotic mythology. That needs to be unravelled in view of Siegfried Sassoon's later involvement with the parliamentary peace group.

It is undoubtedly true that large sections of the House of Commons greeted the Foreign Secretary's virtual announcement that Britain was going to be in the European war with rapturous joy and shouts of delight. Most remarkably, that included the Irish Nationalist benches – only days after it had looked likely that there would be civil war over the Home Rule crisis. However, there was stony silence from the massed ranks of the Liberal backbenches. The lack of enthusiasm here was hardly surprising. After all was not the traditional Liberal watchword Peace, Retrenchment and Reform? One piece of evidence of the Liberal dismay is particularly striking. The MP for Inverness, Annan Bryce, who had been standing at the Bar of the House (the edge of the chamber), which gave him a good view of reactions to Sir Edward Grey, said in Parliament later that day: 'During the whole course of the speech of the Foreign Minister this afternoon, there was not one single cheer from this side of the House.' The careful account in the *Northampton Daily Echo* is worth visiting. This states that the only cheers from the Government side of the chamber were when 'some gleam of hope of England's neutrality seemed to brighten the dark horizon'. And yet there is the oft repeated myth that Grey won near-unanimous enthusiasm for his war announcement. It is reflected in the 2024 novel by Robert Harris, *Precipice*, the background to which is the run-up to the war. The history in this is excellently researched but the account has the regular misconception. Harris writes: 'The Liberal MPs – three-quarters of whom had been peace-at-any-price men a few days previously – were suddenly cheering on the government to declare war against Germany at once.' It was not so. Harris is correct on early Liberal opposition to British involvement in the war but wrong to think that Grey's speech caused it to melt away. A string of Liberals would make passionate pleas in a debate in the evening of that day for British neutrality or at least for Britain to stay out for the moment and to work for the restoration of peace. Later in the war Siegfried Sassoon would get to know some of these MPs.[9] When Britain made its formal declaration of war on Germany at 11 p.m. on Tuesday, 4 April Siegfried was already officially in the Army. He had been given a cursory medical examination, an Army doctor recording:

> Height: 6 ft 1 inch
> Girth when fully expanded: 38½ inches (range of expansion: 3 inches)
> Vision: sufficient
> Age: 27 years 10 months
> 'I consider him fit for the Territorial Force.'

The uniform was ill-fitting. The Territorial Force into which Sassoon was inducted was for home service but that was very swiftly changing. Days later the recruit signalled assent to being sent abroad if required. It was as a private (Sussex Yeomanry) that he signed up because he did not want responsibility. We have a glimpse of Siegfried probably just before the war in the recall of Francis Meynell, typographer, publisher and poet:

> With his ginger hair Siegfried was a very startling sight. I remember him as wearing sandy-coloured tweeds, a yellow waist-coat and a pink shirt.[10]

This is valuable because the then photographs of Siegfried are of course not in colour. As for Francis Meynell, Sassoon cannot then have imagined that he and Meynell, who would be a conscientious objector when conscription came in, would one day be linked not just in the pursuit of poetry but in rebellion against the war.

Before he could leave England, Sassoon suffered a severe arm fracture in a riding accident. He spent the spring of 1915 in recuperation. During this time his attitude to the war changed. It was not going to be over anytime soon. He now felt that a more serious commitment was needed from him. In May 1915 he took a second-lieutenant commission as a platoon commander in the Royal Welch Fusiliers. It should be noted that while Sassoon was punctilious with his spelling 'Welch', often (including in the official stamp-mark on his application form) it is 'Welsh'. His 11 May application's mention of Marlborough College attracted a bold pencil underlining. Sassoon was of the correct social caste for an officer.[11]

He was stationed at Béthune in the Artois region of northern France. This area had seen the big Battle of Festubert in May 1915, as the Allies tried in vain to puncture the German lines. That failure saw the tactics shift to 'attrition', a euphemism for weakening the enemy by cumulative slaughter. Sassoon had recently led a working-party up to the trenches to do defence-strengthening, across a marsh and up the communication trench, in the darkness of night, in which the weather veered between rain and frost. His men had to carry burdens of hurdles and planks, under which they slipped and skidded. SS always looked after the welfare of his platoon. In an 8 January 1916 letter Sassoon reported to his mother that his platoon had enjoyed 'a splendid lot of grub for Xmas, and lots of beer'. Theresa regularly sent her son parcels. Siegfried told her that her latest gift of some gloves had reached him safely. He thanked her 'ever so much'. The gloves had gone, he told her, to one of the men. Perhaps that was not quite what his mother intended. Sassoon looked after his platoon's comforts with fond care. He told Theresa that he had got them a muffler and a pair of leather-palmed gloves each. It was a newsy letter, in a war-grim sort of way. The men had been practising with gas helmets. Sig drew a little sketch, whimsical and skilful. Mustard gas was a novelty of this war. The Germans had led the way in the spring of 1915. British troops would follow suit in this lung-damaging direction in 1917.[12]

He had struck up with another poet. Robert Graves was a 20-year-old captain. The pair had made an expedition in November to a cake-shop in Béthune, where they tucked into buns and compared poetry notes. In his diary log of this event, Sassoon called Graves 'an interesting creature, overstrung and self-conscious, a defier of convention'. He observed that Graves was 'very much disliked'. His new friend had a part-Germanic name from his German mother. He was Robert von Ranke Graves The affinity before the war of Britain and Germany needs always to be remembered. It went far beyond a shared royal family. At the start of the war four British cabinet ministers had gone to German universities. Now Germany was the enemy. Sassoon found some of Graves's verse commentaries on the war, as he observed in his diary: 'very bad, violent and repulsive'. Graves was not yet published. SS thought he should keep it that way for a while.[13]

Physically, the chums contrasted. Both had pronounced noses, but while Sassoon's added to his tall impressiveness, Graves's (he was also tall) went with a face that Sassoon called 'twisted'. Graves was unruly and a show-off. Sassoon was on the introverted side and self-conscious. Siegfried took pains to get his Army dress just right; Robert was sloppy. Graves's *Goodbye to All That* autobiography is a polished classic but it is cavalier with the actuality. It is valuable but caution is required with it. *Goodbye* says that Sassoon showed Graves his 'To Victory' poem during the Béthune tea-shop session, but it was not yet written.[14]

What of Siegfried Sassoon's wartime poetry up to this point? In his 1945 memoir *Siegfried's Journey* he describes his production during his pre-active service period as 'a dozen war-oblivious lyrical pieces'. There was also a mini-epic called 'The Old Huntsman'. Sassoon's first 'war poem' was composed in the summer of 1915 during training. It was called 'Absolution':

The anguish of the earth absolves our eyes
Till beauty shines in all that we can see.

A vision is presented beyond the 'horror of wounds'. There is the solidarity of soldier comrades: 'What need we more, my comrades and my brothers?' There is a nod to the widely proclaimed British war aim of 'fighting for our freedom'. Sassoon is dabbling with a war poet persona, so far finding only received platitudes. He wrote later that, '…my too nobly worded lines expressed the typical self-glorifying feelings of a young man about to go to the Front for the first time.' 'Absolution' would later be well reviewed 'by middle-aged reviewers', as he put it, adding that, 'the more I saw of the war the less noble-minded I felt about it.'[15]

When Siegfried Sassoon got to closer quarters with the front line, a process of change set in. But it was, as he himself said, 'gradual'. He started to represent in his verse his active service environment and experience. After the fortification repair-work he wrote the first draft of 'The Redeemer' (which he later re-wrote).

Here is the squalor and suffering of soaked boots, heavy with clay, as shells burst in the distance and whistling bullets are heard. Suddenly amid the glare of an explosion, he has a vision of Christ. Sassoon (not at this time particularly religious) has feelings of pious devotion. But not for long. One of his troop unknowingly deflates it. The man's feet have gone deep into the mud. He exclaims: 'O Christ Almighty, now I'm stuck!' Sassoon's poetry was taking on new shape, with home front-type idealisation rudely punctured by the vernacular of the sweating and shivering men in the trenches.[16]

Sassoon's poetry was taking on new shape, with home front-type idealisation rudely punctured by the vernacular of the sweating and shivering men in the trenches.[17]

SS had some news when he wrote to Edmund Gosse: 'The Redeemer' had been taken by *The Cambridge Magazine*, 'whatever that may be like'. This publication, which carried a regular digest of the foreign press including German, would become one of Sassoon's regular poetry outlets. It was was a target of anti-pacifist vigilantes in Parliament. It was run by war-dissenting Cambridge University academics but it was not a university magazine. It was published in London.[18]

Sassoon's brother. Hamo, a second lieutenant in the Royal Engineers, had died at Gallipoli in November. A sniper wound turned septic. Hamo had been at school with Siegfried, who had been in the thrall of his confident and competent sibling with his dry sense of humour. Theresa Sassoon wrote to Siegfried: 'I am a most miserable Ash.' Sassoon's message of condolence was short. Words failed on this occasion:

My dear dear Ash –
I can't write anything – We must just keep our chins up, that's all.
Sig[19]

On 18 December 1915 Siegfried wrote 'To My Brother':

... I am in the field where men must fight.
But in the gloom I see your laurell'd head
And through your victory I shall fight.[20]

Here was verse to delight the readers of *Punch* or whatever: little or nothing personal, just the glorious cause. In fact, Siegfried was hit hard by his brother's death. The loss and its meaning took some time to settle. The shift in stance from 'Absolution' came unevenly. On the day that 'To Victory' appeared in the *Times*, Sassoon composed a poem entitled 'Glory: 1916'. This had 'a happy heart', Galahad and 'swords in harmony'. Galahad was the knight of gallantry and purity. Rupert Brooke's 'To turn as swimmers into cleanness leaping' is echoed.[21]

A fortnight earlier Siegfried had committed to his diary a declaration of war-joy:

I am happy, happy...We're safe for another year of war, so next summer ought to do something for me. Anything but a 'cushy' wound.[22]

A 'cushy' wound was one not too serious but enough to remove the soldier from the front lines. The word was heard all the time in the Army.

Sassoon at this time was quite often able to ride his horse through the French countryside. Singing birds and green pastures took him straight back to growing up in Kent and Sussex: riding to meet the hounds; playing cricket with the glory of staying at the wicket for an hour or two as he resisted the bowlers and accumulated a score. He was serious about cricket. It was competitive: so was Siegfried. His journal for 13 January 1916 has a long description of a ride through some villages: white-walled houses, roofs patched with moss, somewhere a peacock, 'four solemn geese'. A couple of children in blue emerge from a house to see who is galloping by. Sassoon loved it. He mused in his diary:

How strange it is that I came to the war prepared to suffer torments and to see horrible sights; and I have found hours in heaven, and noble counties at my feet and love inhabiting the hearts of men.[23]

A division in the landscape between storm and sun reminded him of the conflict. Do we see the merest pre-echo of peace-promotion? On the contrary: days like these had the effect of stimulating Galahadish dreams of vanquishing the foe. A long war was in prospect and that was fine. This world was good.

## Chapter 2

# 'Brother Lead and Sister Steel'

If Siegfried Sassoon's First World War story is a drama, a repeating scene is Garsington Manor in Oxfordshire. Here we must briefly return.

Lady Ottoline Morrell was married to noted anti-war MP Philip Morrell, of a distinguished family of brewers and lawyers. Philip, of Black Hall in Oxford, was a solicitor by profession. He had been encouraged into Liberal politics by Ottoline. He had captured Henley from the Conservatives at the General Election of 1906, losing it in January 1910 but winning Burnley at that year's December General Election. He was never comfortable in politics, but he worked hard as a constituency member – and he was interested in foreign affairs. On 3 August 1914, while Siegfried Sassoon was preparing to receive his khaki, Philip was at the House of Commons in the forefront of those who were trying to keep Britain out of the war. At 6 foot 3 he was conspicuous and he secured a debate, which he led, causing some anger. It made no difference but the neutralists were able to have their say. From the Ladies' Gallery high above the Commons chamber Ottoline watched her husband. She wrote in her memoir that he acted 'splendidly and courageously.'[1]

Philip kept out of controversy during 1915. The consensus for fighting the war to a conclusion was holding comfortably, but a minority of the Labour Party, including Ramsay MacDonald who resigned from its leadership, and a few Liberals, were quietly opposed. November 1915 saw the first beginning of the parliamentary campaign for peace by negotiation. It tried to recruit Philip Morrell but without success. Philip did not want to antagonise his Liberal constituency association in Burnley. The arrival of the first conscription legislation in Parliament in January 1916 provided a proxy outlet for war opponents. Military compulsion seemed to some to be a denial of ancient citizen rights, including Magna Carta (1215) and the Petition of Right (1628). Philip Morrell was one of forty or so parliamentary opponents of conscription. They battled in committee deep into the night to win arrangements for conscientious objectors to war (a new right, which the Government conceded). In May 1916 conscription was extended from single to married men. The rejection was seconded by a Liberal MP who had been on the Western Front. Corporal H. Bertrand (Bertie) Lees-Smith was almost alone among the couple of hundred soldier MPs in not having an officer's commission. One of his arguments was the stigmatisation faced in the Army by conscripted men.

From January1916 Siegfried Sassoon was aware of the Morrells and Garsington, but so far only in respect of Lady Ottoline's appreciation of his poetry. Meanwhile the entry into his life of Robert Graves was having an effect on his composition. Graves's use of deliberately coarse expression was rubbing off on his own poetry. This is demonstrated by 'In the Pink', composed on 10 February. A private soldier's woebegone state in the trenches is made worse by alcoholic poisoning. We hear the man's vernacular:

> Tonight he's in the pink; but soon he'll die.
> And still the war goes on – he don't know why.[2]

Philip Morrell's circle in Westminster would agree that the war had lost its original purposes. They wanted the Allies to state their aims so that a serious effort could be made at a peaceful resolution of the conflict. Sassoon was not as political as that. In *Siegfried's Journey*, he comments that up to this point, though his emotional outlook on the war had been changed by his experience of it, 'it had been impossible to do any independent thinking about it.' Dissent, now starting to show in his poetry, was about his empathy with the suffering rank-and-file troops whom he led. An unpoetic ring of realism characterises 'In the Pink', as in 'five miles of stodgy clay and freezing sludge'. It is very far from the mellifluous tones of 'To Victory'. An epigrammatic style, some way from poetry in its regular sense, was starting to take shape. Sassoon would later remember 'In the Pink' as 'the 'first of my outspoken war poems'. It was refused by the *Westminster Gazette* – as being unhelpful to recruiting. Sassoon later explained that 'In the Pink' referred to 'some typical Welshman, who probably got killed on the Somme in July, after months and months of a dog's life and no leave'.[3]

Siegfried did get some leave. In London his preferred company was gallery proprietor and art critic Robert Ross. Sassoon wrote that Robbie was, 'one of the most attractive and amusing men I had ever met'. Ross actively promoted Siegfried's poetic career. He was knowledgeable and astute. He had been a friend, possibly lover, of Oscar Wilde. A small debonaire man, he was anti-war, a position these days requiring some courage. Sassoon was attracted to him both intellectually and physically. He recorded in *Siegfried's Journey* that Ross 'hated the war, and was unable to be tolerant about it and those who accepted it with civilian bellicosity and self-defensive evasion of its realities.' If Sassoon was going to be an anti-war poet, Ross was his ideal manager, especially as he exercised a pragmatic discretion.[4]

Ross had supported Oscar Wilde amid his persecution. Siegfried Sassoon's own homosexuality had the possibility of putting him on the wrong side of the law if he became active. Wilde was sentenced in 1895 to two years' hard labour for 'acts of gross indecency with other male persons'. Sassoon, like his homosexual friend Robert Graves, was strictly puritanical in his sexual behaviour, but there was always that potential tension regarding the law. SS's verse composition is a male landscape with practically no women. Later in 1916 a soldier acquaintance asked him why his poetry was woman-free. His reply, as recorded in his diary, was that: '[women] are outside my philosophy.' It was a neat side-step but revealing of a narrowness. As regards the troops under his command, Sassoon's sexuality and his humanity overlapped. Both his officerly concerns for his men and his poetry demonstrate a tenderness towards them and a compassion for their suffering in foul weather and on glutinous terrain. He was much aware that he, as an officer with a horse, could escape, as in the canter through the villages which so pleased him, and that his men had the onerous requirement to haul tackle with them whenever their unit moved.[5]

The military stalemate showed no sign of being broken. In the war of wearing down, a big part was played by the snipers. In Britain, readers of the *Daily Chronicle* read about the life of a sniper on the Western Front, who told distinguished war correspondent, Philip Gibbs:

> I picked off twelve in one afternoon. But it's all in a day's work. If I can kill one or two a day, I'm satisfied …I can't help laughing sometimes when I catch one bending, as you might say.[6]

Siegfried Sassoon relates in *Memoirs of an Infantry Officer* that, 'a renowned big-game hunter gave us demonstrations of the art of sniping.' As Sassoon explained, it was a matter of 'reducing the numerical strength of enemy'. He thought that the hunter would be better employed in actually shooting Germans than in lecturing, since his battalion lacked the necessary telescopic sights. Siegfried's emotions about the killing swirled.[7]

He sometimes felt a motive of personal revenge for the loss of comrades. One was David Thomas, a Sandhurst-trained sub-lieutenant ten years his junior who at one time was his regimental depot room-mate. Thomas was heterosexual, with a girlfriend at home. Siegfried did not reveal to 'Tommy' (or 'Tommie') that he was deeply in love with him. Thomas was killed as he worked on a night-wiring operation. Sassoon wrote in his diary on 19 March:

> …They came afterwards and told that my little Tommy had been hit by a stray bullet and died last night. When last I saw him two nights ago, he had

this notebook in his hand reading my last poem. And I said goodnight to him, in the moonlit trenches. Now he comes back to me in memories, like an angel, with the light in his yellow hair, and I think of him at Cambridge last August when we lived together 4 weeks in Pembroke Coll in rooms where the previous occupant's name, Paradise was written above the door...In the half-clouded moonlight the parson stood above the graves, and everything was dim but the striped flag laid across them, Robert Graves beside me, with his white whimsical face twisted and grieving. ...So Tommy left us, a gentle soldier, perfect and without stain. And so he will always remain in my heart, fresh and happy and brave.

For you were glad, and kind, and brave;
With hands that clasped me, young and warm;
But I have seen a soldier's grave,
And I have seen your shrouded form.[8]

Sassoon was getting into the experience of the front line. He wrote in his diary on 31 March about going out at night into No Man's Land: 'Tonight I'm going to try and spot one of their working-parties and chuck some bombs at them.' It was:

...most exhilarating – just like starting for a race. Great thing is to get as many sensations as possible. No good being out here unless one takes the full amount of risks, and I want to get a good name in the Battalion, for the sake of poetry and poets, whom I represent. No Man's Land fascinates me, with its jumble of wire-tangles and snaky seams in the earth winding along the landscape...[9]

He was getting blood-thirsty. The next day he wrote:

I used to say I couldn't kill anyone in this war; but since they shot Tommie I would gladly stick a bayonet into a German by daylight...Now I've known grief for Hamo and Tommie, hate has come [as well as love and sorrow], and the lust to kill. Rupert Brooke was miraculously right when he said, 'Safe shall be my going, Secretly armed against all death's endeavour; Safe though all safety's lost.' He described the true soldier spirit.[10]

Siegfried brooded in his diary on 4 April 1916:

> Stockwell [the new commander of the Battalion] wants a prisoner, and I am going to try and get one for him, but it isn't for that that I am going out. I want to smash someone's skull; I want to have a scrap and get out of the war for a bit or for ever...While I am really angry with the enemy, as I am lately, I must work it off, as these things don't last long with me as a rule.[11]

On 22 April 1916, a Saturday during Easter, Sassoon 'sploshed through the dismal water', as his diary put it, as he made his way to call his platoon together for 'stand-to', the regular gathering for inspection, collection of rations and so on. This occasion stimulated 'Stand-to: Good Friday Morning'. The poem anticipated the satirical verse for which Sassoon would become known. He wrote:

> ...Deep in water I splashed my way
> Up the trench to our bogged front line.
> Rain had fallen the whole damned night.
> Oh Jesus, send me a wound today,
> And I'll believe in Your bread and wine,
> And get my bloody old sins washed white![12]

In the lottery of survival or not a 'blighty wound' could mean the difference between survival into old age in reasonable health or not. Sassoon later said that he considered the poem 'one of the most effective of my war productions'. 'Stand-to' goes on:

> I went and stared at the dug-out door.
> Down in the frowst I heard them snore.

'Frowst' was the stink of soldiers' sweat. Someone 'grunted and swore' when Sassoon called. The cutting-edge detail upped the realism in a way that was new.[13]

Around this time Siegfried Sassoon took a motor-bus to an Army School course at Flixécourt, 'a pleasant little town', as his diary notes, halfway between Amiens and Abbeville, over thirty miles from the front lines. He had a 'clean little room'. Shuttered windows looked down on a steep street. Sparrows chirped and starlings whistled, and nearby a church tower clock struck. Sassoon found a new outlet for feelings of romance in a young officer called Marcus Goodall, who had been with him at Marlborough and loved birds and history. SS wrote: 'Another glorious day. Starlight on the mill-water ...'. His company were told that the 'big push' would have really big results. In one of the classes Siegfried listened to 'a great brawny Highland Major talking of the Bayonet'. He seems to have been inspired:

> For close an hour he talked, and all who listened caught fire from his enthusiasm: for he was prophesying; he had his message to deliver.

The message was:

> If you don't kill [the German], he'll kill you! Stick him between the eyes, in the throat, in the chest, or round the thighs...Get your bayonet into his kidneys; it'll go in as easy as butter. Kill them, kill them: there's only one good Bosche and that's a dead un...Don't waste good steel. Six inches are enough – what's the use of a foot of steel sticking out at the back of a man's neck?[14]

Bayonet training, including 'putting on a killing face' was regular Army experience. If a soldier was out of bullets and at close quarters with an enemy, he could turn his rifle into bayonet mode as he deployed the blade attached to the muzzle. After the bayonet lecture, on 25 April 1916, Sassoon composed a poem, which he entitled 'The Kiss':

> To these I turn, in these I trust –
> Brother Lead and Sister Steel.
> She glitters naked, cold and fair.
> Sweet Sister, grant your soldier this:
> That in good fury he may feel
> The body where he sets his heel
> Quail from your downward darting kiss.[15]

It appeared in the *Cambridge Magazine* on 27 May 1916. It has drawn controversy. Robert Graves, who identifies the instructor as Colonel Campbell, V.C., says that, 'Siegfried later offered it as satire.' Graves implies that the poem was originally composed in the spirit of the tutor. Sassoon was indignant about this. He told one commentator that he had loathed bayonet fighting and that the lecture was 'an absolute horror'. Which of the interpretations is right? Jean Moorcroft Wilson goes with satire, as does Patrick Campbell, who calls Graves's statement 'one of his many inaccuracies'. But Graves has received backing. Jon Silkin is of the view that Sassoon wrote 'a ferocious poem' and retained it because it was part of the record of his emotions during the war. This is persuasive. The timing is telling: immediately after the lecture and at a time when Siegfried was in happy-warrior vein. For the poem to be a satirical put-down of the bayonet tutor would be anachronistic.[16]

On his return from the Army School, Sassoon was emotionally volatile. He did not want to be killed but he did want relief from trench boredom, a feeling that he loathed. Brigade headquarters ordered an attack on German trenches, apparently with no other point than morale-boosting. Siegfried, as he told friends, hoped to be on the raid. He longed for adventure. He wanted to win a medal. One fellow officer advised him against asking Colonel Stockwell to include him in the attack: in a month or two they would 'all be over the top', meaning the start of the big push. Sassoon did admit to himself that it would be 'silly to be laid out by a stray bullet'. However, he was in happy-warrior temper. He wrote an in-the-event-of-my-death farewell letter to his mother (who is turned into 'Aunt Evelyn' in *Memoirs of an Infantry Officer*). In later years he would cringe about the note, with the thought that 'my own fine feelings took precedence of hers.' Farewell letters were part of the young officer cult of insouciant self-sacrifice in vogue in the earlier stages of the war. That attitude of mind had since been shaken by the realities but Sassoon's late arrival at the active service front meant that he was behind the curve. 1,131 alumni of Siegfried's cousin Philip's Eton College fell in the war. One of them, Lionel Sotheby, left an after-death message: 'To die for one's school is an honour…To die for one's country is an honour…Floreat Etona…Farewell.' By early 1916 many of the romantic patriots were dead. Sotheby fell on 25 September1915.[17]

SS did ask to go with the 25 May 1916 raiding party. He greeted the twenty-five men, their faces blackened with burnt cork, and asked Stockwell if he could go with them. 'Certainly not,' said the Colonel: 'Your job is to stop in our trench and count the men as they come back.' The men were given whisky – enough to administer a boost but not to incapacitate them. In his *Memoirs of an Infantry Officer* description of the event, Sassoon makes a number of general observations, including that it was the younger men who were most likely not to be able to cope with the stress of active service. When this happened, they were sent back to Britain if they were officers, with a discreet letter for the senior authorities and thereafter they would drift around their battalion headquarters, doing what work they could. For the rank-and-file, as Sassoon explains, there was no such escape: 'If a man became a dud in the ranks, he just remained where he was until he was killed or wounded. [18]

In the preparations for the assault on the German position, there was the regular joviality of 'Who's for a Blighty one tonight?' After the attack, as wounded members of the party were crawling back, Sassoon's account reports that: 'Among them was a grey-haired lance-corporal, who had one of his feet almost blown off…He said, "Thank God Almighty for this; I've been waiting eighteen months for it and now I can go home."'[19]

The attack was a failure. The German wire had not been cut by the preliminary bombardment, as was so often the case. The human cost on this occasion was eleven men injured and two fatalities. Sassoon's memoir tells that after the raiding party had set off and he sat on the parapet of the trench where his orders were to remain, he heard one of two sentries muttering to his mate, 'They'll never keep that ---- inside the trench.' Siegfried appreciated the compliment. The sentry was right. Sassoon went out into No Man's Land. He investigated bomb-craters and brought in wounded and dead under heavy fire. He was out again on the next night, recovering abandoned equipment. Colonel Stockwell's report states that all the wounded were brought back 'largely owing to Sassoon's bravery'. Stockwell recommended him for a Military Cross. Sassoon's casualty form mentions the granting of the honour. It was recorded by the London Gazette, the official governmental journal of record, on 27 July 1916: 'Awarded the Military Cross for gallantry & devotion to duty in the Field'. Colonel Stockwell's more detailed citation reads:

> For conspicuous gallantry during a raid on the enemy's trenches. He remained for 1½ hours under rifle and bomb fire collecting and bringing in our wounded. Owing to his courage and determination all the killed and wounded were brought in.[20]

Sassoon subsequently wore on his tunic with pride the white and purple ribbon. He admitted later that he had been lucky not to be chosen to go on the raiding-party, since it was near-impossible to get through the wire and he would have been determined to breach it somehow. The Military Cross ranked third below the Victoria Cross and the Distinguished Service Order. The DSO was usually for senior officers, with the MC being generally for officers of the rank of Captain and below. For private soldiers and non-commissioned officers there were the Distinguished Conduct Medal and the Military Medal. (The Victoria Cross was for any rank, officer or not.) Sassoon's ribbon was important to him because of its indication of social responsibility: it was not just a personal triumph.

On the infamous first day of the Battle of the Somme, 1 July 1916, Siegfried Sassoon was 500 yards behind the lines. As Paul Fussell has pointed out, had he been in the initial attack, his survival chances would have been 'slim indeed': about three-quarters of the officers of the battalions in the attack and half the men were wiped out. Sassoon's battalion was in reserve. He had a good view of his section of the front. The toll for the British Army on the opening day was 20,000 dead. It was the start of months of carnage. It is hard to see the Somme and the other 'big pushes' of 1915-1917 as other than life-squandering folly. The Somme operation was lambasted by Winston Churchill, currently out of office, in a memorandum. Churchill was against the industrial slaughter for which 'attrition' was the polite word. An Allied military conference decided that the Germans needed to lose 200,000 men a month. Churchill objected to the aim of winning victory by the means of killing more Germans than the Allied casualty total. David Lloyd George, the War Minister, who would become Prime Minister in December 1916, felt the same way. Not until 1918 would the politicians gain the upper hand over the generals. Churchill's poor opinion of the 'top brass' was shared by Siegfried Sassoon and very widely in the Army. Jean Moorcroft Wilson, in noting that on 10 July Sassoon's battalion was passed by Sir Douglas Haig, Commander-in-Chief of the British Armies in France, speaks of 'a privilege they are unlikely to have appreciated'.[21]

The Somme offensive was on an eighteen-mile front, with thirteen of Sir Douglas Haig's divisions aiming to open up the way for the British cavalry to drive thirty miles into German territory. The opener was the huge bombardment of shells, aimed at destroying the wire in front of the German positions. Famously misconceived was the expectation that the British troops would walk through where the German wire had been. It was largely intact and the superior and deeper German dug-outs, which impressed Siegfried Sassoon when he saw them, generally protected the defenders against the bombardment. The talk of a war-turning mighty blow against the Germans turned out to be fantasy. The battle would last until its abandonment in November, with some opening day objectives still not achieved.

On the first day of the Somme Siegfried Sassoon's section of the line gained some of its objectives. But generally, it was an unmitigated British disaster. Sassoon's *Memoirs of an Infantry Officer* describes his company under the stress of watching and waiting. He was not yet involved but he did some wire-cutting, at considerable risk from snipers. There was jesting, as some of the men prepared for the ordeal of going over the top. One officer was known as 'Asbestos Bill' because of his bulky waistcoat, claimed by its manufacturers to be bullet-proof (Sassoon was sceptical). This had been sent to him by his girlfriend. It caused him to bulge and perspire. Gallows humour naturally included 'Blighty wound' prospects. Before the attack there was the protracted, ear-splitting noise of the heavy guns firing at the German positions. One fellow-officer was left haggard. Sassoon's account remarks: 'I felt no sympathy for him at the time, but I do now.' The company was detailed to occupy a major strategic feature, Mametz Wood. Here is a recurring Western Front place name. It is mentioned in Michael Palin's 2023 book about his great-uncle Harry, who was killed on the Somme on 27 September 1916. The author visited the scenes that Harry had known. He mentions Siegfried Sassoon looking towards the wood and seeing it 'looming on the opposite slope'.[22]

Sassoon's memoirs delineate character types. In his platoon was a nineteen-year-old lance-corporal, whom he called Kendle: 'remarkable for his cheerfulness and his courage, and his cheeky jokes...until the war broke his spirit.' He comments that, 'Many a company had its Kendle.' One officer 'lost all control of himself' and was making 'incoherent utterances'. The man was on his way to tell the commanding officer that his company did not know which way to go to find the Germans. Sassoon threatened him with his gun, sending him back where he had come from, since Stockwell 'would certainly shoot him if he rolled up in such a condition of "wind-up"'. 'Windy' was soldier parlance for being frightened or prone to being frightened. Being windy (or not) when the test came was a big factor in determining reputation. Sometimes results were surprising. Siegfried was not windy but he sometimes wondered whether he might fail to be equal to some future circumstance. His recollection throws in the detail that the man whom he saved from the Colonel was killed ten days later – 'in what I can only call a bona fide manner'.[23]

On 5 July Sassoon was in action. British troops were scheduled to move into Mametz Wood with tools to fortify it. It was supposed to be unoccupied. The intelligence and planning proved to be bungled. The wood was full of Germans. On his way to do what he could in this situation, Siegfried saw the dead of the recent fighting. He wrote in his diary:

> These dead are terrible and undignified carcases, stiff and contorted. There were thirty of our own laid in two ranks by the road, with bloody clotted fingers mingled as if they were hand-shaking in the companionship of death. And the stench undefinable. And rags and shreds of blood-stained cloth, bloody boots riddled and torn.[24]

On the British side of Mametz Wood was a row of trees known as The Quadrangle, in which was a shallow trench abandoned by the Germans. The advancing troops of Sassoon's battalion had occupied Quadrangle Trench. The Germans had left equipment and several bodies in it as they fled. It offered not much protection. About five hundred yards away was an enemy-occupied trench. After daylight, fire from a sniping post at the end of this became severe and five British were killed. Then followed an incident which became Siegfried Sassoon legend. SS's biographers have followed the romance in *Memoirs of an Infantry Officer*. In this Siegfried in a mad impulse captures the German trench single-handed, does not know what to do, and takes a deep breath and charges back the way he has come. The entertainingly unreliable memoirs of Robert Graves have Sassoon reading poetry in the German trench. Sassoon's account in his diary of the Quadrangle Trench operation is sober, a slab of Western Front chronicle rather than an episode of Robin Hood or Bertie Wooster. There is also a straightforwardly factual account in Dudley Ward's *Regimental Records of the Royal Welch Fusiliers*.[25]

What actually happened? The sniper-post on the edge of the German trench was a danger to the British troops. While Sassoon's men were occupying the Germans by firing at their parapet, he himself threw four Mills bombs into their trench. The Germans were taken by surprise and fifty or sixty fled into Mametz Wood, abandoning for the moment the trench. Sassoon counted eighty-five packs left behind on the fire-step. (A fire-step was a muti-purpose construction about two feet high formed out of the front wall of a trench.) Sassoon's diary does not mention a headlong return flight. It merely states that, 'We had got the Quadrangle Trench well held by midday.' That was the object of the operation. It would have made no sense for Sassoon to spend any time at this point in the evacuated German trench. *Memoirs of an Infantry Officer* has Sassoon subsequently deflated when he reports to the commander's field headquarters and is dressed down for his failure to send a message that the trench had been taken and for holding up of the battalion's attack by freelancing. Invented novel-colouring is understandable: a battalion log would have been flat in a novel. Some of the tweaks relate to the market of 1930, fair enough given that the Sherston trilogy is fictional, albeit based on events. *Regimental Records*, calling the Quadrangle Trench operation 'a bombers' fight', reports that Colonel Stockwell declared that 'Stevens and Dadd did splendidly, as did Sassoon also.' There is no suggestion that the bombing of the German trench was a lone Sassoon enterprise. Rupert Hart-Davis's edition of Sassoon's diaries states that: 'For this exploit SS was recommended for a further decoration, but the award was disallowed because the whole attack had been a failure.' This is probably a confusion with a Sassoon event of the following year. It is sometimes said that Sassoon was recommended for the Victoria Cross for the trench bombing. This may be discounted. As well as being highly unlikely, it is nowhere to be found in Sassoon's memoirs or his correspondence.[26]

Sassoon described the trench event with glee to Edward Marsh: 'Eddie, I chased 40 Bosches out of a trench by Mametz Wood all by myself. Wasn't that a joyous moment for me? They ran like hell and I chucked bombs and made hunting noises. I wonder if I shall ever be able to take soldiering seriously?' Marsh no doubt enjoyed hearing of Sassoon as a chortling English amateur running rings around the German professionals. That was very much part of the national script. In fact, Siegfried took soldiering very seriously. He applied himself conscientiously and efficiently to the military arts, and caringly looked after the needs of his platoon. He was popular and well regarded in the Army and an asset to his battalion. Eddie, not being military, was a suitable correspondent for poet-in-the-trenches yarning. That said, there is no doubt that Sassoon displayed the 'Mad Jack' bravery for which he was becoming known and that his bombing did indeed (temporarily) chase a lot of Germans out of a trench.[27]

Sometimes in Sassoon's *Memoirs of an Infantry Officer* candour makes for uncomfortable reading. He states that:

> ...I definitely wanted to kill someone at close quarters...My courage was of the cock-fighting kind. Cock-fighting is illegal in England, but in July 1916 the man who could boast that he'd killed a German in the Battle of the Somme would have been patted on the back by a bishop in a hospital ward.[28]

He wrote to Edmund Gosse on 11 July of the experience of battle:

> You will be glad to hear that I've emerged from the battle without getting damaged...I found that I could really enjoy the fighting after the deafening bombardment had subsided; one gets curiously callous to the terrible things that happen. The grey-faced dead are like so many dolls; their attitudes are seldom noble. I don't know which are the most pleased – our slightly wounded men or the German prisoners. For safety takes them all away from their hell.[29]

Mametz Wood was eventually taken after repeated attacks. Four thousand British troops had been killed or wounded in it. Robert Graves, when he arrived in the area, found the wood full of German and British corpses, and 'not a single tree unbroken'. The wood today, dense with old trees and undergrowth, has a memorial to the dead, and visible traces of craters and trenches. Sassoon and Graves were not the only poets on that battlefield. The Welsh poet David Jones would write memories of the Western Front from December 1915 to July 1916 in his 1937 *In Parenthesis*. As Martin Gilbert notes, the battle on the Somme became 'a daily struggle for small woods and even smaller villages.' Woods like Mametz were the stuff of the delirium of hospitalised soldiers. In the Mametz area operations the words to his men of Lieutenant Colonel Carden are recorded in *Regimental Records*: 'Make your peace with God. You are going to take that position, and some of us won't come back.' Carden was killed in action on 10 July 1916.[30]

Siegfried Sassoon's poetry was not completely about his own side. The body of a young, good-looking German in a ditch made a deep impression of pity on him: 'dead in a squalid, miserable ditch'. This man, Sassoon imagined, had hated the war and longed for peace. He constructed how the German would have viewed his enemy: 'the damned English loomed in scrambling haste.' Patrick Campbell discerns in this, 'embryonic pacifist sentiments'. Sassoon so far was no more than an ordinary follower of politics in the press. He was unaware except in the most general way about the politics around feelings such as he expressed in this poem. Before the end of the year that would change.[31]

## Chapter 3

# Ottoline

On 23 July 1916 Siegfried Sassoon had a temperature of 105 degrees. His servant, a former Lancashire railway worker ('Flook' in *Memoirs of an Infantry Officer*, perhaps for his Lancashire vowels), fetched a doctor. Acute dysentery was diagnosed. SS was sent to the New Zealand Hospital in Amiens. In his ward, a delirious and dying soldier was ranting about a wood. This produced a poem:

> ...The ward grew dark; but he was still complaining
> And calling out for 'Dickie'. Curse the Wood!
> 'It's time to go. O Christ, and what's the good?
> 'We'll never take it, and it's always raining.'[1]

'In Hospital' was subsequently revised and re-named 'Died of Wounds'. Sassoon wrote later: 'I got the idea in the hospital at Amiens, where a youngster raved and died in the bed opposite mine. I think he came from High Wood at its worst.' He had 'hit on a laconic anecdotal method of writing which astonished me by the way it indirectly expressed my passionate feeling about the agonizing episode described.'[2]

Siegfried Sassoon admitted that the nobility of shared adversity in the trenches quickly fled before a yearning not to be sent back to them. But as he recuperated, personal losses weighed heavily on him. It was reported that Robert Graves had been hit in the leg and the chest and had succumbed to his wounds. Siegfried was distraught:

> And now I've heard that Robert died of wounds yesterday, in an attack on High Wood. So he and Tommie are together, and perhaps I'll soon join them.[3]

The report of Graves's death was erroneous. Robert recovered. A death that was for real was Marcus Goodall, which hit Sassoon hard. He wrote in his diary:

> ...Your mirth destroyed and from your lolling head
> The racing thoughts gone out like smoke on air,
> Thinning and whirling and subsiding – where?[4]

Sassoon's notebooks provide a wide-ranging record of his life on the Western Front. As well as his diary entries, there is an assortment of jottings, and there are drawings. A list of dead and wounded comrades appears at one point.

There are military procedure notes, including 'Consolidation of Woods: Establish centres of resistance for all round defence at the corners and salient of the wood. These are the points most liable to counter-attack...' There is a Scheme of Battle: '...In conjunction with the French, the 4th Army will take the offensive on '2' day; will establish as a primary objective a line...' There is roughed out verse. It was in the notebooks that some of Sassoon's subsequently most famous poems were composed. There are reflections by Siegfried on himself, on his fellow soldiers and on the war.[5]

One section is entitled 'Dealings with the men':

> Dislike of N.C.O.'s...My desire for my own comfort. Hardships of men only natural and just; most of them are used to it. The Quartermaster; his socialist talk. Difficult to understand him; endless forced cheeriness of the officers and men. Psychology of self: how the experience affects my character. Feelings of growth?[6]

We find: 'Different types met with':

> 1) Remember one fool who was always airing his philosophic rot. He would say it was the best thing ever known when he came out. Wouldn't go back if was asked to. How splendid the men are. Certainly was a reckless person. How I hated him for the admiration his deeds won him: how I hated shaking hands with him after he got his decorations.
> 2) Another always talking about things I don't understand. Racing, hunting etc. A snob...[7]

There is much that is anti-war in these pages. Particularly striking is a large ink sketch called 'THE SOUL OF AN OFFICER'. This is a diagram rather than a piece of artistry. There is an outstretched figure on the head of which sits a military hat. Issuing from the officer's eyes and mouth are effusions of scribble. We read these in a compartmented triangle (left-to-right):

> Eating and drinking
> commonplace chatter about war – & skiting of own escapes from shells etc
> girls and silly second-rate vulgarity

Poking out on the left is a helmeted German head, with sinister sidelong eye-focus. Out of its mouth issues a tube-like apparition labelled DEATH. Corresponding on the right we see the arms and head of a feminine-looking figure labelled FEAR. The drawing is undated. Its page position suggests late June, days before the start of the Battle of the Somme.[8]

Sassoon was transferred to medical care in England. As he crossed back to Britain in a hospital-ship, he scribbled in his notebook memory fragments:

> Last weeks in war zone. Attack. Getting away with it... Vivid incidents. Collecting souvenirs from dead Germans. Men dying from bullets in head.[9]

He was sent to Oxford, where he had a room in Somerville College, which housed wounded and sick soldiers. In France Siegfried Sassoon had once remarked to a correspondent that he was 'not lucky enough to be wounded'. His illness (of a type known as 'trench fever') proved not to be too serious. It was a blighty-wound equivalent. He made the most of this time, writing on 2 August of the Oxford bells chiming and the sound of a piano floating across the lawn: 'emotional trash' he called it. Always a lover of nature, Siegfried enjoyed the tall chestnuts swaying against the blue sky. Lying in his little cream-white room, he thought 'Who cares?'[10]

He wrote to his Uncle Hamo that he was sharing his ground floor accommodation with a man who had been at school with him at Marlborough. The fellow was 'dull' but Sassoon was amused that his 'papa' was a country parson with grey side whiskers, 'quite the Antony Trollope pattern'. Perhaps papa came to visit? Siegfried was enjoying such visions coming back to his consciousness after the horribleness of the war fields.[11]

As he immersed himself in Fanny Burney's *Evelina*, Sassoon's mind was lifted from the Somme, though pangs for his comrades intervened whenever news of the battlefield reached him. He had plenty of time for his poetry. He worked on using subversive irony to show the difference between home presentation of the soldier and the reality. In 'The One-Legged Man', an Army man rejoices that he is safe home (to an idyllic pastoral scene) and can expect to reach 'the span of comfortable years allowed to man'. The ending packs a punch to go with the title:

Splendid to eat and sleep and choose a wife,
Safe with his wound, a citizen of life.
He hobbled blithely through the garden gate,
And thought; 'Thank God they had to amputate!'[12]

Epigrams became Sassoon's trademark. He noted in *Siegfried's Journey* that poems like 'The One-Legged Man' gave him 'a strong sense of satisfaction that I was providing a thoroughly caddish antidote to the glorification of "the supreme sacrifice" and such-like prevalent phrases.'[13]

Sassoon saw his poems as 'satirical drawings'. They were 'deliberately devised to disturb complacency'.[14]

He was still a poet, not a campaigner. He explored the range of emotions. 'Stretcher Case' has a delirious soldier coming round and finding to his joy that he is not dead but back in Blighty, realising this from seeing posters advertising familiar domestic items:

Large, friendly names, that change not with the year,
Lung Tonic, Mustard, Liver Pills and Beer.[15]

This came from travelling on a Red Cross train.

In Oxford, Sassoon was just six miles from Ottoline Morrell. He was informed of this by Robert Ross who visited Somerville, delighted to find his friend in reasonable shape. Siegfried had been happy to correspond with the lady who was so keen on his poetry but he had not been sufficiently interested to research her. He was startled to learn from Ross that she was 'extremely well known in the literary and artistic world' and was a half-sister of the Duke of Portland and the wife of a Liberal MP who was 'rather conspicuous by taking an extreme pacifist line about the War'.[16]

Lady Ottoline was indeed well known. Miranda Seymour's biography is aptly titled *Life on a Grand Scale*. Ross suggested a trip in a taxi to Garsington Manor. This was done on 10 August 1916. The house, with an estate, dated from the sixteenth century. Around here were to be found a collection of academics and intellectuals doing farm work, rather grumpily. Garsington's conscientious objector colony was an outcome of the conscription legislation of this year. Many had thought that conscription would produce insurrection. It did not but nor (as is sometimes claimed) did opposition fade away. The group in the House of Commons did not fold its tents. The conscription controversy brought Philip Morrell back into the thick of politics – not traditional ones, which were on hold, but the new politics of war. Philip still declined to join the peace-by-negotiation campaign but he was a vigorous anti-conscriptionist.

The right to conscientious objection won by himself and his colleagues was something quite new in any country. It did not necessarily have to be religious. But conscience was narrowly interpreted by the tribunals, which could be harsh in their decisions. Exemptions, where they were granted, often took the form of a direction to serve at the front in the Non-Combatant Corps. Absolute exemption was rare. 1916 was the year of showdown between the authorities and the absolutist resisters, with executions being a possible ultimate outcome. Some men who gained conscientious exemption were assigned to work in the national interest, hence the Garsington. arrangement. Farming was of special importance since the two sides in the war were trying to starve each other.[17]

Lady Ottoline's diary for 12 August 1916 captures the opening of her first encounter with Siegfried Sassoon:

> I was sitting for [Dorothy] Brett in the Studio and was walking down the ladder. Daisy [maid] comes to say "A Mr Ross has come to see you." At the bottom in the Door I see a young soldier – It is Siegfried Sassoon. It seemed all like a quick gay dream.[18]

The journal, dropping into reflective mode, ponders on suddenness and sensation and her reactions on such occasions. The account continues:

> He was very easy to talk to – hesitating in talk but always sympathetic and full of humour. Had tea outside and RR talked mistily.

Ottoline provides more detail in her later memoir account:

> He sat up very erect and turned his head in a peculiar stiff movement to one side. Although he talked a good deal he had a trick of hesitating over his sentences, but still he was full of humour. The lean face with green hazel eyes, his ears large and rather protruding and the nose with wide nostrils made me think of a stag's head or a faun. He seemed very shy and reserved...As I looked at his full face I said to myself, 'He could be cruel.'[19]

The latter thought is perhaps hindsight. What did Sassoon make of the meeting? SS's 1916 diary is silent at this time until late December. As he later explained: 'Those war diaries of mine were written mostly at the Front. My doings while in England didn't seem worth recording.' In France he might be killed any day. Some of the diary gap is filled in by Sassoon's *Memoirs of an Infantry Officer* account of 'George Sherston', but this studiously avoids any mention of the Morrells and Garsington. However, Sassoon's later *Siegfried's Journey* memoir does have an account. His first glimpse of Ottoline was a rear one as she descended the ladder in voluminous orange Turkish trousers. The apparition of Ottoline, arresting with her exotic dress as she tended to be, seems to have been a shock to the system of the socially conventional Englishman. Ottoline was no shrinking violet. Her six feet of height was often topped by a huge hat. Nothing about her lifestyle was understated. Siegfried was embarrassed by her appearance. As well as her outsize headgear there were her paint, powder and purple hair. In Siegfried's view she had no need to be 'a modern Messalina'. He thought that she had 'immense dignity and distinction' as she was: the artificial impositions got in the way of her fine qualities.[20]

The start of Sassoon's association with Ottoline was an afternoon of surprises for him, including that the maid was treated like 'an old friend'. Ottoline cut across social classes, happy to make anyone feel at home. Kate Roiphe has written of her: 'She dressed as if she were about to be painted, and she often was.' Siegfried, arriving in mid-easel session, was straight into Ottoline's environment. He recalled that the artist 'also took a bit of getting used to'. Dorothy (the Honourable, as he would learn) was in corduroy trousers – he had not seen a lady dressed like this before. Garsington was a department of Bloomsbury. It was new territory for Siegfried. We must be careful here however, not forgetting the previously visited reminiscence of Francis Meynell that Sassoon himself before the war liked to dress colourfully.[21]

It was no doubt a relief for Siegfried when a taxi arrived to take him with Ross back to Oxford. However, he was soon back on another visit, telling Lady Ottoline at length of his life, as they walked around the gardens and the pond. The word 'sympathetic' is used more than once by Ottoline both in her diary and her memoir about Siegfried. It is clear that already SS had taken on a special importance in her life. She assessed in her memoir that none of her intellectual friends (except perhaps Lytton Strachey) 'had ever entered into that chamber of my being whence springs the fountain of romance, where a strange and magical coloured light plays upon the intruder'. Sassoon had unconsciously pulled this off: 'tall, thin and wonderful' she called him in her diary, adding that, 'he thrills me.'[22]

A trip to Oxford's Ashmolean Museum was planned. Ottoline's short diary reference to this event shows that her feelings were getting deeply involved with this soldier:

> Brett and I cycled in and met him. We went to Somerville and could not find him. When we were sitting dejected it was such a start of joy when he appeared. We had tea at Black Hall.[23]

For Ottoline, the fleeting nature of the encounters was an agony. Her journal represents this in disconnected bursts. August (undated) has:

> Siegfried Sassoon. I long to get in touch with him. Can't you see…?...I love him…long and long for him…but he cannot feel it or he would come.

On 10 October there is despair:

> I have no letter from SS though I sent him a book and letters…So farewell to that dream. Must I go on my own Path again alone…?

On 11 October she is reflecting on the world that she and others could make: Siegfried would not be in it, since he lived in his own world – 'the language of his own life'.

On 15 October she thinks she knows why there is no contact:

> I am in the dark Tunnel of Silence for SS is mute. He is in love with someone. When he comes out into the light from the tunnel that will be the scenery that I shall see.

He had sent her a picture but no letter. Her diary exclaims: 'Why did you send me that photograph, Siegfried, why?' In her mind an image has taken shape: 'a chalice…full of quite wonderful wine'. She has held it up to him but he has 'dashed it to the ground.' It is 'broken to atoms'.[24]

What was the dream? Ottoline's diary tells that it was a 'mighty' one – 'the fusing together of two souls, two minds'. Miranda Seymour seems right that there was 'only a small physical element' in Ottoline's passion for Siegfried. Ottoline was dubbed Lady Utterly Immoral (the pun helped by the stress in Morrell being on the first syllable), That is unfair. Ottoline liked intimacy, but of a soul-mating kind. She did have real flings and Bloomsbury's ever gossipy antennae picked these up, but she seems to have been unkindly served by history (and by novelists who helped themselves to her life). As her journal shows, Siegfried was her desired partner in the voyage of existence. In her own way, the 43-year-old exponent of creative arts and wife of a politician yearned for the soldier. The pull was potent.[25]

The Morrells' marriage was an open one. It had survived the long liaison between Ottoline and Bertrand Russell. Ottoline was devoted to her husband, but Philip did not satisfy her soulmate needs. She was still searching for love in its widest sense. Siegfried Sassoon was on a soulmate quest too. The Army had provided him with a support community, but he had not yet found on any permanent basis a special individual. His sexual orientation made it unlikely, quite apart from other considerations, that Ottoline could be his solution. Not for a moment did his thoughts go in that direction. There was another divergence. Ottoline hated the war *all the time*. Not so Sassoon. He hated it *some* of the time. Much depended on his mood and where he happened to be. Ottoline was politically against the war. Siegfried's dissent was so far more about the treatment of the solders than the motives and purpose of the conflict.

As Sassoon continued his recuperation leave, he made another Oxfordshire trip. This was to Burford where his uncle Hamo, his mother's brother, was taking a holiday. Hamo Thornycroft was a sculptor of serious fame, whose works included the statue of Oliver Cromwell outside the Palace of Westminster. Next year he would be knighted. Sassoon corresponded regularly with him, writing thoughtful, long, letters. A letter of 18 May is rapturous about the French landscape: 'spacious and lovely… absolutely free and full of light.' Now Siegfried enjoyed with Hamo Oxfordshire in the August heat of harvest time. Only a minority of the British population now lived in the countryside. Romanticisation of it linked in to the notion of the war being a fight to preserve a quintessential rural England. Actually, Britain was to a large degree industrialised and suburban, but idealised country scenery went with the glorious war crusade. In the House of Commons on 7 February 1917 Admiral Sir Hedworth Meux, Conservative, talked of German militarism and atrocities and found an English contrast:

> What have we in England? We find on an early autumn morning a Zeppelin coming down on the coast of Essex and a rural British policeman walking off in charge of twenty-two German prisoners. We have all got to see this War through.[26]

This rather evokes Rupert Brooke's 1912 'The Old Vicarage, Grantchester', written in a café in Berlin, as he ached for England: 'Unkempt about those hedges blows An English unofficial rose.' The Germans were seen as bureaucratic and bossy, while the English were freedom-loving amateur improvisers (but clever enough ultimately to beat the Germans). Siegfried Sassoon's 1930 *Memoirs of an Infantry Officer*, in which at one point he routs the Germans in a bumbling and hilarious one-man mission, fits nicely the English self-image, still potent as it was between the wars and set to continue into the next one. The countryside idyll perhaps appealed less to those who had to toil in it on a daily life basis, but that did not apply to Siegfried, who much enjoyed his meandering with his uncle around Burford.

Sassoon was no Hedworth Meux. Inwardly he was much at odds with Uncle Hamo and his uncle's friend Mr Horniman, a former MP, a pair who were among the countless who thought that the Battle of the Somme was a glorious endeavour. Sassoon wrote:

> It wasn't possible to imagine oneself even hinting to them that the Somme Battle was – to put it mildly – an inhuman and beastly business.

Hamo and Horniman saw the casualty lists of course but horrors as in the recent raid by Sassoon's battalion would be beyond their comprehension:

> Their attitude was to insist that it was splendid to be in the front line. So it was – if one came out of it safely. But I resented their patriotic suppression of those aspects of war which never got into the newspapers.[27]

Siegfried Sassoon saw the difference between the war as the soldiers knew it and the war as it was viewed at home. By the last week of August 1916, he was back in Kent with his mother. Ottoline Morrell sent him a manuscript book for him to make a selection of his poetry. It was, as he described it, 'beautifully bound in orange-vermilion vellum, with end papers of a brocade-like Italian pattern of blue and marigold entwined on a dim-gilt background [with a] hundred leaves of hand-made paper'. Fair-copy transcribing pleasantly occupied him until the middle of September when he was set to go to Garsington to stay, Ottoline having sent him an invitation. Meanwhile Robbie Ross was preparing to submit some of his poems to 'an influential publisher'.[28]

Sassoon knew from his correspondence that his battalion, having been kept out of the line for nearly five weeks, was due to be moved back up at any moment. That meant the likelihood of more news of casualties. Siegfried could never completely relax. The trenches and their perils were a permanent part of him – though he admitted that when fox-hunting, to which he happily returned, he 'did not worry overmuch'.

He received a letter from his battalion's Quartermaster, Captain Cottrill, a professional non-commissioned officer, Lancashire working-class, middle-aged, short, balding, battle-scarred. Sassoon's revelation that he was uncomfortable with the working-class NCOs has been noticed. But he got to like Joe and formed a close friendship, keeping in touch with him after the war.

Now the quartermaster had news of the sort that Sassoon must have feared:

> The old Batt. is having a rough time. We lost 200 men in three days… The aid-post was blown in. All were killed except the doctor who was buried in the debris. He was so badly shaken when dug out that he had to be sent [to England].[29]

The next Cottrill letter had further bad tidings. In progress was the early September Battle of Ginchy. Sassoon's battalion was attacking a German-held village. Cottrill had a list of deaths and serious injuries. The fallen included Asbestos Bill ('died of wounds').[30]

Ottoline Morrell's anguish over Sassoon's unresponsiveness must have been relieved to a degree when he accepted her Garsington invitation. The exact days of the visit are not certain. The relevant chronological run in the visitors' book is: '…Robert Graves 12 September [Tuesday]; Siegfried Sassoon [no date stated – because he arrived with Graves?]; Lytton Strachey September 15-18 …' The Graves and Sassoon visits look like the same event.[31]

For Siegfried, Garsington (with his dog Topper) was bliss. He recalled an antique four-poster bed in a room with 'its old mullioned windows looking across the green forecourt to the tall wrought-iron gates.' Below, the Morrell little girl was playing with the pug Socrates, and a peacock was parading. A maid would knock on Siegfried's door with a can of hot water for his pre-dinner ablutions. There was another side to Garsington beside its charms. That was anti-war talk by people who were politically informed. This evidently had a powerful effect on Sassoon, including (not quite yet but soon) the composition by him of, as he put it, 'scarifying verses against bloodthirsty civilians, profiteers and those who falsely glorified the war'.[32]

There was a drawback for Ottoline. That was the presence of Robert Graves. There was the bond between the two soldiers. That did not suit Ottoline's desire, though actually it seems to have been Robert rather than Ottoline who was jealous. Ottoline, whatever her passion for Siegfried, was above jealousy. She was open-hearted. Her memoir recalls that her impression of Graves was of 'an odd fellow with the face of a prize-fighter'. She found him 'very possessive of Siegfried'. He seemed to resent SS's friendship with her. She found Sassoon:

> very sympathetic and attractive, and my instinct goes out to him for he seems so intimate to me, as if he were a twin brother. He is natural and full of fun…so human and aware of ordinary life, after the intellectuals who walk along half-blind. [33]

Ottoline was close to the colours and senses of nature. So was Siegfried. There was a match there – no surprise that Ottoline liked SS's poem about colours. It was tantalising that he was at an emotional distance. She wrote:

> Sometimes I feel that in him I have found that wonderful companion that I have so much desired, but he is very aloof and obviously doesn't need my friendship.

Ottoline gave Siegfried some pages embodying her dream for Garsington ('touchingly amateurish' SS called it): 'Come then: Gather here all who have passion and who desire to create new conditions of life, new visions of art and literature and new magic worlds of poetry and music.' She wanted 'reason released from convention'. Sassoon's aspirations were more limited. And he knew that fairly soon he would have to return to the Front.[34]

Sassoon was starting to think politically. Garsington was an eye-opener for him, as he later explained in *Siegfried's Journey*. He knew the thinking of soldiers. They muttered and complained about their personal discomforts and about the incompetence and stupidity of those who were running the military campaigns and operations. This was not political. The given was that however rough and badly organised the British and Allied war was, it was their job to keep going until the Germans were defeated. The war was not 'a wicked outrage on humanity' needing to be stopped. In 1916 it looked as if it might go on for ever but for soldiers at the front it was 'theirs not to reason why'. The outlook at Garsington was completely different: there was *every* reason for the war to be halted. They thought about that night and day. The viewpoint of Garsington people was that the war was being waged for unworthy motives and that it was morally incumbent on a courageous minority to speak out against public opinion that backed the prolongation of the conflict. Sassoon had conversations at Garsington with Philip Morrell. Discussion with an anti-war Liberal MP was something new and what he heard was making an impact on him. He was impressed by Philip's 'judicially-expressed opinions'. Here was the start of a growing feeling in this soldier. Siegfried was getting the sense that at last he was learning something of the truth of what went on 'behind the political scenes'.

Siegfried always wore his officer's uniform when he was out and about, and he was proud of it. At Garsington, pacifists gathered in the house round the fire in the evening after they had finished their farm work. Sassoon wrote: 'the conscientious objectors weren't unfriendly but my being in uniform created a barrier.' The fact that Sassoon was a fighting man will have been uncomfortable for men for whom Garsington was their protection against being dragged into the Army against their will. In Siegfried, pacifistic sentiment was starting for the first time to enter his emotional apparatus. In the village was an 'enemy alien' German violinist, no doubt rescued from persecution by Philip Morrell. She entranced Garsington's 'Red Room', causing Sassoon to reflect how 'insane' it was that even musicians should be at war with each other.[35]

Siegfried Sassoon was able to put his emotions about the war into a political context, as he listened to the pacifists' condemnation of 'militarism' and Philip Morrell's assessment of the chances of a negotiated settlement. There was apparently some real hope on this front. Sassoon recalled:

> I gathered that the Germans had made tentative peace overtures through neutral channels and that the Prime Minister was in active disagreement with Lloyd George about it.[36]

Sassoon, sceptical though he increasingly was about the war, was very far from being in the peace camp. On 8 October he wrote to Uncle Hamo from Ringmer in Sussex (where he was staying with an Old Etonian stalwart of the hunt, Norman Loder):

> I suppose they will tell me to go back soon but they don't seem in a hurry about it. I shall have to go to the depot for several weeks before being sent back to France...Isn't the news good? [The Germans] are on the downward grade at last but it will be a slow descent.[37]

Sassoon's correspondence is sometimes a puzzle. He spoke to friends and relations in terms that they liked. Uncle Hamo was a war believer. His patriotism was not clouded by doubt. His nephew knew about the slaughter and the life-changing injuries in the Battle of the Somme. He knew that little ground was being gained. Why was he writing to his uncle so buoyantly? Siegfried was happy to humour his uncle's optimism. His spirits were in good shape. His freedom probably stretched no further than a few more weeks but he was enjoying life. He hoped to get in some fox-hunting and some seaside golf; and there was the pursuit of a big publisher for his poetry.[38]

## Chapter 4

# All Over?

The autumn of 1916 was an unreal interim for Siegfried Sassoon. He remarked in *Siegfried's Journey* that it was a mystery how he convinced medical examiners that there was anything still wrong with him. The gulf between himself and his mother in perception of the war was as yawning as that with his uncle. For Theresa, a Conservative Imperialist, 'the British were St. George and the Germans were the Dragon.' Siegfried meanwhile was cheered by a personal letter from the publisher Mr Heinemann, that he had read the submitted poems 'with great pleasure and admiration' and would be delighted to publish a selection. Robbie Ross asked Sassoon to make the selection himself but said that he would take the responsibility. They needed to 'pacify the oracles', these being Edmund Gosse and Eddie Marsh, both of whom had 'a preference for idealized soldier-poems'. Gosse was a fervent patriot. With the coming of war, he had thrilled to 'the Condy's Fluid that cleans out the stagnant pools and clotted channels of the intellect'. He had told off the librarian of the London Library, partly educated in Russia, for the poor war performance of Russia. There were bumps ahead perhaps but Sassoon's book, to be called '*The Old Huntsman*', was on the tracks and a publication agreement was signed.[1]

A Siegfried Sassoon poem of some significance appeared at this time. 'The Poet as Hero' was published in the *Cambridge Magazine* of 2 December 1916. With its ironic title, it served for the paper as a reply to a reader who protested about its publication of Sassoon (curiously thinking that the poet was rebuking the poor quality of British soldiers). The new poem ends:

You've heard me, scornful, harsh and discontented,
Mocking and loathing War: you asked me why
Of my old, silly sweetness I've repented –
My ecstasies changed to an ugly cry.

You are aware that once I sought the Grail,
Riding in armour bright, serene and strong;
And it was told that through my infant wail
There rose immortal semblancies of song.

> But now I've said good-bye to Galahad,
> And am no more the knight of dreams and show:
> For lust and senseless hatred make me glad,
> And my killed friends are with me where I go.
> Wound for red wound I burn to smite their wrongs;
> And there is absolution in my songs.[2]

Sassoon was expecting to be back on the Western Front. Here is his channel for his emotions. Anger against the war was no good out there but he could direct his rage over his fallen friends into fighting on the battlefield. Siegfried's passion for vengeance for his dead comrades may be compared with that in the famous poem, first published in *Punch* a year earlier, 'In Flanders Fields', by John McCrae, a Canadian physician in the British Army. This has:

> In Flanders fields the poppies grow
> Between the crosses, row on row…

Then the tone changes:

> Take up our quarrel with the foe:
> To you from failing hands we throw
> The torch; be yours to hold it high.
> If ye break faith with us who die
> We shall not sleep, though poppies grow
> In Flanders fields.[3]

The call for vengeance for the slain is addressed to the politicians. This was when the peace-by-negotiation campaign had just begun in November 1915 in the British Parliament, the way being led in the Lords by Leonard Courtney and in the Commons by Arthur Ponsonby. McCrae's attitude was very different from that of Siegfried Sassoon, who was coming to favour the peace-by-negotiation campaign. For Sassoon, vengeance was an emotion to carry him through on a personal level on the Western Front. It was not political or directed against Germany.

Sassoon's leave expired on 17 November. He was summoned for examination to Caxton Hall, Westminster. In the waiting-room, as *Memoirs of an Infantry Officer* relates, his eyes fell on a notice stating 'the scale of prices for artificial limbs, with instructions as to how officers could obtain them free of cost'. This prompted 'Arms and the Man'.

Sassoon was declared fit to return to the Army, not yet for resuming active service abroad, but that would follow. In *Memoirs of an Infantry Officer*, he remarks that he 'pretended to be pleased' as he walked away from Westminster'. He 'wondered whether the politicians had any expectation that hostilities would be concluded by Christmas.' As a reader of the newspapers and a listener to the Garsington talk, he was aware of the speculation. An armistice with a peace conference to follow seemed a possibility.[4]

In December 1916 Siegfried was sent to the Regimental Depot ('The Huts') at Litherland near Liverpool. Here also was Robert Graves. The two shared a hut. At the beginning of January, Graves was passed medically for a return to France, having declined an offer of more home service. At the depot Sassoon caught up with the military chat, including expectations of a decisive blow being delivered against the Germans on the Western Front in the coming year.[5]

SS's duties included training some of the recruits produced by the conscription legislation. Early in 1917 he wrote 'Conscripts', which concluded:

> Their training done, I shipped them all to France,
> Where most of those I'd loved too well got killed.
> Rapture and pale Enchantment and Romance,
> And many a sickly, slender lord who'd filled
> My soul long since with lutanies [lute music] of sin,
> Went home because they couldn't stand the din.
> But the kind, common ones that I despised
> (Hardly a man of them I'd count as friend),
> What stubborn-hearted virtues they disguised!
> They stood and played the hero to the end,
> Won gold and silver medals bright with bars,
> And marched resplendent home with crowns and stars.[6]

The poem appeared in the *Spectator* in February. This is curious since the magazine was on the right of politics and unequivocally with war to the bitter end. Here was a poem quite outside normal war cheering. One has to think that a commissioning editor misunderstood it. At a cursory glance, the poem ends with conscripted soldiers, originally unsuited to battle, having learned well and having thrashed the Huns, marching home with medals jangling. But Sassoon actually is talking about his own poetical history during the war. He is celebrating the way that simple verse techniques have stood up better to describing war than the precocious ones which he had previously been cultivating. The poem is not a celebration of conscripts proving themselves in the war. It is something else. And an implied protest about the slaughter on the Western

Front is deftly slipped in. Siegfried took delight in telling Ottoline Morrell: 'I am really becoming highly respectable.'[7]

'Conscripts' was too clever for some of Sassoon's friends. Graves told him: 'I have to take the "lutanies of sin" on trust because I can't understand them but I'm sure they must be good.' Edmund Gosse got completely the wrong end of the stick, complaining to Siegfried about 'a cruel and unworthy libel on members of the House of Lords'. (He had an interest: he was Librarian of the red-benched House.) Siegfried was amused, but concerned. Writing to Uncle Hamo, he said, 'Of course I meant my own precocities of pre-war days…It's thin ice for me…[Gosse's] well-known liking for people in Debrett [listing the peerage].' The snobbishness of Sassoon's conservative-minded patrons – Eddie Marsh was another – was awkward territory, since the social establishment was full-square behind the war. Hamo tried to explain the poem to Gosse but Edmund denied misunderstanding: 'I blamed it and I blame it still. It is a blot on his work and it shows his limitation.' He thought that Sassoon was 'strangely undeveloped for his age', though he assured Hamo: 'He is a dear attractive creature, wonderfully loveable.'[8]

'Conscripts' shows the development of metaphor in Sassoon's poetry. He comments in his *The Weald of Youth* reminiscences of pre-war that, 'Abstract ideas are uncongenial to my mind…I have always instinctively avoided the use of metaphors.' That had changed.[9]

If the *Spectator* was bamboozled by the Sassoon metaphors, it soon struck back. The next issue made sure that the correct poetic response to the war was trumpeted. It prominently carried a poem by J. Berkeley, Lt-Col:

> If death should claim this mortal shell of me…I pray you shed no tear…I pray you clothe yourself in gala hue… cheering me along, that I pass the SOLDIERS' GATE, whose arch is sacrifice…unburdened by regret, to greet my comrades who have bled for England's sake, and, risen from the dead, rest clear of Honour's debt.[10]

The message was that the sacrifice was worth it because 'honour', the totem word of the war, was upheld. A *Punch* poem of August 1917 entitled 'Jimmy – Killed in Action', carries an injunction not to grieve. The soldier has made his sacrifice and is content. 'Jimmy' apparently was a simple soul who loved horses and laughter. His 'merry spirit' will live on:

> Freed from the power of weariness or pain,
> Forbidding us to mourn – or to forget.[11]

There is humanity here, in contrast to the patriotic formulae of the colonel, but both poems deliver the official line: the worth of the sacrifice of lives in the essential cause of beating the Germans.

The conflict in the Coalition cabinet between War Minister Lloyd George and Prime Minister Asquith, about which Siegfried Sassoon learned during his stay at Garsington, came to a head a week into December with the overthrow of Asquith and the formation of a new Coalition Government by Lloyd George. If the purpose of the defenestration of Asquith was to avert a favourable British response to German peace feelers, it was just in time, since within days the German peace move became official. The *Annual Register* for 1917 states:

> An interesting announcement was made in the House of Commons on December 11, when Mr Bonar Law [Chancellor of the Exchequer] said that the British Government had been informed in September through a neutral diplomatic channel that the German Government would be glad to make a communication relative to peace.[12]

This is what Siegfried Sassoon had been hearing about at Garsington. Around 13 December the German overtures became direct, with what was called 'The German Peace Note' to the Allied governments. But now the Asquith government, which might have negotiated, was gone.

The background was that the Supreme Command of Generals Hindenburg and Ludendorff, who had the upper hand in the power contest within Germany, allowed Chancellor Bethmann-Hollweg to make an offer but on condition that there would be unrestricted submarine warfare if it failed. To come to the negotiating table would make much sense for both sides, but in both Germany and Britain war hardliners were entrenched. Still, there had been real hope of peace until the abrupt fall of Asquith. Siegfried Sassoon might have been developing his literary career in 1917 in a post-war world.[13]

Peace prospects became hopeful on 18 December when President Wilson, in what was called 'The American Note' wrote to the Belligerent Powers suggesting a Statement of Peace Terms. But the new Lloyd George Administration was preparing to repel overtures.

Siegfried Sassoon recorded in his notebook at this time, under the title 'Garsington (The Pacifist View of the War)' sections of letters received by him from Ottoline Morrell. One is dated the day of the fall of Asquith: 5 December 1916. Ottoline, well informed through her circle, had some inside knowledge of what lay behind the political earthquake. She wrote:

> The spirit and purpose of the war (that kept it fine and clean at first) dwindles more and more and gets fainter, leaving it utterly ghastly. It is terrible to know that vast numbers of the men fighting simply loathe it and are kept there by the brutal fury of L.G. and a few others like him. It seems pure insanity. Last week my hopes flared high, for I heard from old Birrell who came down here that the Germans had made definite Peace proposals and he hoped they would come to something. It was this that occasioned the Cabinet row – LG furious at the idea of Peace. LG's triumph is very depressing.[14]

Augustine Birrell, Liberal MP, cabinet minister until two years previously, was moving towards the parliamentary peace-by-negotiation group. His visit to Garsington is in the visitors' book on 2 December 1916.[15]

Under 'More Pacifism from Garsington', the Sassoon notebook has part of a 25 January 1917 letter from Ottoline:

> The Labour Congress and the Papers are simply sickening. How human beings can be so grossly brutal stupid and unimaginative I cannot understand. The possibility of Peace seems to make the devil leap up in people's hearts and to make them lust for more blood to be shed while there is yet time.[16]

The reference is to the annual conference of the Labour Party, which was in progress as Ottoline was writing. It was chaired in Manchester by George Wardle, on Labour's right-wing, who endorsed Lloyd George's declared policy of fighting to the bitter end. The account in the 1917 *Annual Register* shows that Wardle was backed by the majority of the conference. There was loud applause for him. He admitted 'the sacrifices of cherished principles'; and that Labour was split on the war. It states that in Wardle's presidential address, 'A reference to recent peace manoeuvres and the mention of President Wilson evoked an outburst of enthusiasm from the pacifist section.' Woodrow Wilson in the White House was the big hope of British peace promoters. The parliamentary peace-by-negotiation group had only five of the Labour Party's forty MPs in its ranks. Labour's pro-war majority backed the Government's rejection of the German Peace Note. The slaughter was set to continue.[17]

Ottoline's letter continues:

> The Spring offensive is pure devilry – when after all, peace could be made quite advantageously to the Allies. Another poor little harvest of village youths has been called up and has gone off to barracks. They do hate it poor creatures.

Siegfried Sassoon could expect to be in the Spring Offensive. There was still no sign of the military stalemate being broken. Since Germany's military aim was to hang onto the swathes of territory which it had gained in 1914, the outcome of the Battle of the Somme amounted to a German defensive victory. The coming Allied offensive would be a joint operation of French and British troops, with the French General Robert Nivelle in command. This would bring early successes but ultimate failure, a consequence of the death toll being mutinies in the French army.

As Lloyd George took power, an article by Philip Morrell appeared in the December 1916 edition of *UDC* (Union of Democratic Control) magazine. It was called: 'Why the time has come.' Morrell's thesis was that the time was ripe for negotiations to end the war. The peace-by-negotiation group had another member.

The eleven-strong band established themselves on the second-back bench below the gangway on the Opposition side of the House of Commons. The House was (and is) arranged in adversarial fashion, with the Government and Opposition parties facing each other across the central aisle. The gangway on each side (halfway down) was frequently mentioned since it had political connotations. Independent-minded and rebellious Members were to be found below the gangway, towards the bottom end of the chamber that is (at the top being the Speaker's Chair). In the new politics, conscription opponents and war dissenters sat below the gangway. The peace-by-negotiation group were all Liberals and Labour but next year certain Conservatives would support them, including Somerset MP Aubrey Herbert, a soldier of noted physical bravery (wounded at Mons). Speaking about a *Times* editorial of February 1918 setting out how Europe could be reshaped by the war, Herbert said that he would not shed his blood for that: the paper should go and 'shed its own ink'. A number of the peace-by-negotiation parliamentarians came to Garsington. They included Philip Snowden, with whom Siegfried Sassoon would later be in alliance, as well as ex-Labour Leader Ramsay MacDonald. Ottoline Morrell liked Richard Lambert, a Liberal MP who came to Garsington with his wife. The pair decorated the cottage they occupied with Greek mottoes and frescoes, and seemed, she said, 'to be quite happy and content amongst all these young and rebellious Conscientious Objectors'. Lambert had captured a Tory seat in December 1910 thanks to a brilliant campaign speech by Winston Churchill. Out of favour and out of Government, Churchill was currently serving as a military officer on the Western Front, but he would soon be back. Before the end of the war, he would try very hard to recruit Siegfried Sassoon for his team.[18]

The House of Commons peace-by-negotiation bench still had some hope as the new Lloyd George Government established itself. The group made its move on the German Peace Note on 21 December 1916. The lead was taken by Liberal Bertrand Lees-Smith, who had spent eight months on the Western Front before asthma compelled a return to Britain. Lees-Smith presented what Parliament did not usually hear: a rank-and-file Army perspective. The Northampton MP told the Commons that he felt sure that the men at the front would back a settlement, 'provided we can obtain guarantees that our honourable obligations will be fulfilled'. He looked at the consequences of trying to crush the other side:

> Some wish to hold the Central Empires down by a military decision, followed up by economic strangulation. If you do that you will carry forward into peace the hostilities and the hatreds of war; you will divide Europe into two rival camps; you will make armies, navies and armaments more burdensome and oppressive than ever; you will make war more inevitable and deadly than ever.

Calling for a positive Government response to the German Peace Note, Lees-Smith made an appeal to the Liberal traditions of his colleagues:

> Trust yourselves boldly to those decent, kindly, humane forces which are to be found in every man and nation. Put behind you military decisions and Paris conferences; see only terms of peace which will enable you to substitute the possibility of friendship for the continuance of hatred and on those terms of peace erect a league of nations. I believe that those who put their trust in the great moral forces which lie latent in the hearts of man will find that in the long run they have never failed mankind. Trust them once again.[19]

It was almost the first time that Parliament had heard the words League of Nations. The recent Paris Conference of the Allies had been about having a trade war with Germany to follow the shooting one. It is not known whether Siegfried Sassoon picked up this debate. However, his sentiments were those of Lees-Smith. Robert Graves states in his memoir that: 'Siegfried vehemently asserted that the terms [the German proposal for peace negotiations] should have been accepted; I agreed.' Sassoon's diary for 22 December 1916 confirms Lees-Smith's view that the Army would back a settlement of the war by mutual agreement of the two sides:

> ...The War is settling down on everyone – a hopeless, never-shifting burden. Newspapers and politicians yell and brandish their arms, and the

> dead rot in their French graves, and the maimed hobble about the streets. And the Kaiser talks about Peace because he thinks he's won...Nothing before me but red dawns flaring over Ypres and Bapaume. And people still say the War is 'splendid', damn their eyes. And the Army in France can contemplate a 'patched-up peace' because it is so weary of the ways of death.[20]

'Patched-up peace' was the regular phrase for knocking together a settlement – not a great one for either side (because neither had won), but a pragmatic set of compromises, which would restore peace.

Two days later Sassoon reviewed his personal situation:

> Of course I've got to go [back to the Western Front] – I never doubted that; but if I'm there another eight months, and come back *safely wounded* (!) shall I have anything better to say about it all, or shall I be more bitter, and unbalanced and callous? Not much use enquiring. It will be good fun in its way; and reading Sorley's letters has given me a good cheer-up. He was so ready for all emergencies, so ready to accept the 'damnable circumstance of death' – or life.[21]

Fellow-Marlburian, fellow-soldier and fellow-poet, Charles Sorley died on 13 October 1915 at the Battle of Loos. Shortly before his death, he wrote:

> When you see millions of the mouthless dead
> Across your dreams in pale battalions go,
> Say not soft things as other men have said,
> That you'll remember. For you need not so.

That was because the dead could not perceive or respond. The poem ends:

> Then, scanning all the o'ercrowded mass, should you
> Perceive one face that you loved heretofore,
> It is a spook. None wears the face you knew.
> Great death has made all his for evermore. [22]

One of Sorley's poems is entitled 'To Germany':

> ...You only saw your future bigly planned,
> And we the tapering paths of our own mind,
> And in each other's dearest ways we stand,

And hiss and hate. And the blind fight the blind.
When it is peace, then we may view again each other's truer form…
When it is peace. But, until peace, the storm,
The darkness, and the thunder and the rain.[23]

Sorley had been preparing the way for the War Poets. Siegfried Sassoon copied some of the 'mouthless dead' poem into his diary on Christmas Day, 1916.

When Sassoon had been out at the front, he had oscillated between angry-pacifist (hating war and its destruction, as well as the incompetence of the high command) and happy-warrior (rejoicing in the successes that he had achieved and further ones that he anticipated). Out there, no time was available for worrying about being killed; in England there was plenty. Now, Siegfried was 'ceasing to believe in the war itself'. The news of heavy casualties in his battalion, making it almost unrecognisable, added to his depression and foreboding. 'It took a good deal of the heart out of me,' he wrote.[24]

Sassoon was receptive to a new offering from popular novelist and political commentator H.G. Wells. *Mr Britling Sees It Through* is a self-explanatory title. Wells had changed his views since being one of the greeters of a 'war to end all wars'. His new book was nuanced but essentially anti-war, special targets being administrative incompetence in the Army and jingoism at home. His critique evaded the Defence of the Realm Act as being spoken by a fictional character. Siegfried loved the book. He logged its theme in his diary:

> *Mr Britling* says: Everywhere cunning, everywhere small feuds and hatreds, distrusts, dishonesties, timidities, feebleness of purpose, dwarfish imaginations, swarm over the great and simple issues….it is a war now like any other of the mobbing, many-aimed cataclysms that have shattered empires and devastated the world; it is a war without point, a war that has lost its soul, it has become mere incoherent fighting and destruction, a demonstration in vast and tragic forms of the stupidity and ineffectiveness of our species.[25]

That passage hit him as a bolt from the blue: 'For several minutes I sat staring at the words.' It was a political moment. Lights lit. It was 'exactly what I'd been thinking, only I didn't know how to say it!' He compared it with his diary comment on the war as a 'hopeless, never-shifting burden'. Sassoon was edging towards political analysis.[26]

David Jones may be compared. His *Parenthesis* reflects on the change in the nature of the war experience since the beginning of the Battle of the Somme:

> Things hardened into a more relentless, mechanical affair, a more sinister aspect. The wholesale slaughter of later years, the conscripted levies filling the gaps knocked the bottom out of the intimate, continuing domestic life of small contingents of men…In the earlier months there was a certain attractive amateurishness, and elbow-room for idiosyncrasy that connected one with a less exacting past. The period of the individual rifle-man, of the 'old sweat' of the Boer campaign seemed to terminate with the Somme battle.[27]

Now it was the industrial slaughter of 'attrition'.

We find in a Sassoon journal entry for 12 January 1917 that the other day he had sent Ottoline Morrell a book of his poetry. What came back from Lady Ottoline was:

> Have you ever felt as if some clouds of glory had come down, or some bush had turned to burning glory and that the only thing to do was to bow in speechless reverence, almost fearing to look again in case the glory should have vanished. It was this that I felt when your little book entered my room this morning, in its brown cover – hiding its glories. I cannot thank you…I really can only bow myself in wonder and delight at its visitation…Your illustrations make me cry with wonder…They really are quite extraordinary…quite as wonderful as Blake's…[28]

There was more. (The omission dots are SS's.) Sassoon found the superlatives cloying and called the comparison with William Blake 'nonsense'. Half a dozen lines of his comments are heavily squiggled out, labelled, in ballpoint pen of a later age, 'silly remarks about dear O.M.' Siegfried was one of many who only later appreciated Ottoline. It seems not inapposite to quote here the 1938 memorial inscription composed by Ottoline's friends, including Virginia Woolf and T.S. Elliot: 'A brave spirit, unbroken, Delighting in beauty and goodness, And the love of her friends.' That seems fair. Of the qualities mentioned, Ottoline's bravery, which was very real, would be of key importance to Siegfried later in this year.[29]

The following day the Sassoon notebook has an entry with just the title Jan 13th but it is clearly more Ottoline quotation – probably from the same letter. She is upset about D.H. Lawrence turning her into a character in his new book:

> Lawrence (D.H.) sent me the M.S. of his new Novel. It is all very bad – written in that dreadful Physical, Pathological Language – absolutely unreal and disgusting – He has put me in it – a most appalling woman – the very antipodes of what I believe I am like – he makes me out corrupt

> – dead – bedrugged – everything I most loathe – He describes every detail here – It is written with such hatred – I almost think Frieda [the wife of D.H. Lawrence] did it![30]

This has to be *Women in Love*, D.H. Lawrence's sequel to *The Rainbow*, against the suppression of which Philip Morrell protested in Parliament. Lawrence, unable for several years to find a publisher for the book, circulated typescripts, one of which (Ottoline's?) was among Siegfried Sassoon's collection for his Army reading.[31]

The expected happened. Sassoon's diary for 27 January 1917 reports an interview with two grey-haired, khaki-clad military administration men sitting at a table, with blue and white sheets of paper before them. They asked him whether he felt fit enough to go out. He replied that he did. He was passed fit for military service. He wrote in his diary:

> As I went out into the grey street and the bitter east wind I felt as if a load had been lifted from my sullen heart. I'd got another chance to die a decent death. And a d-d uncomfortable one, probably.[32]

The diary entry ends on a note of pleasure as he examined the first batch of proof-sheets of his poetry book *The Old Huntsman*, which looked 'first-class in print'. Back came the desire to live. He had a book of poetry coming out. He did not want to die. Back came the attitude expressed in his diary a couple of weeks earlier when he declared that he had a grip on life and how to describe it and that he hoped that he would not be killed in 1917 since he had a lot to say.[33]

Sassoon had been riding with the Cheshire Hunt and had stayed the night at Wistaston Hall, Crewe. The chatter depressed him. Conversation echoed the newspapers. There was an 'emptiness', with 'Debrett on every table'. A diary page is ripped out here: the next picks up Sassoon in mid-tirade against staff officers at Litherland: a captain (name scribbled out) who had just got back from three weeks' sick leave with his mistress. The officer claimed an injury caused by riding but actually he was suffering from gonorrhoea. He had been there for over a year since being sent back from the front. Sassoon was sour: 'What earthly use are these people? They don't instruct anyone; they simply eat and drink... They aren't even willing to be killed; I can at least say *that* for myself, for I've tried often.'[34]

Following this diary entry is a poem (not published in Sassoon's lifetime):

> England has many heroes; they are known  
> To all who read of German armies beat.  
> One chap got drunk and took a trench alone,

And grinned to cheering mobs in every street.
Though England's proud of him – her stuffed V.C. –
No medal was attached to his D.T. [delirium tremens from alcohol withdrawal].
Think of the D.C.M's and D.S.O's
And breasts that swell with Military Crosses;
They are the pomps of War; and no one knows
Nor cares to count the bungling and the losses.
But I would rather shoot one General Dolt
Than fifty harmless Germans; and I've seen
Ten thousand soldiers tabbed with blue and green,
Who, if they heard one shell, would crouch and bolt.
But when the War is done they'll shout and sing,
And fetch bright medals from their German King.[35]

Sassoon viewed the departure to the front of a batch of trainees: A draft of a hundred and fifty were setting off to France that evening. Most of them, he said, were 'half-tight', except those who had been confined to the guard-room 'to stop them bolting (again)'. A chaplain was encouraging them on their way, making some jollying jokes. He prayed that God would go with them. He would go with them as far as the station. The account reads like the purest of satire, prefiguring *Oh! What a Lovely War.* The commander told the departing men that they were going out to the Big Push, which would end the war. At this some cynical groans were heard. The men marched off to the beat of drums: 'a pathetic scene of humbug and cant'.[36]

He reflected on his swirl of emotions during the past year:

> It all came back to me – the anxious unsettled ideas of last spring and summer: desire of death; emotion at facing danger unafraid; repugnance at the commonplace grossness of the majority and their incessant chatter about 'Blighty' and 'cushy wounds', their little souls wanting nothing nobler than to creep safely home to – what?

He had never found anyone at the front who had got any value out of Christian theology.[37]

A couple of days before Sassoon left the depot (for a short spell of home leave before his return to France) there was another surge of anti-war emotion. He went with a fellow officer to the Liverpool Hippodrome, where there was merriment about tanks. He recalled in *Siegfried's Journey* that it was this that inspired the composition (in February 1917) of the poem 'Blighters', which imagines the music hall audience being terrified when tanks come off the stage into the stalls. Sassoon hated the jingoistic jokes, which he saw as mocking 'the riddled corpses'. Among those who liked the poem was Thomas Hardy. Sassoon's Hippodrome companion was killed at the Bullecourt operation on the Western Front several months later.

Sassoon's frame of mind as he prepared himself mentally for heading back to France was not helped by two intense afternoons with Ottoline Morrell, who of course did nothing to temper his negativity. He was on form with his sarcasm, remarking to Lady Ottoline:

> One gets sent out again like a cabbage to Covent Garden Market. Cabbages are better off because they don't claim to have unconquerable souls, and aren't told that they are making a supreme sacrifice for the sake of unborn vegetables.[38]

He was cheered up by an alcohol-fuelled literary gathering at the house of Heinemann, whose table was apparently unaffected by food rationing. Siegfried later commented that: 'It was just the sort of entertainment I needed – civilized and deliberately disregardful of the war, which my companions detested as much as I did.'[39]

## Chapter 5

# 'A Stupendous Blow'

Siegfried Sassoon's return to France was unpleasant. In his diary he describes feeling 'nervous and rattled' as he left London on 15 February 1917. That wore off when he was aboard *The Archangel*, but his spirits were low. His notebook jottings now turn political: politicians shouting for more guns and men in order to carry out the wishes of Milner, Northcliffe, Lloyd George and Carson. The soldiers are 'sardines', being swept up in nets for the War Office to tin and send away to be eaten. An endpiece remark that some of the sardines are brave and will be given medals, may be seen as a sardonic jeer but we must remember that medals and the ribbons that went with them were of the utmost importance to Siegfried Sassoon. He hoped to win another decoration. The diary passage is about Britain's conversion into a war machine. Lord Milner, an Imperial administrator, now in the War Cabinet, championed the British race and the British Empire, advocating Imperial preference ('tariff reform') and the inclusion of the governments of Britain's dominions in the central governance. Alfred Harmsworth, Lord Northcliffe, was the mightiest press baron, owning the *Times* and the *Daily Mail* and pushing the cause of no-negotiation war to the end. Sir Edward Carson, Irish Unionist lawyer of noted bellicosity, had led the powerful Unionist [Conservative] War Committee of backbenchers, which had been instrumental in the overthrow of Asquith. He brought his total-war passion to being director of propaganda. Liberalism was eclipsed. The civil rights for which Philip Morrell and his parliamentary group forlornly battled were being steamrollered by the machinery which Sassoon, not without some justification, likened to sardine-tinning.[1]

There was nothing to cheer SS on his arrival in France. At the base camp near Rouen he caught, ironically enough, German measles. He spent some days in a 'squalid little' hospital compound, reporting to his diary that:

> Four of my fellow-patients play cards all day; their talk is all the dullest obscenity. The other two are good enough, one a rather charming little Scot in the gunners.[2]

*Memoirs of an Infantry Officer* has the Sherston character seeing on a notice-board:

> ...the names of three private soldiers who had been shot for cowardice since the end of January. 'The sentence was duly carried out.'[3]

This cannot be literally true. Of the three-hundred-plus British Army executions in the war for military offences, only a handful were for 'cowardice'. The vast majority were for 'desertion'. Of the 14 Western Front executions in January and February 1917, eleven were for 'desertion'; two were for 'quitting post' and one was for 'casting away arms'. Announcement within the Army of executions as a warning not to run away from the lines was part of the system.[4]

Siegfried's resilience seemed to have lost its spring:

> While I lie awake starring at the darkness of the tent my terrors get hold of me and I long only for life and comfort, and the weeks before me seem horrible and agonizing. I haven't the physical health to face the hardship and nerve-strain. Nothing seems to matter but a speedy release from the hell that awaits me. Yet I should loathe the very idea of returning to England without having been scarred and tortured once more.[5]

He was of course in the thoughts of Ottoline Morrell. A letter from her dated 1 March berates the new Government. She reports on Neville Chamberlain, Director of National Service. It was beyond the imagination of the world of 1917 that Chamberlain would lead Britain into a second war against Germany little more than two decades after this one. Chamberlain (not yet in Parliament) was in charge of conscription and manpower. He was the wielder of the 'toothcomb' which prised military service avoiders out of 'funk holes'. Ottoline wrote:

> Apparently N. Chamberlain is complete and absolute tyrant over the civil population. Once in his net anyone can be ordered to do what he (N. C.) likes, suitable or otherwise. To raise any objection is to prove himself a slacker. Philip said [Chamberlain] interviewed 200 MPs and gave his views, and very clearly and amiably laid down his scheme, which is to run its course unchecked by Parliament or anyone else...I always hope that such measures will make people revolt and make the War intolerable... but they seem to swallow anything.[6]

The presents from Garsington continued. Before Sassoon left Litherland, his fellow officers were entertained by a rug which Ottoline had doused with perfume. (In one of his letters to his mother, Siegfried remarked that, 'Lady Ottoline's taste in scent is beyond a joke.') The gift was ribaldly remarked on by the others as suggestive. It was multi-coloured, made by herself. Ottoline found her way into Siegfried's verse composition. A letter from Sassoon to Edmund Gosse turns into a little poem about 'a wondrous dame feeding her zoo and keeping them tame – in a place of colour and delight where young men think it wrong to fight.' He admitted that it was feeble: not up to the standards of his publisher Heinemann.[7]

An Ottoline letter of 17 February informed Siegfried:

> I wrote to Bertie Russell and told him you were going out again; he said he would send you his book. I remember he said when he met you here: 'He is obviously a real Poet.'[8]

The Russell book that was on the way to France was *Justice in War-Time*.

Many soldiers went into Rouen to visit the brothels. Sassoon had no inclination. He poeticised unkindly about offering a five franc note and being 'happier with a goat'.

The brothels fulfilled a need, and hygiene was attended to, but even so they produced sexually transmitted diseases on a copious scale. Class divisions applied: red lamp for private soldiers; green for officers. The establishments were semi-permanent fixtures because the lines shifted so little in the military deadlock. Over in Westminster, Bertie Lees-Smith was to the fore in pressing for British soldiers to be banned from attending the 'maisons tolerées'. Ultimately this campaign succeeded, with the brothels being put out of bounds for British troops. This had unfortunate consequences since alternative outlets were found without medical supervision, meaning that the sexual disease rate rose. Liberal morality prevailed over pragmatism with health precaution.

Siegfried Sassoon's notebooks are a mixture of diary entries, reflection pieces, notes and lists. Character sketches include a Rifle Brigade major whose service went back to the Boer War. He had come out to France to take up a command. He was an old cavalryman who talked broad Irish and liked to tell the waitresses off about the quality of the food. He had African and Canadian medals. He bragged about how tough he was with conscientious objectors. He mentioned one called Scott Duckers, whom he could not 'deal with' because the authorities 'were afraid of him': he could only get him five years' imprisonment. He said he would have knocked the man about if he had been allowed to. Duckers is known to history. He was a solicitor, an anti-war activist. He made a legal challenge to his military call-up. A police sergeant and colleague arrived at his Chancery Lane office as he was about to leave to attend a case at Lambeth Police Court of a conscription resister. He invoked solicitor's privilege: that he could not be arrested while on the way to court for a client. He took the opportunity of presenting the sergeant with a copy of *Liberalism – Its Principles and Proposals*, a 1902 work of Herbert Samuel, who in 1916 was Home Secretary. The eponymous principles included rejection of conscription. The police officer explained to Duckers that, 'people talk very differently when they get in the Cabinet.' A week later Duckers was fined £2 and ordered to be handed over to the Army. Wearing his solicitor's silk hat and black coat, he was taken to the recruiting station at Scotland Yard. When he refused to cooperate, he was put in a detention cell of extreme squalor with five other prisoners. He was court-martialled and sentenced to twelve months' hard labour, commuted to 98 days detention. Thus began the regular cat-and-mouse repeating sequence of call-up, arrest, court-martial and imprisonment. Liberal MP Edmund Harvey penned a foreword to Duckers's book on his experiences, written during a brief interval of freedom:

> For the moment it may seem that the inconvenient protest of an unpopular minority has been effectively suppressed. But in the end the clamour of the Press, the outcry of the platform and the eloquence of the pulpit cannot prevail against the still small voice of truth in prison.[9]

Duckers was not released until nearly the end of 1919. His especially cruel treatment was apparently the result of the vigorous persecution of him by the officer mentioned in Siegfried Sassoon's notebook. In *Memoirs of an Infantry Officer*, Sassoon was no longer complimentary about the captain/major, describing his treatment of conscientious objectors as 'frankly brutal'. He added a personal note:

> I hadn't formed any opinion about Conscientious Objectors, but I couldn't help thinking that they must be braver men than some I'd seen wearing uniforms in safe places and taking salutes from genuine soldiers.[10]

He was surely correct. In June 1916 over thirty resisters were shipped to Boulogne and court-martialled. Sir Douglas Haig was apparently going to have some of them shot but after concerns were raised, the then Prime Minister H.H. Asquith intervened to stop it. They were still sentenced to death but their sentences were commuted to long imprisonment. The courage of the men drew admiration from soldiers. Philip Snowden told the House of Commons on the subject of conscientious objectors:

> I know these young fellows. They are the present-day type of those men to whom we owe all the liberties we have today. They are men who are prepared to go to scaffold for the sake of their principles. They are the

> men who will stand against the wall and face the muskets rather than be conscripted into the Army against their conscientious view.[11]

As Siegfried Sassoon started to readjust to the noise of war, his cynicism sharpened. He wrote in his diary on 4 March 1917:

> There is a sort of unreasoning, inhuman gaiety in the air which is beyond description. The English are supposed to be mad in their way of treating the War as a joke, but I think it is only their inherent stupidity and unwillingness to face things. I sometimes feel that everyone (even the Base-Colonels) will suddenly go stark mad and begin shooting one another instead of the Germans. The whole thing is so monstrously implacable to all human tenderness. All the while there is the spectacle of Youth being murdered.[12]

Sassoon, now in the Second Battalion, was sent to Chipilly, a camp on the Somme. Disappointingly, Robert Graves was not there, having been invalided back to England.

While Sassoon was re-establishing himself in France, in London Parliament was digesting sensational news. On 15 March 1917 it was announced that a revolution was under way in Russia. Tsar Nicholas Romanov had abdicated. The advent of the new Provisional Government, with a mixture of liberals and socialists, was welcomed rapturously by the peace-by-negotiation group in the Commons. Its members looked particularly to Alexander Kerensky, the Minister of Justice. Kerensky, who would become Prime Minister in July, had identified himself with a policy of peace-by-negotiation with no annexations. The new Russian government's programme was, as Martin Sixsmith has noted, 'impeccable liberal idealism': the release of political prisoners, civil liberties, an end to religious and ethnic discrimination, and the abolition of the death penalty and the Tsarist police. The Commons peace group saw great opportunities. Russian socialists wanted to join with socialists in the other Allied countries in meeting their counterparts on the other side of the war divide with a view to peace-making. The British Government wanted none of this but with Russia as Britain's war partner and good relations needed, there was some hope that the planned conference (Stockholm was the intended venue) might actually happen.[13]

On 22 March 1917 Siegfried Sassoon's diary reported that, 'Vague news comes of the German retreat.' In February and March 1917, the German forces pulled back to the so-called Hindenburg Line, 25 miles in the rear. This was a surprise but it was not really an Allied breakthrough, more a German strategy, aiming to create a defensible buffer-zone. The much talked up Allied Spring Offensive featured the Battle of Arras. The city of Arras, in the Artois region of northeast France – the birthplace of Robespierre – became a focal point of fighting. Sassoon was on the way to the action. *Memoirs of an Infantry Officer* has: 'That way to the Sausage Machine!' some old soldier exclaimed as we passed a signpost marked *Arras, 32 k.*'[14]

Sassoon's correspondence with his mother might suggest that any romance of war was thoroughly out of his system:

> Out here the conditions make it almost impossible to think independently. The average mental attitude of the officer isn't at all stimulating. They can hardly be said to think at all – which on the whole, is the best way of getting along comfortably. War is a most deadening performance when the first excitement and strangeness has worn off. [15]

But we know that Siegfried's mood shifted. He thanked Theresa for 'the various parcels'.

The following day Sassoon wrote to Uncle Hamo. He related to the sculptor a visit to Amiens cathedral: 'The glass looked more gorgeous than ever: a miracle of colour.' In the letter war prospects get a diplomatic mention, with Siegfried's awareness of Hamo's full support of the cause and its prosecution. SS hoped that, 'these Germans will go on retreating.' He mentioned reports of 'acute food shortage' in Germany, commenting that, 'It is difficult to know how much to believe,' Then he said: 'A rather cynical view about the war seems to prevail among our troops.' Siegfried's decent honesty and family regard meant that he had to tell his uncle about widespread negative feelings among the troops. He did so with no hint that he shared them. The letter concludes:

> It's hard to get any comprehensive view of what's happening in the campaigns and in men's heads.[16]

That was no doubt true – and the German pull-back was a puzzle. As to what Siegfried thought about the war, Hamo will have been little the wiser.

On 7 April Sassoon was not far from Arras. Soon he would be in action. The approach of battle brought on a burst of happy-warrior exulting in his diary. After a good meal of coffee and eggs he said that if he had the choice between 'England tomorrow and the battle', he would choose the battle without hesitation. He could not understand why this was so, but: 'My feeling of quiet elation and absolute confidence now is something even stronger than last summer's passionate longing for death and glory.'[17]

Siegfried Sassoon wrote a ten-page account of this time for Dudley Ward's *Regimental Records*. He also wrote a contribution to Captain James E. Dunn's

*The War the Infantry Knew*. Dunn was the medical officer of Sassoon's battalion. *Regimental Records* has Sassoon's information that he was in command of No.8 Platoon, which contained 8 Joneses. He describes an extremely uncomfortable and unpleasant camp, the officers' chamber being cold, draughty, smoky and ill-lit: 'Orderlies would bring in a clutter of tin plates and mugs; machonachie stew [vegetables, potatoes and beef in thin broth] was consumed in morose discomfort.' The tea drink was 'that nasty concoction'. Sassoon's platoon seldom mustered more than 20. His regimental log is uncomplimentary about the calibre of some of his men:

> A recent draft had added a collection of undersized half-wits to the depleted battalion. Several men in my platoon seemed barely capable of carrying the weight of their equipment. In my case platoon training commenced with the platoon commander teaching a man how to load his rifle. Afterwards I felt that the poor devil would have been a less perilous ingredient of my command had he been left in his first ignorance.[18]

This uncharitable recollection comes as a jolt. It exemplifies Siegfried Sassoon's many-sidedness. His register depended on his audience. Here he is making a military assessment in a regimental history. *Regimental Records* elsewhere calls Sassoon 'a very stout man'. This is not what we are expecting, but 'stout' here means strong, not fat: Siegfried was slim. Suddenly we see SS as the tall, tough Army guy, a surprise because we know him as a poet, and poets are proverbially sensitive flowers. Siegfried *was* sensitive but it was a sensitivity that he could channel into going out onto the battlefield thirsting to split the skulls of those who had terminated the lives of friends whom he loved. His preparatory school nickname was 'The Onion'. That turns out to be rather uncannily appropriate. Sig was the man of layers. He was proud of his physique, and with it went leadership, practicality and appreciation by his Army superiors. The above quoted passage suggests some condescension towards those not thus blessed.[19]

In his piece for Captain Dunn's collection, Sassoon describes two officers:

> Casson, aged 23, had been at Winchester and Christ Church [Oxford]; he was a sensitive, refined youth, and an amusing gossip. Evans was about the same age, but had not 'enjoyed the same social advantages'. He was very noisy and garrulous, always licked his thumb when dealing cards, and invariably answered "Pardon?" when any remark was made to him. That "pardon" became a little trying at times.

Sassoon was not immune to the social snobbery endemic in the Army fraternity. It was not Victorian times: 'officers and their ladies'; 'NCO's and their wives'; 'private soldiers and their women', but there was a hangover from those days. Siegfried Sassoon is always very careful to call himself 'an officer'. His comparison between Casson and Evans concludes:

> Equally good when tested, these two merged their social incompatibilities in the end; both were killed on September 26th.[20]

Evans is Rees in *Memoirs of an Infantry Officer*, where Sassoon mentions that he 'kept up his courage by talking incessantly and making jokes about the battle', adding however that 'he couldn't get the nonchalance into his eyes.'[21]

Second Lieutenant Casson is mentioned elsewhere around this time in Sassoon's Dunn collection account:

> ...Casson and I walked up the hill; I wanted to get him accustomed to the unpleasant sights. There were a lot of our yesterday's dead lying in front of the trench. They lay there in all their equipment, most of them shot in the head. When Casson was at Winchester he did not anticipate he would ever be walking about on a fine April evening among a lot of dead men.... Detached from the fighting, we had merely gone for a short walk after tea, so to speak, and I couldn't help feeling as if I'd been showing Casson something obscene. (Nine years afterwards the whole business has become incredible. Unfortunately young Casson is not alive to share my sense of the incredulity of that little evening walk.)[22]

Melancholic foreshadowing marks also an account of 'a convivial evening' spent by several officers during this journey:

> ...Ralph Greaves drew pleasant sounds from a piano. He played as though he were saying goodbye to all music for ever. Three weeks later he had lost one of his arms.[23]

On 9 April 1917 as Siegfried Sassoon slogged towards to Arras, a fellow-poet was killed by a shell on the Battle's first day. Second Lieutenant Edward Thomas, 39, who used to review books, was a new arrival on the Western Front. He shared with Sassoon a deep love of the south country. A cultural roots Welshman, Thomas had adopted Hampshire. At Easter 1915 Edward regretted the unattended flowers in the wood, no longer gathered by young men and their sweethearts. He hated the hypocrisy of the war and the newspaper jingoism.

But he volunteered. He felt that powerful emotion that caused some, including Sassoon, to see the war as a defence of their beloved countryside. Thomas's celebrated poem 'Adlestrop', in which an express train makes an unscheduled stop at a Gloucestershire village station, has an exquisite poignance from the date of its composition, June 1914. Before enlisting, Thomas had put in a claim for a civil list pension. He was backed by Walter de la Mare. Edmund Gosse counselled Thomas's fellow poet against exaggerated promotion of him. Thomas's work was 'creditable', but: 'I have met with little of his that deserved the epithets "rare" and "beautiful".' The Gosse favour which Siegfried Sassoon enjoyed was not lightly earned.[24]

On the march Sassoon was put in charge of a fatigue party carrying boxes of trench mortar bombs to an ammunition dump. They were heavy and the terrain was difficult. Normally, officers did not do load-carrying: they supervised their men doing this. Sassoon, very unusually, carried bombs himself. It was a signal of his empathy with those whom he commanded, as was his obtaining of supplies of cigarettes to cheer them up. He was a popular and liked officer.

On 12 April Sassoon's diary gives an impression of conditions. His Second Battalion had been ordered to the front the previous afternoon. He was in a tiny dug-out with two others. It had a stove but rations were getting short. He and Casson had just finished the last orange. SS had the regular complaint of 'trench mouth' (bleeding gums and ulcers) but he was feeling 'fairly fresh' – probably because of the prospect of action. (At least he did not have 'trench foot' which meant the failure of the toes as a result of loss of circulation due to prolonged exposure to water.) All around was the rumbling of the guns. It was bitterly cold. There was nowhere to lie down. Sleep was near-impossible.[25]

On 14 April 1917 the journey to the action station was over. What Sassoon found in the Arras zone horrified him. He recalled:

> We were among the debris of the intense bombardment of two weeks before; concrete emplacements were smashed and tilted sideways; the chalky soil was everywhere pitted with huge shell-holes, and there were many dead bodies – I can remember looking down, as I blundered and gasped my way along, and seeing a mask-like face floating on the surface of the flooded trench. This face had detached itself from its skull. I can remember two mud-clotted hands protruding from the wet ashen soil like the roots of a tree turned upside-down; one hand seemed to be pointing at the sky with an accusing gesture. It was a yellowish corpse-like day.[26]

It inspired 'The Effect', which Sassoon would compose in the coming summer:

"He'd never seen so many dead before."
They sprawled in yellow daylight while he swore
And gasped and lugged his everlasting load
Of bombs along what once had been a road.
... "How many dead? As many as you wish.
Don't count 'em; they're too many.
"Who'll buy my nice fresh corpses, two a penny?"[27]

William Heinemann, considering this for a Sassoon anthology, found the last line 'quite impossible'. The full poem however would appear in the Heinemann June 1918 Sassoon collection *Counter-Attack*, with a preface:

> "The effect of our bombardment was terrific. One man told me he had never seen so many dead before." – War Correspondent.

Soldiers usually kept their experience to themselves when they went home. David Jones's *In Parenthesis* title for his memoir speaks to the keeping by soldiers of 'a kind of space between'. What went on within the brackets was not suitable to be shared outside. But the sealing was not watertight. Nor was the suppression and the sanitisation of war detail always effective. There were occasions when trench experience reached the public, including by way of House of Commons debates, with MPs speaking uncensored under parliamentary privilege. On 5 January 1916 Sir Hamar Greenwood, one of the active service Members on leave to attend the conscription debates, told the House:

> The frightful [First] Battle of Ypres occurred over a year ago now, yet you can still see the bodies sticking out of the mud. You can see the grizzled hands of English soldiers anywhere along the Ypres salient sticking up out of the mud at point after point.[28]

Sassoon's 2nd Battalion had taken over from the 13th Northumberland Fusiliers. Siegfried had the duty of posting sentries. He noticed a company in a panic: 'N.C.O.s and men jostling one another in their haste to vanish through a narrow doorway, which led down to the bowels of the earth'. His *Regimental Records* account speaks of 'this rabble', whose two officers had 'no idea except to get everyone downstairs as soon as possible'. *Memoirs of an Infantry Officer* describes the men as being 'in a state of wind-up'. The operation in progress was in the build-up to The Second Battle of the Scarpe, 23-24 April, which was part of the 9 April to 16 May Battle of Arras. The ultimate result of the attack by British troops on German defences near the city of Arras would be a stalemate, with heavy casualties on both sides.

Sassoon wrote up his diary on Sunday night, 15 April, sitting in what was known as the Hindenburg Tunnel. *Regimental Records* has details of this feature:

> In this part of the Hindenburg Line there was a long gallery beneath the main trench, fitted with bunks and other conveniences. There were entrances, alternate wide stairs and inclined planes for stores, every forty to fifty yards. Within the part of the tunnel occupied by the battalion were units and detachments of two brigades, jostling amid new mud and old refuse, improvised and intended latrines, British and German dead. A dreadful place.[29]

German defensive engineering was better than Allied construction. This tunnel was particularly elaborate, but full of horror.

SS's diary entry, covering this and the previous day, well conveys the human cost of this kind of warfare. He had been told to take command of a hundred bombers (out of the 270 men in the battalion) to act as reserve for the First Cameronians in the next day's attack. The Cameronians were set to bomb down the two Hindenburg Lines. In a previous attempt to do this they had been driven back. Sassoon did not know whether he would be needed in action. He expected that it would be 'bloody' if he was. He had not slept for more than an hour at a time for half a week, but he was feeling 'pretty fit and cheery'. He was always energised by the prospect of action. He had been deeply disturbed by 'the most ghastly sights' since his battalion had arrived there. The dead bodies lying about the trenches and in the open were 'beyond description', particularly after rain. British shelling and bombing had left a number of mangled, shelled-twisted Germans around the place. And everywhere there were British corpses, most of them shot through the head. Sassoon fully expected to be killed the following morning.[30]

There was a barrier in the tunnel, with Germans on the other side. This, so Sassoon was informed, would have to be climbed over. 'Could anything be less pleasant?' he put it in his *Regimental Records* description. The underground part of the attack was later cancelled. SS had 'not the faintest idea', as he put it, of what he had to do. He was required to send in a written plan to battalion headquarters. Fortunately, he met up with Ralph Greaves, who was better informed and wrote out a schedule for him.[31]

Siegfried Sassoon's *Regimental Records* log runs from 3 a.m. on Monday, 16 April. He was with the Cameronians' Colonel underground when news came that the Cameronians had been 'driven back after advancing a little way'.

Sassoon put on his helmet and announced that he was 'going to take 25 men up to the show'. He and his Sergeant, named Baldwin, got out of the tunnel and led their twenty-five, finding their way to the leader of the Cameronians, who told Sassoon that Germans were all around and that the Cameronians were out of bombs. Sassoon goes on:

> Feeling myself to be for the moment an epitome of R.W.F. [Royal Welch Fusiliers] prestige, I became unnaturally jaunty and unconcerned. 'But where are the Germans?' I asked. 'I can't see any Germans!' He looked a little embarrassed. My behaviour became more and more patronising and complacent. 'All right,' I remarked, 'You needn't bother – we'll see to all this!' Or words to that effect.[32]

Leaving Sergeant Baldwin to organise the collecting of Mills bombs, Sassoon made contact with a Corporal Smart of the Cameronians, who had a bag of bombs. The two advanced along the trench. Sassoon was shocked to come across 'a young, fair-haired Cameronian private lying propped against the wall, in a pool of his own blood, his eyes open staring vacantly at the sky'. He went on with the corporal, throwing bombs and advancing, the corporal 'much more artful and efficient than I'. (Sassoon's companion evidently moved more cautiously.) 'Between us', says Sassoon's account, 'we created a considerable demonstration of offensiveness.' The objective (as reported by the corporal) was reached. Sassoon comments: 'I had caught an occasional glimpse of a retreating German, but the whole thing had been so absurdly easy I felt like going on still farther…My overstrained nerves had stirred me to such a pitch of febrile excitement that I felt capable of the most suicidal exploits.'[33]

His adrenalin rush was enhanced by revenge motivation for the young Cameronian. Sassoon paid the price of a classic mistake. During a lull he poked his head out of a narrow evacuation which he had been exploring. He described in *Memoirs of an Infantry Officer*:

> No sooner had I popped my silly head out of the sap than I felt a stupendous blow in the back between my shoulders. My first notion was that a bomb had hit me from behind, but what had really happened was that I had been sniped from the front.[34]

Siegfried Sassoon was 'no good for about a quarter of an hour'. When he came round, he wanted to make a new attack. He could not because the operation was halted. Elsewhere it had failed. His section in *Regimental Records* ends: 'I was back in the tunnel within four hours of leaving it.'[35]

A major omission on the part of the Sassoon biographers is reference to the account of the operation in the memoir of Frank Richards, *Old Soldiers Never Die*. A signaller with the Royal Welch Fusiliers throughout the war, Richards relates:

> ...The following morning one hundred bombers of the Battalion under the command of Mr Sassoon were sent to the Cameronians to assist in a bombing attack on the Hindenburg Trench on our right. A considerable part was captured but was lost again when the enemy made a counter attack. During the operations Mr Sassoon was shot through the top of the shoulder. Late in the day I was conversing with an old soldier who had taken part. He said, "God strike me pink, Dick, it would have done your eyes good to have seen young Sassoon in that bombing stunt. It was a bloody treat to see the way he took the lead. He was the best officer I have seen in the line or out since Mr Fletcher...If he don't get the Victoria Cross for this stunt I'm a bloody Dutchman; he thoroughly earned it this morning." This was the universal opinion of everyone who had taken part ...He hadn't been long with the Battalion, but long enough to win the respect of every man who knew him.[36]

The failed attack was on Fontaine-les-Croiselles, a village 15 kilometres south-east of Arras. Siegfried Sassoon's diary summary of this time is laconically entitled 'The Sleepless Days'.[37]

# Chapter 6

# Hospital Reading

The injured Siegfried Sassoon was returned to England for recuperation. He was sent to the 4th London General Hospital, as it was called in the listing of hospitals in England receiving the war wounded and ill. This one was on Denmark Hill. Sassoon's 20 April 1917 'Arrival' report has, under 'Cause of Return': 'G.S.W. [gunshot wound] (Right Shoulder)'.

Sassoon of course had his notebooks. On 23 April he wrote 'In the Ward: Morning'. This is a journalist-mode physical description incorporating a social and psychological survey of the ward's inmates. It was a large, light room with tall windows. Siegfried lists flowers: daffodils, primroses, red lilies and tulips. Evidently thought and effort had gone into making this environment as pleasant as possible. This was a ward for officers. The class division into officers and rank-and-file which so permeated the Army did not neglect hospitals. Sunshine slanted through the windows onto the forty white beds. The men were smoking and reading newspapers – these no doubt with vast amounts about the progress or otherwise of the various war fronts, with the regular optimistic spin. A gramophone was blaring raucously down the ward. SS was not an enthusiast for its pop offerings. Music selection was judicious: sentimental songs like 'Somewhere a voice is calling' going with the evening glow of the lamps. In the morning the noise was vibrant: 'Everybody's doing it' and 'At the Fox-trot ball'. Some of the officers were shuttling to and from their ablutions and shaving. In the Army permitted moustache size went conventionally with rank: full-bushy-handlebar was frowned on below the top brass. Lip bristles were a badge of rank. Sassoon's account speaks of 'contented faces'. The men were out of the killing fields, for a while at least. 'War-shop chat' was for later in the day. In the morning the energy and desire for that were not there.[1]

There were no bad wounds in the ward. The hospital specialised in neurological, battle-stress cases. Sassoon called his fellow-patients: 'the lucky ones, whom a few days of peace have washed clean of the squalor and misery and strain of ten days ago', but perhaps they were suffering inwardly more than he realised.

On 24 April Siegfried wrote to Hamo. His uncle will have been startled when an Army note jumped out of the envelope: **Kit of S. Sassoon 2RWF Wounded.** His nephew's letter had the detail:

> I was very nearly your late nephew. The sniper only just failed to make a good job of it. The bullet missed my jugular by a fraction of an inch and the spinal column by not too much.[2]

His letter was in unusually frank mode:

> I think another dose of the war will just about send me dotty. I get the horrors at night when I see the corpses again; last week was beyond anything I had been up against before.

This was not Sig's usual cheery-soldier chat. Hamo's nephew was in post-battle trauma. It was the experience of so many. The outcome of the war would be a generation of ex-soldiers – those who survived – for whom, behind the conventional stiff upper lip of not talking about it, mental disturbance was commonplace.

Among the letters that reached Sassoon was one dated 21 April from Robert Graves, writing from No. 4 Officer Cadet Battalion, Wadham College, Oxford. Robert was now an instructor. Lung weakness made him unfit for further active service. The cadet training job was suiting him well and he was dreaming about Siegfried joining him:

> At last I am comfortably settled down here, and by Heaven, it's a good game now that I'm cured of the desire to go back to France. I know I'm more use here and would only crock up if I tried a fourth time and if it wasn't for you being out there again I'd feel this was too good to be true. Get a cushy quick and I'll work this sort of a job for you here. Anyhow, get sent to Somerville if you get over to Blighty at all: in time to read your reviews with me.[3]

The news of Sassoon caught up with Graves a day later. He wrote again. His scheme for his friend was firming up:

> Sassons, if you can tell me about your sickleave, etc., and when you'll be fit for light duty I could get you a job in a cadet battalion: possibly here but certainly somewhere nice (Cambridge?), through my colonel.[4]

Sometimes in the hospital it was as if Siegfried Sassoon was still on the Western Front. His notebook has 'In the Ward (ii)'. This is the night. The gramophone is off. The lights are out. It is not completely dark because fires glow here and there in their grates, casting shadows. In the beds, huddled drowsy figures are outstretched. Now come the visions. The account has: 'Then the horrors come creeping across the floor.' Sassoon sees around the ward 'parcels of dead flesh and bones'. Faces glare at the ceiling. 'A livid grinning face' peers at him, clutching his sheets. The apparition is silent. The corpses look at him reproachfully. He is lucky with his safe Blighty wound. He is where they wanted to be when they were listening to the din of the bombardment before the start of the attack. He, by contrast with them, is 'in the kindly immunity of the hospital'. The scene has a terrible finale:

One boy, an English private in full battle order, crawls to me painfully on hands and knees, and lies gasping at the foot of my bed; he is fumbling in his tunic for a letter; just as he reaches forward to give it me his head lolls sideways and he collapses on the floor; there is a hole in his jaw, and the blood spreads across his white face like ink spilt on blotting-paper.[5]

Sassoon cannot sleep. He wishes he could.

For some who had been on the battlefields the flashbacks would never completely cease. Harry Patch, last surviving British Western Front soldier (several months in 1917) would be troubled by sudden light at night in his care home when he was well over a hundred years old.[6]

Sassoon was at Denmark Hill for a couple of weeks. His reply to Robert Graves gave vent to his indignation about the Western Front:

> It makes me mad to think of all the good men being slaughtered this summer, – and all for nothing. The bloody politicians and ditto Generals with their cursed incompetent blundering and callous ideas will go on till they are tired of it, or have got all the kudos they want. I wish I could do something to protest against it. If I shot the Premier or Douglas Haig – (or even Frankie Lloyd!!) they would only shut me up in a mad-house. If I refuse – as a protest – to go out again to commit suicide, they'll accuse me of being afraid of shells. Do you believe we shall be any better off by the end of this summer of carnage? We'll never break their lines. So far, in April, we've lost more men than the Germans. The Canadians at Vimy lost appallingly. Yet the official communiqués lied unblushingly about the casualties.[7]

Who is the presumably very important Frankie Lloyd? Biographical delving turns up a surprise. He was a British (later American) film director, prolific in the 'silent' (but sometimes noisy) era. How could Lloyd be responsible for the killing fields? Until 2018 there would have been no answer to this question – plenty about the filming of the Battle of the Somme, that new development in media of this war, but nothing about soldiers watching films. But a recent television documentary has revealed the almost entirely forgotten Western Front industry of keeping soldiers happy with cinematograph shows in unused buildings behind the lines. The equipment did not have to be shifted about too much with the near-static lines. Thousands queued to see the latest releases. Officers viewed with the men. Anyone out there would have known who Frank Lloyd was. His offerings had romance, glamour, suspense and adventure. The ferried in film-reels distracted soldiers from thinking about being killed, mutilated or mentally damaged. They would find distraction as they squashed in to catch The World and the Woman, Sins of her Parent, Heart of a Lion, or whatever. The movie-houses were the circuses in Western Front bread and circuses.[8]

Before he put his letter in its envelope, Sassoon added a thought:

> I am sending a copy of *The Old Huntsman* to Sir D. Haig – Rather a joke – He can't stop me doing <u>that</u> anyhow and of course he'll use it in his W.C.

Two days into his stay at the hospital Siegfried Sassoon wrote in his diary 'To the Warmongers'. It opens: 'I'm back again from hell with loathsome thoughts to sell.' It has: 'For you our battles shine with triumph half-divine.' 'You' are the establishment who were keeping the war going. This was Sassoon's most political poem so far. In 1925 Sir Edward Troup, after a career as Permanent Secretary to the Home Office, wrote a book on his department. It concludes with a reflection on the King coming out of the Home Office on each anniversary of the Armistice to lay a wreath at the foot of the Cenotaph and to share with his people remembrance of 'The Glorious Dead' of the monument's inscription. The phrase constitutes the final words of Troup's book. Here in this poem is Siegfried Sassoon's refutation, delivered in April 1917, of glory in slaughter.[9]

The phrase 'The Glorious Dead' is of uncertain origin. The suggestion that it came from Rudyard Kipling is unsupported. The words were apparently selected by Sir Edwin Lutyens, the architect of the Cenotaph memorial (which was erected between 1928 and 1932) but it seems that Lutyens was not the author. The source is unknown. Wherever the phrase came from, hypnotic though it may be, the thesis that the carnage of the First World War may be seen as glorious is refuted by Siegfried Sassoon's poetry. Sorrow and tribute are powerfully there but the notion of glory out of the killing-fields, which was so heavily promoted at the time, is surely dispelled by Sassoon's testimony.[10]

News was reaching Sassoon of what was happening to those left behind. He told Robert Graves in his letter: 'It's b---y about the 2nd Battalion.' Among the recent casualties was a young officer called Robert Hanmer (wounded), on whom SS doted. Hanmer's attractions included his fair hair and boyish simple tastes.

Sassoon fantasised about rescuing Bobbie in battle. He had known Hanmer in the pre-war world of hunting.

In Sassoon's hospital poetry, a general makes an eponymous generic appearance. A couple of soldiers meet him on the road to Arras, the grim route that SS knew well. The chief is pleasant to the pair, greeting them with Good Mornings. Harry and Jack appreciate this as they slog along their way, burdened under their equipment packs (which of course officers did not have to carry). It seems to be a happy sort of poem. But the pleasant scene is followed by an ominous pause of a blank line. Then we learn that The General 'did for' Harry and Jack with his plan of attack. The extra line after an apparent concluding couplet lands the Sassoon end-punch. His colloquialisms are effective in delivering the Army common-man. 'Did for them' was originally 'murdered': Sassoon took advice to alter this. *Memoirs* is spiced with sarcasm about generals. At one point, the 'George Sherston' narrator touches on scenes at a top brass military conference at a chateau, where creature comfort is not spared. Some of the participants are making their way to luncheon, taking 'a little relaxion after their intellectual effort'. Sherston hopes that they will loosen their belts to make room for the food.[11]

Where did Sassoon's poetic satire come from? He wrote in *Siegfried's Journey*:

> Nothing I had written before 1916 showed any symptom of this development. It was as if I had suddenly found myself to be an expert boxer without having undergone any training…I merely chanced on the device of composing two or three harsh, peremptory, and colloquial stanzas with a knock-out blow in the last line. And having brought off my effect once or twice, I was urged by Robbie to do it as often as I could.[12]

With time on his hands in hospital, Siegfried Sassoon read Bertrand Russell's *Justice in War-Time.* Russell had been anti-war from the start. He had been prosecuted under the Defence of the Realm Act for an anti-conscription pamphlet, as well as being dismissed from his post at Trinity College, Cambridge. He was also banned by the authorities from lecturing in South Wales on political philosophy. Sassoon acknowledged Lady Ottoline's gift of the book on 26 April:

> I am reading the book which makes me feel worse than ever about the useless slaughter which is going on. O <u>it's monstrous!</u> The papers are crammed with lies about the battle.[13]

The book was a series of essays. Russell wrote:

> …All the Great Powers of Europe have precisely the same objects: territory, trade and prestige. In pursuit of these objects no one of the Great Powers shrinks from wanton aggression, war and chicanery… We and [Germany] alike have been immoral in aim and brutal in method, each in the exact degree which was thought to be to the national advantage. If either they or we had loftier aims or less brutal methods, the war might have been avoided.[14]

He examined critically the policy of the Entente in the years up to 1914. He argued that British foreign policy ought to be more democratic. The concealment (suspected) of a military understanding, with commitments, between Britain and France, had been bitterly resented before the war by Liberal backbenchers and by Labour. Russell thought that the first step of British foreign policy should be 'to announce that the British Empire is large enough, and that we intend not to occupy any new parts of the earth's surface.' At this time the secret treaties and agreements, including the Treaty of London of 1915 (which brought Italy onto the Allied side with territorial promises) and the Sykes-Picot agreement of 1916 (which aimed to divide the Middle-East between Britain and France) were no more than suspicions but they were strong ones. The pacts would be revealed in Britain later in 1917 by the *Manchester Guardian* newspaper, following the second Russian revolution and the opening by the Bolsheviks of the government archives. Siegfried Sassoon will have heard Philip Morrell and others talking at Garsington about what was suspected regarding Allied behind-the-scenes agreements.[15]

As ever, Ottoline Morrell was thinking about how to brighten Siegfried Sassoon's environment. In his letter Siegfried told her:

> Flowers arrived last night. I like the smell [of the] leaves best. Here it's all war-jabber and raucous gramophone. But the people are very sweet to me – and the sunlight comes in at the 24 tall windows, and dazzles the flowers that shine in crowds along the Ward.[16]

Sassoon told Ottoline that he had 'done the best "horrible" poem I shall ever do'. This was about his experience in the Hindenburg tunnel. It ends with a description of himself climbing up the steps through the darkness into the twilight, 'Unloading hell behind him, step by step'. 'Hell' echoes an Ottoline Morrell journal entry of 20 February 1917. In bold ink, standing alone, is: **Hell – Black Dirty Hell 1917**. This year, 'Hell' was a word in regular currency. Sassoon's Hindenburg Tunnel poem is untitled in his notebook. It would later become 'The Rear-Guard'.[17]

A publication sceptical about the Government's war purposes (though its editorials were discreet) was the *Nation*, which was influential in Liberal circles. The journal was starting to publish Siegfried Sassoon. Robert Graves was amused (but no doubt pleased) that he and Sassoon were in the same issue. The column was headed 'TWO POEMS BY SOLDIERS'. These were SS's 'Died of Wounds' and Graves's 'The Last Post'. Meanwhile Sassoon's first book (apart from his privately published ones) was due out soon, with some of his anti-war poetry in it. If a good write-up could be landed in the *Nation* for *The Old Huntsman*, it could seriously stimulate the book's sales prospects.[18]

*The Old Huntsman* had been held up by a paper shortage. The German blockade and the sinking of ships were having serious effects: not only food was rationed. But now Sassoon's poetry collection had a launch date, 8 May 1917. This would turn out to be the week when mutiny broke out in sections of the French Army.

*Huntsman* was dedicated to Thomas Hardy. Sassoon states in *Siegfried's Journey* that:

> The collection which Mr Heinemann had accepted contained very little that could offend sensitive opinion. Most of it was idyllic and graceful, and the war pieces were mainly descriptive. …There were less than a dozen poems in satiric vein.'

This categorisation is disingenuous. Did the fact that another war against Germany was in progress influence Sassoon's representation? Anyone flicking through the book would soon see that some of its content aimed to shock. The first eleven pages are the 'The Old Huntsman' pastoral epic pre-dating the war poetry. Thereafter the majority of the poems are from Sassoon's war output. The first such, 'Absolution', with 'We are the happy legion', will not have troubled the war faithful. The next, 'Brothers', seems to be onside with glorification: a 'laurell'd head' and 'victory' and the vow 'I shall fight'. The next, 'The Dragon and the Undying', presents a 'Dragon lusting to break the loveliness of spires'. This depiction of war's destructiveness is still not really negative: we hear that the dead are 'dawn-lit trees'. There is no rocking of the orthodoxy. The next poem, 'France', with 'harmonies from Heaven' and 'voices of victory and delight' is entirely respectable. And then there is 'To Victory' (strategically dedicated to Edmund Gosse), with no subversive content. A non-war poem follows, expressing Sassoon's distaste for cocktail bars. Then the mood darkens·

With 'Golgotha' we have a 'huddled sentry', guns booming in the 'whistling night' and 'the brown rats, the nimble scavengers'. Then it is downhill for glorious-war. Page 20 has 'A Mystic as Soldier', bewailing that God now has to be sought where 'death outnumbers life'. Enthusiasts for the elimination of Germans can be encouraged by 'The Kiss' on the next page, provided that it is not interpreted satirically. Then the book settles into savage satire, with 'In the Pink', 'Blighters, 'Two Hundred Years After' and 'The One-Legged Man'. Some non-war early lyrical verse is tucked in, but the nature of the intended message leaves no doubt. The final poem, 'A Letter Home' dedicated to Robert Graves, is mystical.

Siegfried wanted to survive and he wanted Robert to survive. In 'A Letter Home' he is expressing defiance of the battlefield lottery. Such is the ending note of the collection, but it is the anti-war poems that set the book's message.

Among the epigrammatic poems are several of those that Sassoon composed in the late autumn of 1916 in England while observing the Home Front scene. The cleverly titled "They" (31 October 1916) is about the war-trumpet churchmen:

> The Bishop tells us: "When the boys come back
> "They will not be the same; for they'll have fought
> "In a just cause: they lead the last attack
> "On Anti-Christ; their comrades' blood has bought
> "New right to breed an honourable race.
> "They have challenged Death and dared him face to face."

The boys reply that none of them are the same. The change is not what the bishop had in mind:

> "...George lost both his legs; and Bill's stone-blind;
> "Poor Jim's shot through the lungs and like to die;
> "And Bert's gone syphilitic; you'll not find
> "A chap that served and hasn't found some change."

It ends:

> And the Bishop said: "The ways of God are strange!"

The poem is meant to disturb. 'Bought' is a deliberate variant on 'won', 'bought it' being military slang for being killed. 'Syphilitic', a nod to the sex industry around the Western Front, makes its first appearance in English verse. Sassoon described in *Siegfried's Journey* how he came to write the poem. Robert Ross had read to him a speech in the paper by a bishop who claimed that young men who went to the front came back with their souls purified. The poem came to

Sassoon 'in a fine frenzy' as he was falling asleep. He scribbled it down, polishing it the next day. He called it 'the most publicly effective poem I had yet written.'[19]

Another sardonic composition that makes it into *The Old Huntsman* is 'The Tombstone-Maker':

> ...He eyed the Cemetery across the road –
> "There's scores of bodies out abroad, this while,
> "That should be here by rights; they little know'd
> "How they'd get buried in such wretched style."

With a neat twist, the poem makes room for one of the numerous items of war mythology:

> I told him, with a sympathetic grin,
> That Germans boil dead soldiers down for fat;
> And he was horrified. "What shameful sin!
> "Oh sir, that Christian men should come to that."[20]

This story is illustrated by an April 1917 cartoon in *Punch*. The German Kaiser, in full regalia not forgetting a spike-topped German helmet, has before him an undersized, timorous-looking new entrant to the German Army. Looking at the lad, he points grimly in the direction of the window. Through it we see a factory-like building with a polysyllabic German name beginning kadav-. The Kaiser tells the youth: 'And don't forget that your Kaiser will find a use for you – alive or dead.' This must be the supposed German 'corpse factory', a plant allegedly for processing dead soldiers (the Germans' own as well as Allied corpses that came their way) into lubricating oil and pig-food. The source seems to have been a Berlin newspaper's use of the word 'kadaver' in a report on the utilisation of animal carcases, this being wrongly interpreted in Britain as referring to human bodies. At House of Commons question-time on 30 April 1917 a Conservative MP wanted the reports circulated in eastern countries, including Germany's Turkish ally, where they would have a high shock value. Governmental intelligence was instructed to produce a pamphlet. Leonard Outhwaite chipped in to ask whether the Government was aware of the 'anxiety and misery' caused by the reports for British people who had lost their sons on the battlefield and feared that their bodies might be processed. Outhwaite did not believe the stories, but he was ready to try any line that might get the slaughter stopped.[21]

Robert Graves had a preview of *The Old Huntsman*. 'Died of Wounds', he said, 'knocks me more every time.'[22]

Sassoon's injury was nearly healed. He expected to go to a convalescent home for three weeks. In due course he would have to return to France, unless an alternative appeared. He remarked in his letter to Graves that all his hospital visitors were urging him not to go back. He called that 'only a beautiful dream':

> I'll have to go on till they kill me dead. But the thought of going back now is agony, just when I've got back into the light again – "Oh Life, O Sun!"

SS is quoting from Graves's poem 'Escape', commemorating his survival after being reported dead. He himself was not in a good way. He told Graves that he was 'beastly weak and in a rotten state of nerves'.[23]

Away from the Western Front, and with the stimulus of his political education at Garsington, Siegfried Sassoon was taking opportunities to become more knowledgeable about the politics around the war. Bertrand Russell's book helped. On 2 May Sassoon was allowed out of the hospital for the first time. He lunched with Robbie Ross at the Reform Club and talked there to H.G. Wells and Arnold Bennett. He liked Bennett. In his diary he called him 'very affable'. Writing to Uncle Hamo, he described the novelist as 'a jolly creature, with his kindly cockneyfied air, and inimitable way of pursing up his mouth after delivering some oracular remark.' Hamo, perhaps surprisingly, liked his nephew's book. He called it 'stunning'. He was particularly impressed by the war poems.[24]

Sassoon also took a bus to Piccadilly Circus to have a restaurant meal with his fellow bomber Julian Dadd, who was on leave. Julian and Siegfried were amused to find their bottle of Hock reduced in price because of its German association. Germanophobia was in full spate. Dachshund dogs were shunned; German-type food names were changed; the Royal Family shed Saxe-Coburg-Gotha in favour of Windsor. De-Germanification was a patriotic passion. At the fighting front it was ridiculed. Liberal MP and Western Front artillery officer Richard Denman wrote to a newspaper in his Carlisle constituency:

> Your virulent armchair warrior would probably suffer some shocks if he overheard conversations of soldiers, or had to censor their letters. Today I saw in the London papers a paragraph telling how a sentimental lady, after listening to *Parsival*, rose in the concert hall and shouted, 'I protest against German music being played while Englishmen are being slaughtered by the Germans'. I read this out to three fellow-officers. One of them laughed at the excellence of the joke. Another remarked, 'how --- silly'.[25]

Sassoon and Dadd would have agreed. At their meal they talked war shop:

> Old So-and-so had been wounded; poor old Somebody had been killed in the Bullecourt show; old Somebody Else was still commanding B Company.

Dadd's cheeriness was belied by 'the haunted unhappy look which he had acquired since the Delville Wood attack last autumn'. Second-Lieutenant Dadd would survive the war but a brother had fallen on the Somme and another brother had been lost at Gallipoli. He himself would be voice-damaged by a bullet in his throat. Decades later he would commit suicide, one of quite a large number of First World War veterans who took their own lives long after the war. At this meal, as the two men talked, while 'remaining loyal to the realities of our war experience', as Sassoon put it, each kept their 'separate psychological secrets' to themselves.[26]

Individuality within the war is expressed by a poem that Sassoon wrote later this year, entitled 'Their Frailty'. Someone had a 'Blighty wound': making him 'safe'. That made war fine. Mothers, wives and sweethearts didn't care so long as 'he's all right'. With the limits to soldier bonding, Dadd could not share the inner depression with which a Delville Wood engagement had left him.[27]

Sassoon left the restaurant 'without having uttered a single anti-war sentiment'. His thoughts had to be kept within his brain – except in certain company. Meanwhile the Archbishop of Canterbury delivered a pronouncement regarding the Christian injunction not to labour on Sundays. In view of the food shortage as a result of the German submarines in the Atlantic and the need for intensive agriculture, the head cleric issued permission for 'a temporary departure from the rule' in view of the emergency. 'Silly old fossil', remarked SS.[28]

# Chapter 7

# The Brasseys

Siegfried Sassoon had leave until 27 June 1917. After leaving the Demark Hill hospital he was relocated to a Marylebone hotel for 800 officers in recovery. There, he had to attend lectures on trench warfare. Among those rounded up were men who had lost limbs or their eyesight. Sassoon hated 'an awful place – very strict regulations', he told his mother. He asked a doctor if he might go to the country to continue his recuperation. The request was successful thanks to his having a letter from a Countess who headed an organisation whereby country houses received convalescent officers as guests. Sassoon was sent to the home of an elder statesman, Thomas, Earl of Brassey and his wife Sybil, Lady Brassey. This was Chapelwood Manor, at Nutley, Sussex, not far from Sassoon's own family home. He escaped the military environment of the Marylebone hotel after only three days. [1]

Sassoon wrote to Ottoline Morrell on 9 May:

> I am here for three weeks – The house belongs to the Brasseys and is nice country. Only 2 other officers here thank God.[2]

*The Old Huntsman* had been published the previous day. SS had received advance copies a week before the end of April. He told Lady Ottoline: 'My book should have reached you by now. I told Heinemann to send one to you as soon as they were ready.'

He had news:

> I have been recommended for a D.S.O. What tosh these decorations are! But I hope I get it. It will all help to make my position stronger when I start playing hell with the British Smuggery.

Here is the first inkling that Sassoon was conjuring plans for making some sort of protest. After he had completed his letter an omission struck him. He added at the top of the first page, upside down:

> Of course I got your bag. It is lovely – I received it just as we were off to the battle and that put it out of my head, so I forgot to thank you. Ungrateful wretch I am.

The succession of Garsington gifts was evidently continuing. One has to think that, while obviously Siegfried could not give thought to receipt of Ottoline's present while he was preparing for the Hindenburg Line fight, the bag might have earned more than an afterthought PS. Ottoline was used to SS's unresponsiveness. It did not stem her continuing thoughts about him. She will have seen immediately when she took in her hand the envelope from Chapelwood who the writer was. On it is the double-S, the one S on top of the other, a Sassoon signature that in later years of established fame he would have engraved in relief on desk seals. We may imagine Ottoline's heart bounding when she saw the autograph.[3]

When Siegfried wrote to his mother on 12 May he had significant news. He had been offered a job as instructor to a cadet battalion at Cambridge. Evidently, he had followed up Graves's idea, and a post was being made available for him. The letter continues that he did not know whether to take the job or not. He shared his joy at his present move, telling his mother that his lodging in 'a most delightful house' with 'old Lord Brassey and his nice middle-aged wife', suited him down to the ground. He was enjoying hearing a cuckoo at dawn as he woke, and a scolding blackbird in the garden trees, familiar sounds heralding the loved chorus of nature. And yet part of him wanted to be back at the battle. He put the paradox in *Memoirs*: he would like to be back in the trenches for a few hours, since they were more interesting than Lady Brassey's rose-garden. The war had 'a sombre and unforgettable fascination'. He had become one of 'its bondsmen'. He would like again to take part in 'some exciting little exploit'. He could not deny that the emotional experience through which he had lived in France was intense.[4]

We may note here Sassoon's diary:

> May 13, 3.30 a.m. (in a white bedroom at Chapelwood Manor)
> This notebook began not many miles from Arras in the bloody month of April, when guns began to bellow. And now my disciplined wanderings have sent me to a very pleasant country house, where perfect good taste prevails, and nobody sleeps in the clothes he wore last week and this.[5]

Lord Brassey ('Lord Asterisk' in *Memoirs of an Infantry Officer*), 81 years-old, eldest son of a railway magnate, was a former Liberal MP and had been Civil Lord of the Admiralty (and he was the founder of the *Naval Annual*). He had also been Governor of Victoria. There was another circumstance of Lord Brassey. He was an advocate of peace by negotiation. There were not many such in Parliament. It was a most remarkable chance that Siegfried Sassoon, already introduced to the Morrell family of peace promoters, found himself lodging with this particular member of the House of Lords. Brassey is mentioned in the memoirs of the German liberal politician Prince Max of Baden, who wrote regarding the early summer of 1916: 'A man like Lord Brassey comes down openly for a peace of understanding with Germany.' Brassey is mentioned by Arthur Ponsonby in a letter to fellow peace group MP Charles Trevelyan on 2 June 1916. Ponsonby told Trevelyan that he had set a new group of MPs going in the promotion of the cause and that they were hoping to get some more peers too: Brassey was a target because of his peace inclination.[6]

It is no surprise with Lord Brassey's Admiralty history, that he was, or had been, inclined to the peace-making camp. In the years before the war there was little Admiralty enthusiasm for the sending of a British Expeditionary Force to conduct land operations in Europe. In 1911 a switch of personnel in the cabinet had been required as a result of the Agadir crisis. Winston Churchill, who was keen on a British European land war, was moved from the Home Office to the Admiralty, to replace Reginald McKenna, who shied away from a British continental war. Traditional Admiralty thinking was that Britain and its Empire were best kept safe by British world naval supremacy, and that land war adventures should be avoided.

Siegfried Sassoon scribbled down in his diary his close-quarters observations of Thomas Brassey. He noted Brassey's physical decline: 'serene old age going downhill too fast'. The peer was bent-double with rheumatics. Sometimes he seemed to Sassoon to be querulous, in childish fashion. And yet the once great statesman was still there. He could be oracular and urbane. 'Death presses him hard' was Sassoon's prognostication, and indeed Brassey would be dead in February 1918, but he was not finished yet, nor was he necessarily done with politics. He went to London frequently and he was in touch with parliamentary affairs. Siegfried Sassoon's biographers and others have missed the importance of this politician.[7]

What about Brassey's anti-war tendency? *Memoirs of an Infantry Officer* preserves a dinner remark which puts the Earl clearly in the dissenter school:

> As for Belgium, he invoked the evidence of history to support him in his assertion that its 'redemption' by the Allies was merely a manifestation of patriotic obliquity. The inhabitants of Belgium would be just as happy as a German Subject-State. To the vast majority of them their national autonomy meant nothing.[8]

This highly doubtful view was blasphemy as far as the establishment's crusade was concerned. Day and night the requirement of the liberation of Belgium from the Germans was proclaimed, with (real) German atrocities in the early days of the invasion of Belgium regularly revisited, with much play also of the extensive catalogue of foul German deeds, many of them mythical (but of course by no means all), in the Bryce Report, published in 1915. This looked like a royal commission but was not, since it gathered unsubstantiated tales without verification. Germanophobia was easily stoked. Many of the stories were debunked after the war. A misfortune of this was that in the Second World War there was scepticism at first about reports of the holocaust. What about atrocities on the Allied side? Siegfried Sassoon would have something to say on this subject, as we shall see. In 1914 Sassoon, in common with most people, had followed uncritically the ethical *casus belli* of the Allies' war as the defence of 'plucky Belgium' against the aggression of an over-mighty brute. As was later admitted by some promoters of the war, the primary British war motive was not chivalry for Belgium (a cause that appealed more to backbench Liberals and Labour) but to look after the interests of the British Empire. It should be added that the parliamentary peace-by-negotiation group was solidly and unequivocally behind the liberation of Belgium as a necessary requirement of a peace settlement. Its members were confident that this could be achieved.[9]

A possible indication of Lord Brassey's negativity on the war is to be found in a Sassoon letter to Edmund Gosse in which he describes Brassey as 'very woeful on the subject of the war', but SS does not elaborate. The views of Brassey's wife, Sybil, Lady Brassey, were very different from those of her husband. The daughter of an earl, she was Thomas's second wife. She did not share her husband's desire for a negotiated settlement. Her zeal was for clear-cut victory. She made her attitude on the war clear to Siegfried Sassoon. In his diary, SS has a piece entitled 'A Conversation', dated 15 May 1917. There are no names but it cannot be other than an exchange with Sybil. It makes for fairly breath-taking reading. The conversation starts with Siegfried declaring his status: 'Twice he had been to the war, and twice he had come home wounded; and now his friends had half-persuaded him to take a "safe job".' Siegfried was evidently on the way to accepting the cadet-trainer post. The account continues:

> She listened to him, with her grey hair and tired white face, kind, aristocratic and emotionless, leaning a little forward over a piece of embroidery. She represented the patrician distinctions that he had fought for – the climbing woods and green fields that soldiers learn to love when death is over them. She was a Great Lady. And he was only a poet; but he knew that life was

> taking shape in his heart, and reputation a thing of small value compared with his hidden passion for utterance and truth and beauty.[10]

The notion of the soldier making his sacrifice in defence of a quintessentially English landscape was a potent one. Siegfried Sassoon had his moments of being touched by it. His August 1916 meandering around Burford's Oxfordshire fields inspired a thought preserved in *Siegfried's Journey*:

> It was the first time that I had fully realized what it meant to be well away from the war, and [the] serenity [of the English scene] seemed well worth preserving by such obscure personal efforts as one had managed to make.[11]

It was not at this time his driving passion. This was 'longing for life', not 'mystical joy in the idea of sacrifice'.

The 1914–1915 cult of insouciance in the face of death in battle of public-school educated young men, which saw a holocaust of this class, had caught up with Sassoon late. He had lived it and nearly died it but he was now in favour of life. Lady Brassey rejected his viewpoint: She combined belief in the supremacy of aristocracy, the war-to-the-finish crusade and life-beyond-death spiritualism. The combination of faiths worked for her. Sassoon dared to tell Sybil that for him life was preferable to the Roll of Honour. Siegfried's Chapelwood sojourn had produced a remarkable quirk. Having come to stay at the house of a man who the previous year had been courted as a good prospect by promoters of peace-by-negotiation, he was assailed by the man's wife with the argument that victory over the Germans was more important than the lives and limbs of young men – unless they were heirs to a serous title, with 'a place'. That was her exception – because the aristocratic lines had to ensure their transmission with their estates into the next generation. As for the war dead, there was Lady Brassey's belief in continuing existence in a spirit world. Séance holding thrived, providing comfort for some of the bereaved in their trauma. Sassoon has some soldier ghosts in his poem 'Two Hundred Years After':

> ...But when he'd told his tale, an old man said
> That *he'd* seen soldiers pass along that hill;
> "Poor, silent things, they were the English dead
> "Who came to fight in France and got their fill."[12]

Sassoon was scornful of supposed communing with dead soldiers. A book had come out called *Raymond*, by the scientist Oliver Lodge, whose son had been killed in 1915. The book has Lodge's claimed communication with Raymond through mediums and Raymond's detailed reports on his life in the beyond. Sassoon wrote in his diary on 23 January 1917 about 'a bitter attack on Oliver Lodge's spook book in the *Daily Mail*'. He commented:

> Stuff like *Raymond* repels me utterly, having discovered the fatuity of it in my own case, and watched that pathetic, foolish clinging to the dead which goes on among so many women who (like my own mother) have nothing else to distract their minds from war and wretchedness.[13]

It is difficult not to think that Sassoon's patronisingly dismissive attitude towards his mother and her life reflects the male-centredness of his world.

At Chapelwood, Sassoon had a particular reason for thinking about his dead brother, Hamo. He had a letter from the retired form-master of Marlborough's Army Class. John Bain wrote poetic laments to honour fallen alumni. Over seven hundred old boys and staff of Siegfried's school lost their lives in the First World War, the death-rate being matched in the honour rolls of other leading public schools. Peter Parker, the historian who explored the extraordinary sociology of the public schools at war, says that Bain 'filled the columns of the *Marlburian* with sporting elegies of his former pupils.' These were sincerely meant but, as Parker puts it, employed 'an egregious banality of imagery and expression' (a grimmer game'...'old England called'...'death or glory'...'a nobler fame than bat and ball'). Siegfried's reply to Bain was friendly: 'Your verses have touched me deeply.' He was glad of the invitation to help to perpetuate the memory of his brother. He told Bain: 'I know how enormously it will please my old mother [Theresa was sixty-three] – who is nearly worn out with war and worry.' Theresa was a follower of spiritualism. Siegfried wanted less of the retired teacher's bland sentimentality (as in asking him to get rid of 'lovely') and more artistic edge. He suggested (in view of Hamo's marine burial): 'sleeps beneath an alien sea'.[14]

Sassoon brooded on the cadet training job. He told a friend: 'Haven't done anything about Cambridge.' The dilemma was left hanging. He had not actually been offered the post but apparently it was there for the taking if he applied (provided that his superiors assented). In his diary of 21 May, SS viewed it as taking a job in England, 'till "my nerves" are right'. Sybil Brassey with her blunt charm told him that she did not want him 'dangling about, writing poetry'. This diary entry signals a possible direction, about which hints were starting to appear:

> ...I think I'd better go back to the First Battalion as soon as possible, unless I can make some protest against the War.[15]

Two days later Sassoon wrote to literary acquaintance Henry Festing Jones, telling him that he was 'convalescing here with some success'. He said that he expected to go back to France about August, adding: 'though I hate the show and am convinced we are losing and that all this loss of life is sheer waste.' There is no mention of a possible protest here. The rebellion scheme was at an early and unformed stage. It was no more than a possibility.[16]

The recommendation of a new medal is mentioned a number of times in Sassoon's correspondence around this time. Evidently, his dazzling performance on the battlefield on the day of his wounding had much impressed his commander. On an unidentifiable Saturday in May, Siegfried wrote to Roderick Meiklejohn, a civil servant friend who was in the Robbie Ross circle:

> No news of medals but the Colonel writes to thank me "on behalf of the Battallion" [sic] – Lord knows what that's for!![17]

He knew very well. He told John Bain: 'I've been recommended for a D.S.O. (which of course will not materialise).' For so junior an officer this would be special. The Army thought highly of Sassoon. The bluster of self-deprecation in his correspondence and the comedy of his memoirs blur this – and the importance to him of his military reputation.[18]

# Chapter 8

# Speckled Eggs

Reviews of *The Old Huntsman* started to come in during Siegfried Sassoon's time at Chapelwood. The *Times Literary Supplement* on 24 May was not a propitious opener. Siegfried wrote to his mother:

> The *Times* review is a very bad one, and absolutely misses the point of the book, (probably on purpose.) The poem they quote is one of the weakest, though quite pretty. I am afraid it will make a good deal of difference to the sales, but Hardy's letter to me is quite enough to make all the reviewers look silly, (if they could only read it).[1]

Thomas Hardy was a Sassoon appreciator. He told SS: 'I much like the grim humour of "The Tombstone-Maker" and "They" [and] the pathos of 'The Hero'.[2]

The TLS reviewer failed to mention the war poetry. In a letter to Edmund Gosse, Sassoon spoke of 'an inferior reviewer who discreetly ignores everything unpleasant'.[3]

He told his uncle:

> They quote one of the weakest poems (a pretty trifle about Jesus and his Mama) – they ignore all the bitterness, which I believe to be truth – and label me as a devout and amiable Amateur.

He went on: 'Never mind; I will be a wicked poet, I will! Just to spike them!' The failure to engage the literary establishment was stoking rebellion. Sassoon confirmed the importance to him of Hardy's endorsement:

> Thomas Hardy's letter was the great event for me. It affects me more than any review could do, because he praises the grimmer verses which I know to be the significant ones. [4]

The TLS had not uttered its last word on *The Old Huntsman*. A fortnight later it carried another review – by Virginia Woolf. This one glowed. Both the lyrical poems and the epigrammatic war ones were highly commended: SS's realism in describing war was 'of the right, of the poetic kind'. Sassoon's Garsington/ Bloomsbury connection was helping him. Ottoline Morrell was watching the reception of the book and when Siegfried told her of his disappointment about the underwhelming first TLS appraisal, it is likely that she told Woolf, who was a TLS reviewer. If so, it did the trick.[5]

A reception that mattered considerably was the one accorded to the book by the doyen of liberal arts papers *The Nation*. Its editor H.W. Massingham, who underwent a shaking of his belief in the war during 1917, promoted poetry with 'no fuss, no pleas, no nonsense', his biographer tells us. H.W. himself reviewed *The Old Huntsman*, on 16 June 1917. He delivered his verdict in an article entitled 'INDIGNATION':

> It is no reflection upon [Sassoon] to say that these war-verses are not poetry, that they have nothing to do with poetry…Nor are they simply a convenient instrument for vehement rhetoric and declamation. In a word, they are epigrams, thrown deliberately into the harsh, peremptory, colloquial kind of versification which we have so often mistaken for poetry. And, to our mind, Mr Sassoon is quite right to select this method to fulfil a purpose in which every line throbs and of which every line is acutely conscious. For into this epigrammatic content, he is able to discharge the hot fluid of honest rage and scorn, heartfelt bitterness and indignation, which must read so very unconventionally, so very disagreeably to those civilians who have been so comfortably nurtured upon the war-poem of the past…[6]

Massingham does not address the question of whether upsetting the war script might be seen as unpatriotic. Sassoon was not a politician. He was a poet who happened to be a soldier. It was the quality of the work that was being examined. This passed the Massingham test with some credit.

In the review are generous excerpts from 'The One-Legged Man', 'Conscripts', 'They', 'Blighters' and 'In the Pink'. Though Massingham keeps off overt political comment, his view is there in a passing general remark:

> Truth about the actual conditions of the war is objectionable because of the deadly criticism that, like the dagger under a cloak, underlies it.

The Western Front was literally unspeakable. Siegfried Sassoon was testing the taboo. Massingham thought that Sassoon's experimental mode worked, and that it was legitimate. He was measured. The war-verses were 'by no means the fruit of genius', but they were 'dignified by the truth of anger and suffering that swells them, to a power which should do us good…' The editor also registered his protest against reviewers who by reason of patriotic tact, hostility, or whatever, ignored Sassoon's war compositions. These poems, he said, were 'like speckled eggs within a furry nest of seemly Nature-poems'. We may guess that the reviewers who were fascinated by the nesting material while not noticing the eggs were playing it safe in the jingo climate.

The issue of *The Nation* in which the review appears has much consideration of the war. Optimism was in the air. The Battle of Messines-Wytschaete Ridge had dealt the Germans a huge blow, quite literally. Nineteen mines were exploded under their frontline, with a collective explosive power of five hundred tons. Ten thousand were thought to have been killed or buried alive (screams being heard by the advancing British). The reverberations of the detonation were felt in parts of southern England. The Germans withdrew to a new line further east. But within a week the stalemate was back. As ever, there was no real breakthrough, as the cumulative slaughter continued. The *Nation* mulled over 'The Meaning of Messines', celebrating the result but adding a rider: 'We must jettison our Imperialist aims.' These were still kept from the public, but there were the suspicions. One who had no doubt about them was Siegfried Sassoon, thanks to his Garsington connections. By now he was on the brink of making the jump from poetry into politics.[7]

After its wobbly start, *The Old Huntsman* gathered some praising reviews, as well as personal applause from Sassoon's friends. Robert Graves was trying to get all Oxford's bookshops to stock it. How would Sassoon's important patron Eddie Marsh view it? Marsh was close to the war establishment. He liked idealised soldiers in literature, and as he grew older, he was becoming politically more conservative. However, Eddie was reported by Robbie Ross to be 'quite enthusiastic' about *Huntsman*. It was confirmed when Marsh wrote to Sassoon inviting him to contribute a goodly number of pieces to the next in his series of *Georgian Poetry*. Poetry of the Sassoon-type was hardly conducive to the national war message. The Government wanted ever more men to train up for the trenches. The order of the day was 'combing out' of those who had escaped service. Such was the political thrust in the summer of 1917. But in literary circles, Siegfried Sassoon's representations of battlefield horror and its human costs were being well received.

Not all the reviews of *The Old Huntsman* were friendly. A hostile assessment appeared in *The New Witness* on 28 June. The editor of this magazine was Cecil Chesterton, a socialist-turned-nationalist and an anti-Semite. The journal was aggressively vigilante, fiercely opposed to any move towards peace-making. Chesterton had led the mob which wrecked the meeting on 29 November 1915 at London's Farringdon Memorial Hall which was meant to launch the Union of Democratic Control's peace-by-negotiation campaign. *New Witness*, the *Daily Express*, *Daily Sketch*, *Evening Standard*, *Morning Post* and *John Bull*, were among regular inciters of disruption of gatherings of war dissenters. In effect, the orchestrated hooliganism was an extra arm of the Defence of the Realm Act in making sure that any serious challenge to the war was suppressed. The *New Witness* reviewer of Siegfried Sassoon was C.K. Scott Moncrieff. He had been in the Battle of Arras, winning the Military Cross: an exploding shell damaged his leg; after being hit he continued to direct his company.[8]

Why was Moncrieff in the proto-fascist environment of *The New Witness*? Perhaps he needed a living after being stood down from the Army. Perhaps he was in sympathy with the journal's outlook. At school (Winchester) he had been in trouble for publishing a homosexual story. Like Sassoon, he was gay at a time when the practice of homosexuality was illegal. But while Sassoon was non-practising, Moncrieff was a bold risk-taker in his lifestyle. He bravely spoke in court for a homosexual friend who had already been imprisoned.[9]

The *New Witness* review of *The Old Huntsman* is entitled 'The Bayreuth-Baghdad line', an anti-Semitic nudge alluding to the (as yet incomplete) railway line from Baghdad to Berlin, and to Siegfried Sassoon's Baghdad-Jewish ancestry. Elsewhere in the article is a phrase of James Elroy Flecker, 'nothing but a lot of Jews', in to make a verse-craft point but looking suspiciously placed. Moncrieff praised *Huntsman*'s non-war poems: 'Again and again in the short lyrics and the sonnets he touches perfection.' The war poems were 'regrettable': they were out of place in poetry. 'The Hero' was 'disgusting'; 'They', Moncrieff considered, 'adds nothing to the corpus of English poetry.' On 'The One-Legged Man', he thought that had he himself lost a leg as a result of his Arras injury (which he nearly did), he would not have 'made a song about it'. The critique of Sassoon's war poems is political as well as literary:

> There is none of that rare Spirit of Comradeship, that Joy of Battle, that Diviner Air which Mr Osborn breathes in Aldwych on the morning of a "Great Advance". [10]

E.B. Osborn edited a 1917 anthology of Army-authorship poems, called *The Muse in Arms*. He was literary editor of the (Conservative) *Morning Post*. Robert Graves was later derisive about Osborn's collection: the soldiers were 'all very gallant and idealistic but with hardly a poet among them'. This is unfair (and a clever conceit because Graves is in the Osborn collection) but E.B.'s introduction (and to some extent his selection) promotes the familiar notion of the moral and spiritual superiority of England over Germany, with Agincourt harked back to and the regular thread of the school games field as the training ground for military virtues.[11]

Osborn has short shrift for German war poets: not many published ones, he says, and 'nearly all flagrant rhetoric…moved by hatred of other people's countries…' In fact, German trench poets, not a large group, varied in their approach and were certainly not characterised by chauvinism and national glorification. But it would be unjust to dismiss Osborn's book as mere jingo. And Osborn rhapsodised over *The Old Huntsman* in a review for the *Morning Post*:

> If this is not a great poet, true as well as new, then I have wasted a lifetime on trying to find what is, and what it is not the sovereign stuff.[12]

Osborn's book is mentioned in Siegfried Sassoon's letter of 30 April to Robert Graves. Apparently Graves had sent Sassoon a letter to him from Osborn. Sassoon wrote:

> Thanks for Osborn's letter. Heinemann was approached about the Anthology last February and was against giving them anything. I shied at it – not wishing to strike heroic attitudes among patriot poets of the Grenfell-type. But if you think it will be a good thing, I will agree to it. I am therefore sending a note to Osborn telling him I will be pleased to let him have two poems (if Heinemann is agreeable), but stipulating that the poems shall be my own choice – If he uses any, they shall be ones like "Died of Wounds" or "Bert's gone syphilitic".[13]

'The Grenfell-type' evokes Julian Grenfell and his brother Billy, sons of famous society hostess Lady (Ettie) Grenfell, of Taplow Court, Berkshire, which was the haunt of many a leading social light, including Eddie Marsh who revelled in its gossip and tittle-tattle. It was at Taplow (sometime after the war) that Philip and Siegfried Sassoon were introduced to each other. Billy Grenfell was killed on the Western Front on 30 July 1915, leading his men in the face of machine-gun fire. Julian had already died there on 25 May 1915, from a brain injury sustained by a shell. His celebrated poem was 'Into Battle':

> …Life is Colour and Warmth and Light
> And a striving evermore for these;
> And he is dead who will not fight,
> And who dies fighting has increase.
> The thundering line of battle stands,
> And in the air Death moans and sings;
> But Day shall clasp him with strong hands,
> And Night shall fold him in soft wings.[14]

Here is the message that in the fight against the foe, death is worth it – and not so bad. However, unlike on the home front, the righteousness of 'England' and her cause are not spelled out: this could be any war. Grenfell admitted to adoring war. He wrote, it should be noted, a more subversive poem. His 1915 'A Prayer for Those on the Staff' is addressed to a red tabs officer. It concludes:

> ...See that his eggs are newly laid
> Not tinged as some of them with green
> And let no nasty drafts invade
> The windows of his limousine.[15]

That staff officer whom Grenfell had in mind was probably Philip Sassoon. The memoir of L. E. Jones picks up a moment when Philip caught the needle that bristled among service troops against the red-tabbers safely ensconced behind the lines. Philip then was personal secretary (A.D.C.) to General Rawlinson. Jones's regiment was uncomfortably camped in the grounds of Rawlinson's chateau at the time of the Battle of Loos. Out of the building stepped Philip:

> A very slim, very dapper young officer, with red tabs on his collar and shining boots, began to descend the steps.

From the shrubbery a voice rang out: 'Pheeleep! Pheeleep! I see you.' It recalled a cry that used to be heard in Balliol College in undergraduate days when one of Philip's social set, Julian Grenfell, used to torment him by cracking a whip when he saw him entering the quadrangle.[16]

Robert Graves has three poems in E.B. Osborn's book. In his 'Big Words', a soldier has declared himself 'ready to die':

> But on the firestep, waiting to attack,
> He cursed, prayed, sweated, wished the proud words back.[17]

In 'Escape', the poet wants to survive:

> "...Life, life! I can't be dead, I won't be dead:
> Damned if I'll die for anyone," I said...[18]

The Osborn book gathered Siegfried Sassoon's 'Absolution', written in his happy-warrior days, but also his, especially 'horrible', 'The Rear-Guard'. The collection is revealing. Mark Rawlinson has noted that, 'Of the forty-six poets represented in *The Muse in Arms*, fourteen were *late* poets.' The happy warriors of 1914 and 1915 were in many cases dead. The Somme marked the end of cheery optimistic valour. As Osborn himself observes, the poetry after that was different. That is reflected in his book even if the volume looks to a degree like a throwback to the earlier years of glorious crusade. The mood was changing. As Samuel Hynes stresses, the shift must not be oversimplified. There was anti-war poetry and art before the Somme and glorifying material after it. However, 1916 was pivotal. It was when the realities of war caught up with the poets and the artists. The post-war viewing of the war was starting to take shape.[19]

The reactions of the great to Sassoon's book were mixed, but leaning towards favour, though Edmund Gosse was, in Sassoon's words, 'terribly windy' about the anti-war poems. The Poet Laureate Robert Bridges, politically conservative, was reported to be 'a rare and grudging praiser'. Bridges was completely with the national crusade. He was one of Charles Masterman's literary team of war propagandists. The Robbie Ross circle's view of Bridges may perhaps be adduced from the remark by Ross on hearing that Bridges's house had burned down, that he imagined that the cause would be 'dry rot'.[20]

While Siegfried Sassoon's head was full of poetical protest about war, his mother had other things on her mind. Siegfried's letter of 26 May tells her:

> I wish you wouldn't worry about money. Send me the cursed bills and I'll see they are paid <u>at once</u>. Why should you worry yourself about things which don't matter a damn? "The County Court" is, I believe, quite an amusing show to appear at.[21]

Here is the off-handedness of the man who emptied a German trench.

# Chapter 9

# 'Wilful Defiance of Military Authority'

On 2 June 1917 Siegfried Sassoon wrote to Hamo, having been put on the spot by his distinguished uncle:

> The "Herald" is a paper I have never seen, and only vaguely heard of. I can assure you that I'm just as annoyed as you are! The verses weren't written to be used by people with the Herald point of view. They express the "fed up" feelings of an ordinary foot-soldier on his way to the line.[1]

Sassoon's 'Base Details', published in the *Cambridge Magazine* on 28 April, was in the current issue of George Lansbury's socialist, anti-war weekly *The Herald*. It was in the corner of a page chiefly occupied by TRADE UNION AND LABOUR NOTES, under news that ex-Inspector Syme, a campaigner for fairer conditions in the police force, had been re-arrested after being released from prison. Beneath 'Base Details' is the biographical detail: 'Lieutenant Sassoon, who recently received the Military Cross, has again been wounded and is now in a London hospital.' The poem, composed on 4 March, is about staff officers, 'scarlet majors' well behind the battle front, dispatching troops up the line to their deaths, meanwhile 'guzzling and gulping' at nice hotels, reading the Roll of Honour and saying with a sigh: 'Yes, we've lost heavily in this last scrap.' The concluding lines pack the Sassoon punch:

> And when the war is done and youth stone dead,
> I'd toddle safely home and die – in bed.[2]

'Base Details' arose out of days spent by Siegfried Sassoon in Rouen. For staff officers, the pleasures of trips into town were not clouded by the thought of having to go back into the line. 'Toddle' was 'waddle' in the *Cambridge Magazine*: Sassoon changed it to more realistic vernacular and to suit the tipsy state of the officers after refreshment.

Hamo was apparently furious that his nephew's verses should appear in a socialist organ. The *Daily Herald* had been founded as a strike paper in 1911. During the war it was reduced to a weekly *Herald*. Regarding the poem, Sassoon recalled in *Siegfried's Journey*:

> I went up to London resolved to write something more definitely antagonistic than satiric epigrams in *The Cambridge Magazine*, wherein I had made a lively appearance with the lines called Base Details.[3]

A new Siegfried Sassoon poem at this time called 'In an Underground Dressing-Station', about a dying soldier writhing in agony, demonstrates the development of Sassoon's increasingly radical output, graphic and with the realism of snatches of authentic conversation. This poem concludes with pathos rather than bite:

> The surgeon seemed
> So kind and gentle, saying above that crying,
> "You *must* keep still, my lad." But he was dying.[4]

Sassoon sent the poem to his friend E. J. (Edward) Dent, a music academic at Cambridge University who was involved with the *Cambridge Magazine*. Siegfried wanted it in the next issue. He believed that while it was 'too horrible', 'these healthy shocks do people good.' He shared with Dent his latest news from Arras The battalion had lost twenty-five officers since he had left them, eleven being killed; and there had been six more deaths on 28 May, that 'show' having been 'a hopeless failure', with none of the bodies recovered. The fatalities included 'two youngsters I liked very much': there was 'a bad pain in my heart today'.[5]

Sassoon convinced Dent. 'In an Underground Dressing-Station' was in the next *Cambridge Magazine*. So was 'Editorial Impressions', a satire on the taking of star writers on selectively devised tours of the trenches, from which they came back reporting that all was 'going well' and wrote about 'the amazing spirit of the troops'. Politicians also had these horror-avoiding viewings of cheerfully muddy soldiers on the Western Front.[6]

Sassoon states in *Siegfried's Journey* that after leaving Chapelwood Manor (on 4 June), he stayed at his London club. In fact, when he was not with his mother in Kent, his London residence was 40 Half Moon Street, Mayfair. He used notepaper thus printed and it was his listed home address in Army records at this time. In this house, former lady's maid Nellie Burton let rooms to 'single gentlemen'. Nellie was a bohemian, a different sort of bohemian from Ottoline Morrell. She was apt to appear in a mauve dressing-gown, cigarette in hand. The memoir's tweaking of the SS abode was no doubt in consideration of the author's respectable reputation.[7]

A difficulty now occurs in following the story of Siegfried Sassoon. At this point in *Memoirs of an Infantry Officer* there is what appears to be an extended piece of invention. The reason must be that something was needed to plug the gap caused by the author's decision to exclude Garsington Manor and the Morrell

Siegfried Sassoon c. 1916. (*Alamy*)

Lady Ottoline Morrell portrayed in 1919. (*Alamy*)

Philip Morrell.

Garsington Manor 1917.

Siegfried Sassoon while on an Army school course in May 1916 at Flixécourt, where he heard the Campbell lecture on bayonet fighting.

Robert Graves c. 1916. (*Alamy*)

Mametz Wood. (*Alamy*)

Shulbrede Priory (Sussex) where troops appeared in 1917 around the home of a war critic MP. The drawing is by Arthur Ponsonby whose home it was. (*Courtesy Ponsonby Family*)

A 12 July 1916 *Punch* cartoonist's view of the Battle of the Somme, reflecting British home front perception of an Allied triumph.

A FIRM CHIN IN ANNIE'S DEFENCE.
COMMANDER WEDGWOOD.

A *Punch* drawing of Josiah Wedgwood (speaking in July 1917 in defence of an Indian Home Rule campaigner).

Edward Dent. (*Alamy*)

Leonard Outhwaite.

John Middleton Murry. (*Alamy*)

PUNCH, OR THE LONDON CHARIVARI.—July 14, 1915.



THE ENEMY, M.P.

Mr. Punch. "THESE SELF-ADVERTISING PRO-GERMANS MAKE ME SICK. WHAT WE WANT IS A CENSORSHIP OF PARLIAMENTARY REPORTS."

*Punch*'s view of war dissenters in the House of Commons and of press coverage of their speeches.

Hastings Bertrand (Bertie) Lees-Smith as a corporal. (*Courtesy Alistair Lees-Smith*)

A *Daily Dispatch* cartoon prediction of heavy defeat for Siegfried Sassoon's candidate Philip Snowden at Blackburn in the General Election of December 1918. The ballot papers all have crosses by the names of his opponents.

family from his narrative. The fictional filler is fairly elaborately constructed. It is worked around H.W. Massingham, the (real) editor of *The Nation*. In *Memoirs* Sassoon meets Massingham at the National Liberal Club and tries to persuade him to put in his magazine the realities of the war: he will supply the details. Massingham explains that he cannot do this because of censorship and because of the rule that soldiers cannot write about their war experiences. Instead, he directs Sassoon to Bertrand Russell, of whom SS knows nothing (which is considerably untrue).[8]

As editor of *The Nation*, H.W. Massingham had to be careful. His magazine was a hub of liberal dissent regarding the war, but he avoided an overt anti-war position. Even so, *The Nation* had its fingers burnt. On 29 March 1917 the War Department banned overseas sales of the magazine. The immediate reason was a comment in the paper on 3 March 1917 on the pull-back by the Germans of their Western Front line in February. The editorial said that Germany was 'still the master of surprises…The greatest retreat on the West since the Marne has taken place; but in this case almost all the honours go to the enemy.' Although there was hostility in some of the press towards the *Nation* for 'peace mongering', the journalist community rallied against the ban (which in October was withdrawn on the grounds that the magazine was now behaving itself). The affair demonstrated the hazards facing any major publication which challenged the Government on the war.[9]

*Memoirs of an Infantry Officer* presents its narrator as a plain-man ignoramus, receiving from H.W. Massingham a political education. In reality Sassoon was much better informed than most, the reason being his time spent at Garsington with Philip Morrell. Before the war Morrell had been on the Persia and Russia subcommittee of the backbench Liberal Foreign Affairs Committee. He was dismayed by what he learned about Russo-British economic exploitation of Persia, which squashed the democratic aspirations embodied in the parliament of the Persian constitutional monarchy. Persian oil was key to British economic needs because of the switch of the British Fleet from coal to oil. Morrell knew about oil. He had spoken in the House of Commons on 17 June 1914 against the Government's taking of share capital in the Anglo-Persian Oil Company. He will almost certainly have talked to Siegfried Sassoon about oil, which was important to British foreign policy and continued to be in this war. But the Morrell family's part in the Sassoon story was excised in SS's composition of his Sherston memoir.[10]

The subject of war aims had recently been addressed by the *Bradford Pioneer*, an Independent Labour Party paper inspired by Labour MP Fred Jowett, one of Philip Morell's parliamentary associates. Jowett assessed the recent entry of the United States into the war, militarily highly significant of course though it would take a long time for its effect to work in. Jowett warned that:

> American financiers may begin to cast longing eyes on the east. Persia, Palestine, Syria, Arabia may all require 'developing'.... With so many plums ripening, all sorts of new complications will come along if the war goes on much longer and America becomes the predominant partner in it... War is not good for morals.[11]

Before the American entry into the war the British parliamentary peace-by-negotiation group had hoped that President Woodrow Wilson would be a mediator. In the war Wilson would try to discourage the acquisitiveness of Britain and France, but to no effect. Siegfried Sassoon would get to know Jowett's *Bradford Pioneer*. The paper would play a role in his story.

We must here turn to the diary and the memoir of Lady Ottoline Morrell. These describe a short stay by Siegfried Sassoon at Garsington. This visit would be the catalyst for what turned out to be a whirl of events. It may be adduced from Ottoline's diary that Siegfried arrived at Garsington on Friday, 8 June and departed on the Sunday. Sassoon's *Siegfried's Journey*, which makes some amends for the omission of the Morrells from *Memoirs of an Infantry Officer*, still reduces the visit to a day trip.[12]

On the Friday before he set off to Garsington, Sassoon lunched with Arnold Bennett at the Reform Club. Bennett recorded the meeting in his diary:

> He expected some decoration for admittedly fine bombing work. Colonel had applied for it three times but it could not be granted. Sassoon was uncertain about accepting a home billet. I advised him to accept. He is evidently one of the reckless ones. He said his pals said he always gave the Germans every chance to pot him. He said he would like to go out once more and give them another chance to get him, and come home unscathed. He seemed jealous for the military reputation of poets. He said most of war was a tedious nuisance, but there were great moments and he would like them again.[13]

This does not sound someone about to reject war. The 'great moments' that Sassoon wanted to repeat would very likely include killing Germans. Siegfried was far from being a pacifist. But as he engaged Bennett with his joy-of-battle chat, heavily at the back of his mind will have been what he was going to say later in the day when he got to Garsington. Did he talk with Bennett about rebelling? There is no hint of this. In his conversation, his gripe seems to have been the failure of officialdom to award him a second decoration.

Some clue about Sassoon's multiple identities is given in *Siegfried's Journey*, as he looks back from the perspective of 1945:

> What bothers me about that kaleidoscopic young man is the remembered inconsistency of his responses to various individuals. Never the same with any two people from one lunch or dinner to the next, he now strikes me as deplorably chameleonic.[14]

And so to Paddington station. Siegfried's brain will have been active as the express steamed through the countryside to Oxfordshire. Did he chat in his compartment with fellow passengers, who will have noted his uniform? Did he brood? Or was he re-living his luncheon conversation with the celebrity novelist? Or all of these? Such detail has to stay in the imagination.

Sassoon's arrival at Garsington is reported in Ottoline Morrell's journal. The diary is a tease and not just by reason of Lady Ottoline's eccentricities of script. The document is disjointed jottings, in contrast to the connected narrative of her later memoir (in which she acknowledges that her diary entries were sometimes 'wild and rather chaotic'). The diary record concentrates on her feelings towards Siegfried and his reactions to her rather than his dilemma over the war.

Ottoline wrote up her diary on the Sunday evening after Sassoon's departure: 'SS has been and gone.' She records a harrowing scene. When she showed Siegfried to his room he 'poured out' anguish: 'What should he do? He hated war but he had to go on with it, etc, etc.' She thought that for him it was 'a comfort to say it all out'.[15]

Ottoline's later memoir provides more coherent detail on Sassoon's dilemma. He said:

> How could he possibly train others to go out there knowing what they would have to go through. 'They will all be killed or maimed.' He has suddenly become aware of all [the war's] horrors, and feels caught in a trap, passionately longing to make some protest against it.[16]

It is obviously about the cadet training post at Cambridge. A letter from Robbie Ross to Edmund Gosse touches on the matter: it was the sort of post that Sassoon wanted, but he had delayed writing to Cambridge until Robbie chivvied him (and actually posted the letter for him). Sassoon refers to the subject in a letter to E.J. Dent written from Half Moon Street on 6 June. He asks Dent to arrange an interview for him next week by a Colonel Edwards ('this Military Don'). This must be Colonel H.J. Edwards, Officer Commanding, Cambridge Officer Training Corps. The colonel was an expert on Polybius. Sassoon observed to Dent:

> I suppose Col. Edwards understands that I am <u>not</u> "unfit for foreign service". I shall undoubtedly get pushed out again by August in the ordinary course of events. I don't think I mind much what happens![17]

In reality Sassoon minded very much, hence his agonising. He told Dent that he now had only three weeks of leave left, 'then light duty'. With a return to the Litherland Army base now close and a decision on the home front post needing to be taken, it is easy to see how glad Siegfried was of the chance to ventilate his predicament. But it did not resolve the questions. Sassoon's anguished indecision is evident from Ottoline Morrell's diary regarding the day after his arrival at Garsington:

> He wandered about alone, Restless…wandering. I thought he wished to avoid me but I think it was only restlessness. He went round and round like a distraught spirit. [18]

The planned protest is mentioned: 'SS and I went a walk in the Evening after tea to the Wood and he talked more about his plans of rebelling.' There is no detail. Ottoline's focus is on her personal feelings for Siegfried and whether he was equivalently interested in her:

> My feeling for him all the time was that my soul was never his – he wishes to avoid me, even wishes to avoid shaking hands – but that he does feel me intimate with him.

She was becoming reconciled to the failure of her grand design for Siegfried:

> I feel much happier about him – for I expect little now. What the future may be I don't see.[19]

She reflected after Sassoon's departure:

> It went all right. He is very vain and his nerves are all in a terrible state from the war. It makes him violently self-centred. He can only think of himself and his own affairs.[20]

In his weekend at Garsington Sassoon talked to Philip Morrell. The MP advised against making a demonstration: 'It would only be a nine-days wonder...the pathetic absurdity of a solitary second-lieutenant raising his voice against the architects of a world conflict.' A scene lodged in Sassoon's memory:

> Staring at the sunset as he leant on a farm gate, in his wide-brimmed black hat, [Philip Morrell] looked somehow defeated and ineffective, a compromising pacifist who had lost hope of dissuading mankind from its madness. It was the face of a man with fine aspirations, but his handsome features had no potency behind them. Kind and magnanimous, he lacked intellectual toughness.[21]

If Sassoon felt some bitterness it is understandable. It was Philip who more than anyone had brought him round to his present view about the war. But a soldier rebelling against the Army was not Morrell's way of doing things. He came from a legal family. He was steeped in political process. Mutiny was not for him. There was also a personal factor. Three months earlier Philip had blurted out to his wife that he had made two mistresses pregnant – a former maid of Ottoline, and his secretary. He was in extreme agitation. Ottoline was deeply hurt. The marriage was a Bloomsbury-type ('living in squares and loving in triangles' in the Dorothy Parker quip), but the open marriage was by arrangement. Philip had hidden his liaisons. Any publicity of the trouble would be disastrous for the parliamentary peace group. They suffered enough fake news without a love scandal: 'loose-living peace crank', the press would say. For a week or so Philip seems to have had a complete breakdown. He harangued Garsington visitors incoherently. News went round Bloomsbury. Lytton Strachey, a Garsington regular who was a conscientious objector, had it from Clive Bell:

> '[Philip] took leave of his senses, sat in his bed gibbering, moping, mowing, and babbling of green fields, until at last he returned to sanity...I never knew that one could go mad for a weekend – like catching a cold.'[22]

Siegfried Sassoon will not have known these personal circumstances which made it just about impossible for Philip Morrell to be associated with a public protest by a soldier against the war at this time.

Sassoon signed the Garsington visitors' book on the Sunday morning of his departure: 'Siegfried Sassoon June 10th', with the regular twirl under his name. The pen strokes are his standard signature but it looks like an uncharacteristically feeble signing. Do we see the draining of his reserves with his emotional turmoil (that lonely pacing of the paths) during his day and two bits at Garsington? If so (it could of course have been just an indifferent pen nib), that is understandable. But anyway, Siegfried was starting to see the way forward. It was one that was harder in some respects than the Western Front.[23]

Ottoline Morrell, the other tortured soul of the Garsington weekend, did give Siegfried Sassoon some help regarding his plans for a protest, the idea of which she warmly supported. On the Tuesday (12 June) she recorded in her diary:

> I had to go up to see the [doctor] and so I asked Bertie [Russell] and [John Middleton] Murry to Lunch and then B took SS to his rooms…SS and Murry came to tea and talked and talked together.[24]

John Middleton Murry, writer, editor and commentator, was socially self-made, the son of a clerk. He won a scholarship to Christ's Hospital School. When he moved on to Brasenose College, he feared that he would be tormented: he had heard that the place was full of 'bloods' (upper-class bullying rowdies) but after an initial mild encounter, they left him alone and he made friends as he developed a precocious literary career. What about Murry and the war? JMM was now twenty-seven. Conscription went up to forty-one. Absolute exemption was extremely rare and refusal of service meant jail. Murry knew some of the artists and intellectuals who were working on the Garsington estate. In his autobiography, he analyses his feelings towards 'The Machine'. He was not worried about being a 'navvy' (though he would not like it), but he hated the idea of losing his freedom. He had an exemption for poor eyesight but the authorities were re-checking him. The Machine needed ever more men. (Next year conscription would go up to 50.) Murry needed to find a war-related posting to secure him. This he had done, not far from where he lunched with Russell, Sassoon and Lady Ottoline.[25]

Ottoline Morrell says in her memoir that Murry was working for the Foreign Office translating foreign newspapers. In fact, he was a War Office employee. He was editor, as his memoir recalls, of 'an impressive sheet called *The Daily Review of the Foreign Press*'. He had a relationship with Katherine Mansfield, whom he would later marry. When Katherine first visited Garsington Manor, Ottoline was suspicious of a novelist looking for material. Relations warmed but Ottoline was vexed by the sense that, witty and entertaining though Katherine was, she kept her real self behind a mask. In the cultural hothouses of Bloomsbury and Garsington there was needle in the parlour games. There was much going on emotionally and intellectually as worlds intersected. Among those in residence at Garsington when the uniformed Siegfried Sassoon arrived with his dilemma, was Aldous Huxley. Ottoline noted that Huxley felt neglected, and 'was certainly not at all cordial or nice to Siegfried'.[26]

Ottoline Morrell's memoirs have information about the 12 June meetings of herself, Murry and Bertrand Russell. The lunch venue for the group was the *Eiffel Tower* (on the corner of Charlotte and Percy Streets in Fitzrovia). This could not have been more appropriate for the planning of a rebellion against the establishment, since this restaurant was a haunt of bohemian artists and avant-gardes. The Vorticists sometimes met here, until – ironically – the war finished their art movement of violent challenge to the status quo, and their magazine *Blast*. It was a place where Ottoline was comfortable. Ottoline's diary is not quite clear on whether Sassoon was there but he had apparently been with her there earlier in the year. Sassoon and Murry, wherever exactly they were together, apparently greatly took to each other during this day. Ottoline wrote in her diary a week later:

> ...Murry had a letter from SS who told him how much he liked him. That shows he can say Nice things...and that obviously he does not like me – or doesn't feel them for me.[27]

Murry was not a politician; he was not part of the anti-war and anti-conscription movement; he did not have the personal indignation about the conduct of the war that Siegfried Sassoon had. But he did agree with Sassoon's objections to the Lloyd George Government's policy of pressing the war to the bitter end and its failure to look for a negotiated settlement when there were opportunities; and to the imperialism of Allied war aims. And he liked a challenge. He had to leave hastily at the end of the lunch because he was late getting back to his War Office work.[28]

Ottoline Morrell was hurt by Siegfried Sassoon's treatment of her. She wrote in her diary:

> I have done so much for him – Given so much to him and he has Never once said I thank you to me. It is certainly my fate to give and give and slave for people and to get nothing back. It is very disappointing and hard fate.[29]

Siegfried seems scarcely to have registered her feelings. Years later Ottoline read *Memoirs of an Infantry Officer*. The old hurt was compounded, as she expressed in her memoir:

> He has never said a word of thanks to me, and after all I have done a good deal for him. I was rather surprised that in writing of this time he should have entirely omitted any mention of our help.[30]

Sassoon could be very caring about others, but there were large blind-spots in his male-focussed view. Ottoline Morrell in her memoir reconstruction of these days wrote:

> Siegfried is terribly self-centred, and it seems almost as if when he does a valiant action, such as this protest, that he watches himself doing it, as he would look into a mirror.[31]

SS was too consumed with his fictionalised autobiography to give thought to how his editorial snipping of his life history in order to suit the market might affect the woman who had been at his side in his hour of crisis.

Sassoon's planning of his protest and his application for the cadet training post are oddly interwoven. Sassoon's *Memoirs of an Infantry Officer* claims that the job was 'illusory': that he was 'safeguarding himself against what people would say', meaning that putting in for the position was a device, and that he had no intention of actually taking up the post. If he were accused of using rebellion as a means of avoiding being sent back to active service, he could point to the home posting as showing that he would not have been returned to France anyway. But is clear from all SS's contemporary correspondence that the Cambridge job was in play for real. And there was the circumstance of Sassoon's friend Robert Graves, with whom he was so much in parallel, having taken just such a post and having urged SS to do similar.[32]

Sassoon's trip for his Cambridge interview, on Wednesday, 13 June, was combined with a catch-up with E.J. Dent, who was returning to Cambridge from London on that day. The friends arranged to meet at Liverpool Street Station. Dent recorded in his diary:

> I meant to return to Cambridge by the 12 train: but when I got to Liverpool Street I found that the Station had been bombed 5 minutes before and my train was on fire. Siegfried was there, to go to Cambridge with me about a job in cadet instruction. We went off to Kings Cross. We had an hour or more at Hitchin and walked into the town. S was in a very agitated and nervous state – the heroics of pacifism – and evidently a good deal upset by the air raid: he had been in the City and had heard the bombs etc. I was in the Tube and did not…[33]

Edward Dent had much in common with Sassoon and he was happy to put SS's anti-war poems into the *Cambridge Magazine*. However, the acerbic musicologist evidently found his friend hard work. Dent fails to make it into any of Sassoon's accounts. The journey to Cambridge is featured in *Memoirs of an Infantry Officer*, without Dent, with Sassoon's alter-ego George Sherston close to the bombing raid that Dent mentions. Heavy aerial attacks on London by German planes were a new horror, worse than the Zeppelins. On 13 June 1917 fourteen German bombers flying at 12,000 feet dropped over a hundred bombs, killing 162. In *Memoirs*, the author-narrator displays business-as-usual sangfroid as he gets on with drawing a cheque in a bank as the bombs explode nearby. Sherston views the blooded corpse of an elderly man and muses on the difference in the nature of danger as compared with that on the Western Front. Then he crosses to St Pancras to take an alternative route to Cambridge. The tweak of Kings Cross to the next door St Pancras in *Memoirs* marks this as a novel rather than a literal record. *Memoirs* has female bank clerks running down the stairs shrieking. This recalls one of the regular arguments against women having the vote: that they were emotionally ill-equipped to make political decisions. Dent's diary seems to suggest that it was Sassoon who was worked up about the bombs. On the battlefield he was one of the bravest and most composed. This was different. It unsettled him. The appointment with Colonel Edwards had to be postponed until the next day. It went well, Dent's diary reporting that, 'S interviewed Edwards to his satisfaction.' In *Memoirs* Sassoon picturesquely, and probably fictionally, punts a canoe down to Grantchester. The successful outcome of the Cambridge application was that at this point in time all SS's options stayed open. He could take up the post; he could walk out of the Army while making a public protest; or he could return to the Western Front.[34]

Siegfried Sassoon would need the permission of his commanding officer at Litherland to become a home-based trainer of cadets. He wrote to the (fairly elderly) Colonel Jones-Williams. The colonel raised no objection, but told Sassoon that he would be 'sorry to lose him' and hoped that when he was 'quite fit' he would return. The tone was friendly. Jones-Williams congratulated Sassoon on his 'splendid work at the front'. He told him that he was in favour of a bar to add to his M.C. The letter ends: 'I read your book with interest the other day. Wishing you the best of luck.' This senior officer was hardly SS's intended audience.[35]

Sassoon had a letter from another senior officer on the subject of the training post. Major Edward Reginald Kearsley, Adjutant of the 3rd RWF – to which Siegfried was now attached – seems to have had an amiable relationship with him, since he signed 'Yours, Reggie Kearsley'. The adjutant (who was about to move elsewhere) said of the Cambridge job:

> …I think you would be awfully wasted there; why not get a staff job at home where you would have a chance of exercising your ability and getting promotion? These cadets are such horrible youths and the training is

> very elementary. You need not worry yourself by thinking that you ought to go out again; you have made a great name for yourself and have been out quite long enough…We were all very glad to hear that you were not badly wounded.[36]

The major provided Sassoon with details regarding application for training to go on the staff. It is clear that SS was very highly regarded in the Army.

Evidence of the careful attention he paid on training courses is to be seen in his notebooks. From Sassoon's record of lectures, we see the class-based assumption of the trainers: officers would be men with an educated vocabulary and with powers of concentration, whereas the rank-and-file and non-commissioned officers would be less educated, with limited vocabulary, and incapable of sustaining concentration for long. Among the tips for talking to a platoon that Sassoon records, is to use simple language, and to slip in the Army slang with which they would be familiar. The men should be told that when they had captured a trench their safety would depend on their work there: deepening it, building a firestep, or whatever. It should be impressed on them not be distracted from that – for example by examining 'a pair of Boche field-glasses lying about'. The Sassoon notebook logs the instructor's advice to speak slowly to the men, to ask easy questions and not to speak for more than fifteen minutes.[37]

Major Kearsley did not want Sassoon to throw away his life in the course of further dazzling exploits. He thought that the officer's military abilities could be channelled into staff work. Sassoon was most clearly viewed as promotion material. But while SS was keen to have his achievements recognised with honours, he was not interested in the military promotion ladder. His career was as a writer. The Army was an interim. The cadet instructor post, if he took it, would be a means of not going back to the killing fields (the line advised by his friends). It was not a career move.

Ottoline Morrell's diary mentions that Siegfried Sassoon and J.M. Murry were to dine again on the Thursday of the Cambridge trip week. At the Tuesday meetings a plan had taken shape of a carefully framed statement embodying a protest by Sassoon. This, Bertrand Russell said, should be short and should express Sassoon's conviction that the war was 'being unnecessarily prolonged by the refusal of the Allies to publish their war aims'. The need for publication of war aims was a key tenet of the peace-by-negotiation campaign. Murry was designated as the statement drafter. Bertrand Russell would then check it. He would act as Sassoon's 'impresario'.[38]

The reality of war aims on both sides was a critical matter for peace prospects. Aims were shifting all the time without the changes being acknowledged. In March 1915 there had been the Allied acceptance of Russia's claims to

Constantinople. There was the 1915 Treaty of London with its agenda for the benefit of Italy. The return by Germany of Alsace-Lorraine to France (taken from France by the German Empire in 1871 after the Franco-Prussian War) as an Allied war aim – first formally declared by France in December 1914 – was now tacitly accepted by the Allies. And there was the 1916 Sykes-Picot secret agreement on the Allied side to partition, in effect, the Ottoman Empire among the Allies. All this was behind-the-curtain dealing. There was of course also the large matter of undeclared German aims: how much of the territory seized by Germany in the early stages of the war did it aim to keep? The parliamentary peace-by-negotiation group, with whom Siegfried Sassoon was now liaising, wanted all war aims openly declared on both sides. The war had changed in its nature almost out of recognition from that on which the original two sides had entered in 1914.[39]

In *Siegfried's Journey*, Sassoon describes the 14 June drafting session with Middleton Murry in South Kensington. With Murry was Katherine Mansfield. The room was candle-lit and the weather was sultry. SS was self-conscious, as he often was when he was out of his usual zones. Murry was 'sympathetic and helpful' in getting the statement about the war into shape. He condensed and clarified the language. Katherine Mansfield said nothing to Siegfried, except to ask him: 'Do you ever think of anything except the war?'[40]

Murry's editorial skills will have been valuable. In the remarkable succession of chances that was leading the way to a rebellion on the part of Siegfried Sassoon, the circumstance of the literary circle around Ottoline Morrell is a key one.

Bertrand Russell's final check was done next day. What were Sassoon's impressions of Russell? In *Memoirs of an Infantry Officer*, as 'Thornton Tyrrell', Russell is 'small, clean-shaven, with longish grey hair brushed neatly above a fine forehead'. In a much later Sassoon diary memory of Russell, the philosopher and political activist is 'precise, rather pedantic, fairly high-pitched, slightly harsh in tone'. Russell warned Sassoon that, 'This act of yours, if you stick to it, will probably land you in prison.' But that, he said, need not discourage him: 'Of course your action would be welcomed by people like myself who are violently opposed to the War. We should print and circulate as many copies of your statement as possible.' In June of the previous year, Russell had been prosecuted for writing a pamphlet about the operation of the tribunals which dealt with applications for exemption from military service. These were the subject of scorn in Parliament from Philip Snowden, who told MPs:

> The Market Bosworth tribunal chairman said: 'This man [a conscientious objector] puts his own skin first'; it was the first of the breed he had met. Then the tribunal went on to exempt, in the national interest, all the members of the local hunt.[41]

Siegfried Sassoon may or may not have followed the controversy over the tribunals, but we may imagine that the tribunal decision to spare the Market Bosworth foxhunters from Army service would have gone down well enough with him. Bertrand Russell's pamphlet brought him a £100 fine. He refused to pay and would have been jailed had not his friends produced the money. Before the end of the war, Russell would be in prison. The war establishment was not kind to dissent. Sassoon was made aware of what could be in store for him.[42]

Sassoon's fair copy (undated) of the statement, in his diary notebook, reads:

> I am making this statement as an act of wilful defiance of military authority, because I believe that the War is being deliberately prolonged by those who have the power to end it. I believe that this War, upon which I entered as a war of defence and liberation, has now become a war of aggression and conquest. I believe that the purposes for which I and my fellow soldiers entered upon this War should have been so clearly stated as to have made it impossible for them to be changed without our knowledge, and that had this been done, the objects which actuated us would now be attainable by negotiation. I have seen and endured the sufferings of the troops, and I can no longer be a party to prolonging these sufferings for ends which I believe to be evil and unjust. I am not protesting against the military conduct of the war, but against the political errors and insincerities for which the fighting men are being sacrificed.[43]

In a later version, dated July 1917, which would be the final one, there are additions:

> I am a soldier convinced that I am acting on behalf of soldiers.

And (at the end):

> On behalf of those who are suffering now, I make this protest against the deception which is being practised on them. Also I believe that it may help to destroy the callous complacence with which the majority of those at home regard the continuance of agonies which they do not share, and which they have not sufficient imagination to realise.[44]

It is easy to see why the production of this fairly short statement was so lengthy a process. Each word had to be weighed. The Army's conduct of the war could not be criticised. Peace-by-negotiation campaigners regularly found that any word said by them against the war was turned against them as if it was an attack on the British soldiers at the front. Many soldiers agreed with the peace campaign but the official line implied that the troops backed, to a man, fighting until the complete defeat of Germany.

On subject of war aims, Siegfried Sassoon had some background notes in one of his diary books:

> England was asked in April [1917] by the Russian New Govt to state definitely her war aims and to publish the secret treaties made between England and Russia early in the war (the Pact of London). We refused to state it[45].

Sassoon will have had some inside knowledge by way of Garsington. The treaties would remain secret until after the second Russian revolution.

Siegfried's emotions had been at a high pitch through the events that produced his statement. He both relieved and clarified his feelings by writing a poem entitled 'To Any Dead Officer'. He had been shaken to fury when he heard of the death in a typically futile attack on a German position of an officer named Edmund Leslie Orme, who had been close to him. In this composition irony is seasoned with a telephone voice and some contemporary slang, a deliberate contrast with the sonorous elegies glorifying soldier deaths. The speaker is trying to get through to a dead comrade in the beyond: 'Good-bye, old lad! Remember me to God...Are you there...' It concludes: 'Cheero! I wish they'd killed you in a decent show.' The poem's reproach is for the politicians who declare that the war must go on until 'Prussian Rule is trod under the heel of England'. Here is the propaganda of a decent country (Britain) needing to go on to the end in a war to win a crushing victory over an oppressive one (Germany). The opponents of war argued that conscription and the suppression of dissent were turning *Britain* into a 'Prussian state'. With censorship and surveillance and the Defence of the Realm Act and the Official Secrets Act, it was difficult to publicise opposition to the war.[46]

Having completed his statement, Siegfried Sassoon sat on it. He went to his mother's house in Kent. *Memoirs of an Infantry Officer* admits 'procrastination', mixed up with the suspense. He met Robbie Ross at the Reform Club, merely saying that he had been accepted as a trainer of officer cadets at Cambridge. Did he tell his mother about the statement? Presumably not.

Siegfried's childhood home was a neo-Gothic house, named Weirleigh, in the village of Matfield on the High Weald of Kent, several miles from the little town of Paddock Wood. It was hop-growing country. The Sassoon family dwelling was embedded in Siegfried's psyche, as was the surrounding countryside, though his family was not involved in farming or estate management. Here now he waited and dithered.

He was of course in Ottoline Morrell's thoughts. On 20 June she wrote to Siegfried:

> I wonder how you are – Are you glad to be at home or do you find it too sedate? I saw Bertie in London yesterday and he showed me your Statement which I thought extraordinarily good. It really couldn't have been better, I thought. Very condensed and said all that's necessary. It is tremendously fine of you doing it. You will have a hard time of it and people are sure to say all sorts of foolish things. They always do but nothing can really tarnish or dim the value and splendour of such a True Act. Nor rob it of its fruition. Such deeds always bear splendid fruits however much people may carp. It is beastly being a woman and sitting still, irritating. Sometimes I wish to go out and do something outrageous.[47]

As ever, Siegfried's welfare and comfort were to the fore in her musing. She told him that, 'Poor Julian [the Morrells' daughter] has had Measles…I do hope she didn't give them to you.' Ottoline was one of the political circle that had formed around Sassoon. She was with him in what would probably be a very great personal sacrifice in the campaign to halt the slaughter.

At this time Sassoon, though not writing up his diary, was making some political observations in his notebook. They illuminate what his demonstration was about. He wrote:

> …The Jingo[e]s define [the war] as 'an enormous quarrel between incompatible spirits and destinies, in which one or the other must succumb'. But the men who write these manifestos do not truly know what useless suffering the war inflicts.[48]

He was exercised about age and the war:

> Of the elderly male population, I can hardly trust myself to speak. They glory in senseless invective against the enemy. They regard the progress of the war like a game of chess, cackling about "attrition", and "wastage of man-power" and "civilisation at stake". In every class of society there are old men like ghouls, insatiable in their desire for slaughter, impenetrable in their ignorance.

It was a subject that inspired some Graves satire. Robert imagined the generations reversed:

> 'Well dear father, how proud I am of you prepared to make the supreme sacrifice! I only wish I were your age…As it is, I can't be spared; I have to stay behind at the War Office and administrate for you lucky old men.'[49]

Sassoon wrote in his notebook about soldiers and the home front. 'The Army is dumb', he said:

> The soldiers who return home seem to be stunned by the things they have endured. They are willingly entrapped by the silent conspiracy against them. They have come back to life from the door of death, and the world is good to enjoy. They vaguely know that it is 'bad form' to hurt people's feelings by telling the truth about the war. If only they would speak out; and throw their medals in the faces of their masters; and ask their women why it thrills them to know that they, the dauntless warriors, have shed the blood of Germans. Do not the women gloat secretly over the wounds of their lovers? Is there anything inwardly noble in savage *sex instincts*? [50]

Siegfried Sassoon's difficulty with women is evident. He seems to have forgotten Asbestos Bill's girlfriend caringly parcelling up for him a protective waistcoat.

The notebook analysis has: 'Soldiers conceal their hatred of the war; civilians conceal their liking for it.'

He cites a recent TLS review:

> "How vastly the spiritual gain of those who are left behind outweighs the agony and loss of those who fight and die…the everlasting glory and exaltation of war."[51]

He comments:

> This is the sort of thing I am in revolt against. But I belong to "a war-wearied and bewildered minority which regards 'victory' and 'defeat' as rhetorical terms with little precise meaning".

In the literature about Siegfried Sassoon, SS's political views regarding the war have had scant coverage. A major biography considers that his statement was 'quite startlingly naïve…muddled…ill-informed'. This account of the Siegfried

Sassoon initiative takes the view that Sassoon was essentially correct and that the establishment was wrong. Sassoon was no political ignoramus. In the plentiful time available to him in the spring and the summer of 1917 he had benefitted through learning from well informed political brains, most notably Philip Morrell and Bertrand Russell, this at a time when, it may be said, the world was in the grip of quite extraordinary folly.[52]

On 21 June, Siegfried Sassoon took issue in his notebook with an article by Hilaire Belloc in the magazine *Land and Water* (a war commentary journal with a jingo slant). Belloc was arguing from the point of view of British rectitude, while maintaining that the war would be over in 'the next few months'. Sassoon had seen enough to know that it was not going to end this year. (Here was a plank of his rebellion, which does not appear in his statement.) He wrote:

> I am revolting against the war being continued indefinitely; I believe that Carson, Milner, Lloyd George and Northcliffe intend the war to continue at least two more years. To carry out the scheme of 'crushing Kaiserism and Prussianism' by means of brute force, the war must go on two more years.

He looked at war aims:

> If [Government leaders] stated our terms definitely...the German people would insist on the war being stopped...We are aggravating [the Germans'] obstinacy and will to resist by our own intolerant arrogance. It is obvious that nothing could be worse than the present conditions under which humanity is suffering and dying. Will Englishmen be any happier because they have added more colonies to their Empire? The agony of France! The agony of Austria-Hungary and Germany! Are not those equal before God?[53]

About this time Bertrand Russell wrote to Siegfried Sassoon to tell him that he liked the end product of the statement 'very much indeed'. He reiterated that he would help to publicise it.[54]

Sassoon had not seen Robert Graves since January. Graves's cadet-training post at Oxford, which he thought he liked at first, had not worked out well for him. Giving pep-talks to young soldiers, when the horrors of his own experience of the war lay heavy on his mind, imposed mental stress. He took to tranquillizing himself with a strychnine tonic. The result was that he fainted and fell down a staircase. He was sent back to the sanatorium at Somerville College, and then to Osborne House on the Isle Wight, a military convalescent home chiefly for victims of shell-shock. There he joined a prank club of officers who did japes like devising a doll in imitation of a drowned sailor to frighten the locals. On

24 June Sassoon wrote to Graves on his mother's headed stationery: 'Bloody note-paper ain't it?', he bantered. He told Graves that he had been down there for a week and was 'fairly well pleased with life'. He said that seeing so many people at Half Moon Street had tired him out.[55]

Kent was one of those English coastal counties to which the noise of the guns in France carried. Sassoon told Graves: 'I can hear them thudding. It nearly drives me dotty sometimes.' He reflected:

> I don't know whether I want to rush back and die with the 1st Battalion, or stay in England and curse everyone to Hell for their stupidity. But the former method is only playing up to their own gallery ideas; and the latter is pretty hopeless. My name has gone in for Cadet-work. But I won't say I am going to do it. [56]

Here is an on-balance indication that the present likelihood was that Sassoon was going to do the cadet training work. He makes reference to a literary sensation: 'The pacifists all urge me to produce something red-hot a la Barbusse but it can't be done.' In December Henri Barbusse's novel *Le Feu*, based on his experiences as a soldier on the Western Front, had made a big talking-point. It was indeed 'red-hot'. An English translation (*Under Fire*) had come out earlier this month. Sassoon's disclaimer that he intended to follow Barbusse seems to suggest that his own fire of rebellion was cooling. The impression is that a week after writing his statement, Sassoon was preparing quietly to set it aside.

There was no change in his feelings about the war. He remarked:

> ...T. Hardy is the only honest great writer in England now. I wish he would say something against the senseless attitude of the majority of people about the war.

There was a catty comment about the delectable Hanmer:

> I suppose you heard that darling Bobbie has got the M.C. Now he will have something else to polish beside his hair...

Siegfried had a letter at this time from Joe Cottrill. The quartermaster was a regular correspondent. His lengthy letters greeted SS as 'Dear Old Kangaroo' or 'Dear Kangar', perhaps because the hyperactively busy Sassoon hopped about. Joe, working-class Lancashire, was a proud non-commissioned officer of many years' service. The friendship was warm, surprising perhaps in view of Sassoon's notebook comments about NCOs. Chumminess with working-class soldiers did not come naturally to Sassoon. Before the war his life had been a round of leisured pursuits, his poetry being a dream rather than an occupation. But the war and the social mixing that it involved was broadening him. His friendship with Cottrill would last. Joe, who was unaware of the statement, was concerned that Sassoon might be punished for his poetry book:

> I hope trouble doesn't strike you in sailing too near the wind – telling the Truth. The public have been spoon-fed so long on their special pap that when they read or hear the truth they cannot believe it. Men are beginning to ask for what they are fighting – whilst they are fighting and struggling vainly over here day after day, night after night (especially night), their poor unfortunate dependents are being slowly starved to death at Home – not because food is scarce but because they cannot pay the prices a wise 'Controller' – in the interests of the profiteers – lays down. [57]

Economic suffering for the under-privileged classes was real. The previous year Sylvia Pankhurst, leader of the anti-war wing of the women's suffrage movement, took twenty old-age pensioners from London's East End to tea on the terrace of the House of Commons at the invitation of a Liberal MP. She wanted to draw attention to the privations of those who had to depend on the old-age pension. Food prices had risen 65% since the start of the war, but the five shillings (25p) a week pension was unchanged. (A patriotic peer suggested that it might be suspended to help the war effort.) Some elderly people were being forced into the workhouse. Sylvia reported that her guests blinked at '... real butter plastered thick on dainty thin slices of bread and cubes of sparkling white sugar supplied without stint'. It was another world from the queues and belt-tightening of the East End – and the industrial Lancashire that Joe Cottrill knew (as next year would Siegfried Sassoon in a turn of his life yet to come). At the comfortable end of the social scale, Sassoon's diaries report the luxurious dining of the staff officers. Siegfried was shifting politically. By the end of the war, he would be on the same side as the quartermaster.[58]

Sassoon sent Robert Graves his poem 'To Any Dead Officer'. Graves's endorsement was always important to his confidence. SS waited nervously for the postman to deliver the Graves verdict. It arrived in a letter dated 30 June. 'Without doubt a great poem', pronounced Graves: 'Poor little Orme, he'd have been pleased with it.' He offered some technical improvements, but stressed that these were optional: the composition was 'excellent'.[59]

Siegfried fell on Robert's seal of approval, writing back almost immediately (Monday, 2 July). He plunged straight in:

> Hooray! I've been in a state of wind-up about it until I got your verdict which I always take as final. I will try and make Massingham print it, and it really ought to stir people up a bit. But I wouldn't read it aloud for <u>any</u> money. It's a bit too much – but the pathos isn't overdone – it <u>couldn't</u> be with such a subject.[60]

He turned to the subject of the reviews of his book, but before he signed off, he let slip a hint that something big was afoot:

> I wish I could see you, Robert, because I've got something fearfully important to tell you – you will only be able to say that 'it's quite characteristic', though you may not approve. (I'm <u>not</u> engaged to be married.)

The rebellion was back on. Sassoon was going ahead. He yearned to share with his friend what he was doing, but he could not do so yet. What had decided Siegfried? One has to think that it was the realisation that Graves's training of cadets for the slaughter fields (in a similar post to his prospective Cambridge one) had stressed him intolerably and in a fairly short time put him in hospital and then a sanatorium.

Graves got Sassoon's letter during the latter part of the next day, Tuesday, 3 July. It happened that in the morning he had written to Sassoon news of John Masefield telling Eddie Marsh that 'Nichols [Robert Nichols, a best-selling soldier poet], Graves and Sassoon are singing together like the morning stars'. Graves also mentioned to SS that he had heard that he, Siegfried, was going to a cadet battalion at Cambridge. He posted his letter and then Siegfried's new one arrived.[61]

When Graves read it, he was highly alarmed, especially about 'characteristic'. He wrote back immediately with a continuation of the letter he had sent Sassoon earlier in the day. He asked him what this 'characteristic devilment' was: 'Are you standing as pacifist MP? That's the most characteristic thing I can think of next to your bombing Lloyd George.' He wanted Sassoon to visit him at Osborne House: 'Do say you're coming.' Graves was acute in guessing that SS was doing something political. The kinship of the behaviour of Sassoon on the battlefield and Sassoon making a political move is apparently confirmed in a pre-publication draft of *Siegfried's Journey*: 'The impulse which caused me to perform the protest exploit was identical with that which led me to behave with reckless daring in the front line.' This part of Sassoon's make-up went back into his early life. He recalls in his memoir *The Old Century and Seven More Years* that at his preparatory school he was known as 'The Onion…I suppose that I wasn't considered altogether prudent.' His daredevil riding in point-to-point races before the war may be taken as another of the parallels.[62]

On 4 July, the expected Army summons arrived. In the early evening a postal vehicle clattered up to the house with a telegram from the Adjutant at Liverpool. It read: 'Join at Litherland immediately.' Sassoon's superiors had no idea of the rebellion that he was planning. His Army record states that he was promoted to Lieutenant on 1 July 1917. There was no suspicion of anything untoward. This officer had done well and his promotion was deserved. For Sassoon, the time had come. Now things moved swiftly. He stayed put but he wrote on the same day to Bertrand Russell, enclosing the telegram:

> You will see by the enclosed wire that I have got them annoyed by overstaying my leave a week. So we must get the Statement published as soon as possible, and all will be over bar the shouting. I shall probably have to go up there (to the R.W.F. depot) and interview all the people who know and respect me. It's pretty bloody. I shall be in town tomorrow and will come and see you on Friday morning [6 July].[63]

On this day Sassoon wrote to his commanding officer, posting two days later:

> I am writing you this private letter with the greatest possible regret. I must inform you that it is my intention to refuse to perform any further military duties. I am doing this as a protest against the policy of the Government in prolonging the War by failing to state their conditions of peace.
>
> I have written a statement of my reasons, of which I enclose a copy. This statement is being circulated. I would have spared you this unpleasantness had it been possible.
>
> My only desire is to make things as easy as possible for you in dealing with my case. I will come to Litherland immediately I hear from you, if that is your wish.
>
> I am fully aware of what I am letting myself in for.[64]

'This is the first step,' Sassoon noted in his journal, in which he copied the letter.

Bertrand Russell immediately became active. Siegfried Sassoon had willingly put himself into the firing-line of the Army. He was likely to be court-martialled if he did not back down. For the peace cause, there had to be coordination with parliamentary sympathisers and the press. The mainstream press was impossible in the ordinary way since it was either hostile or unavailable. Taking the side of a soldier who was wilfully defying the Army would damage a paper's circulation.

And there was the Defence of the Realm Act. The way forward was the House of Commons, since its proceedings were protected by parliamentary privilege, as was reporting of them. Russell had a mental shortlist of several MPs who might declare for Sassoon in the House. He sent a letter to Ottoline Morrell on 7 July: 'I wrote to Ponsonby but he was away so I have not yet heard from him.' Arthur Ponsonby returned and Russell saw him on 9 July, but by then Bertie Lees-Smith was lined up to read out Sassoon's declaration in Parliament. It would take some pluck when anti-war utterances were seen by some as practically treason, but Lees-Smith was protected by being a soldier who had done active service. Russell told Ottoline that Ponsonby agreed on Lees-Smith being 'the right man to take up [Sassoon's] case in the House', adding:

> I don't want to appear in the matter myself, as S.S. is not an out-and-out pacifist, and it would be a pity if he became identified with those who are.[65]

In his correspondence with Ottoline Morrell, Bertrand Russell mentions the House of Commons Civil Liberties Group, called by its members simply 'The Group'. This had about forty MPs. The organisation came into being to oppose the conscription legislation of 1916. It stayed in place and widened its remit to take in more generally the defence of civil liberties, including Habeas Corpus, Magna Carta and the Petition of Right. The story of these MPs has been largely overlooked by history. Their campaigns, including for imprisoned conscientious objectors, fill many pages of the wartime Hansards. Russell said to Ottoline on 13 July: 'I imagine the Group will discuss [Sassoon] and P[hilip] can settle with them.' Presumably he meant Philip Morrell coordinating with the Group. We may be sure that the Group did discuss Sassoon's case. Unfortunately, the minutes of its meetings have not survived, except for an unofficial record of one of these, on 27 June 1916, made by Catherine Marshall, Parliamentary Secretary to the Joint Advisory Committee of the No-Conscription Fellowship, the Service Committee of the Society of Friends and the Fellowship of Reconciliation. Marshall attended meetings of the parliamentary group.[66]

Sassoon and Russell duly met, probably at the latter's 57 Gordon Square home. On 7 July Russell gave Ottoline news of the outcome:

> I have seen SS twice and was very nice to him! You are quite wrong in thinking that I don't like him – I saw some faults, but not of a kind I mind; and his courage is really wonderful... S.S. had quite decided, and has now taken the irrevocable step – at least he was just going to when I left him yesterday. So now the matter should be spoken of everywhere – the more

> the better. I think he is happier than he was. I talked to Massingham about him, took him to see first Francis Meynell and then Lees-Smith. [67]

Here were the planks of the rebellion: getting the statement printed (by Meynell) and getting it read out to Parliament (by Lees-Smith).

Francis Meynell, as has been noted, was previously known to Siegfried Sassoon. Meynell calls Sassoon in his autobiography 'a young officer known for his valour in the trenches, accepted by the aristocracy as a proper huntin' man'. He states: 'With Bertrand Russell he came to see me at the Pelican Press [which Meynell founded], bringing a careful typescript of his reasons for his mutiny.' Meynell turned Sassoon's statement into a one-page leaflet. Many copies could now be produced. Examples that turn up around the archives testify to its circulation. The police were watching. They seized and confiscated batches ready for distribution wherever they found them.[68]

One copy of the statement rests in the papers of Catherine Marshall at Carlisle Archives. The document is partially discoloured, probably because Marshall's papers were for some years after her death in decaying hampers in a Lake District shed. The heading is: 'This statement is made by Second-Lieutenant Siegfried Lorraine [sic] Sassoon, M.C., 3rd Batt. Royal Welsh [sic] Fusiliers.' Next to M.C. is an ink addition, probably by Marshall: '& bar'. This must have been inspired by Sassoon himself. With Colonel Stockwell's recommendation of a DSO for Sassoon for his bombing on the Hindenburg Line not having gone through, Colonel Jones-Williams at Litherland was evidently backing a bar (a silver bar on the ribbon surmounted by a small crown), Sassoon must have been expecting that this would come through in due course. There is an ink note at the foot of the sheet: 'Mr Sassoon desires wide publicity for this statement.'[69]

If a further military award were to arrive, it would, as Siegfried Sassoon told Ottoline Morrell, strengthen his position in a confrontation with the Army. The thought occurs: what if the cherished and rare red and blue DSO ribbon had come Siegfried's way? Would he have been tempted to pull out of his protest? Medals, because of what they meant, were very high in SS's motivation register.

Sassoon's notebook has a list of intended recipients of his statement:

> Thomas Hardy O.M.
> Lord Brassey
> J.F. Hope M.P.
> H.B. Lees-Smith M.P.
> C.K. Ogden
> Arnold Bennett

E. Carpenter
H.W. Massingham
Lord Henry Bentinck M.P.
Horace Hutchinson
J.A. Spender
Harold Cox
E. Marsh
H.G. Wells

A fifteenth name, Lytton Strachey, is crossed out. Sassoon does not at this stage seem to have been personally acquainted with Strachey, whose iconoclastic *Eminent Victorians* would be published next year. He will have known of Strachey from Garsington. Like most of the Bloomsbury circle, the copiously bearded author was against the war.[70]

There are puzzles. James Fitzalan Hope, later Deputy Speaker of the House of Commons, was a Conservative MP and a Government whip. Sassoon's biographers are silent about him. Hope's papers have not survived. The chances of his agitating for a settlement of the war were surely negligible, one might think. He does however turn up in a letter which we will note later.

As a war sceptic, Lord Brassey is an understandable inclusion. So is Charles Ogden, editor of the *Cambridge Magazine*. The linguist and philosopher, in his late twenties, was exempt from military service because of childhood rheumatic fever.

Edward Carpenter was the author of *The Intermediate Sex* and *Towards Democracy*. Siegfried Sassoon read these books in 1910-1911 and became a friend. The elderly Carpenter, a gay rights campaigning pioneer, was an all-round social and educational reformist. In a letter of August 1911 thanking Carpenter for a book ('which I shall read with great interest, though my German is rusty'), Sassoon was contemplating a visit to Carpenter's Derbyshire home, near Chesterfield.[71]

What about Arnold Bennett? The novelist could not be expected to warm to soldier insubordination. He had been to France at the behest of the authorities, writing 'Over There' pieces upbeat about the war. In 1918 he would take charge of the French department of British propaganda. For a few weeks towards the end of the war he would head the work of the Ministry of Information.

H.W. Massingham could be expected to be privately sympathetic. Likewise, Ottoline Morrell's brother Henry Bentinck, who before the start of the war had been one of a small (and vanishing) group of Tory neutralists.

Eddie Marsh was of the holy battle persuasion but he needed to be told.

H.G. Wells, brilliantly provocative author of the current talking point *Mr Britling*, was perhaps the best hope for Siegfried Sassoon's cause.

J. A. Spender was editor of the influential Liberal *Westminster Gazette*. Spender was a highly unlikely backer of a revolt against the war. In the July 1914 crisis he broke ranks early on Liberal neutralism. He was a just-war editorial crusader.

Harold Cox was an ex-Liberal MP, brother of Agatha Cox, Hamo Thornycroft's wife. On 18 March Sassoon expressed a wish that the 'clique' of Hamo, Harold and another Thornycroft brother-in-law might prove useful in the promotion of *The Old Huntsman*. Cox was a right-wing libertarian, an outlier who had opposed the welfare reforms of the Liberal government.[72]

Horatio 'Horace' Hutchinson was a sporting celebrity: a top golfer and a sports writer.

Siegfried Sassoon sent out the statement copies on Saturday, 7 July. Various notes were included. That received by Harold Cox is in the archive of Cox's brother-in-law, Hamo. Sassoon wrote:

> I am handing the enclosed document to my commanding officer. No doubt I am entirely wrong. Poets usually are! I hope you will give me credit for being honest, anyhow. I am afraid Uncle Hamo will never forgive me.[73]

Nervousness and self-deprecation are found everywhere in the accompanying letters. Eddie Marsh had: 'I could do nothing else'. And Charles Ogden: 'This is a bloody performance but I suppose someone has to do it.' Behind the fluttering however there was steeled determination. Siegfried Sassoon was ready to face a court-martial. He asked Ogden to publish the statement 'after it has appeared in Hansard'. This was the strategy of the Berties, Russell and Lees-Smith. With parliamentary privilege, there could be no prosecution under the Defence of the Realm Act or whatever for disseminating what was said in the House of Commons once it was on the official record.[74]

The posting of the letters was both mundane and momentous. Into the box went the letter to SS''s commanding officer and those to the selected circle. In *Memoirs of an Infantry Officer* Sassoon relates that: 'I walked down the hill to the pillar-box and posted my letters with a feeling of stupefied finality.'

Most recipients took a little time to digest their mailshots but Robbie Ross wrote back instantly:

> Dearest Siegfried, I am quite appalled at what you have done. I can only hope that the C.O. at Litherland will absolutely ignore your letter. I am terrified lest you should be put under arrest. Let me know at once if anything happens.[75]

He will have thought of the fate of Oscar Wilde.

A note came from Bertie Lees-Smith. 'Dear Sassoon' is the surname mode of writing to a colleague:

> Thank you for your letter. Will you let me know as soon as any definite action is taken against you – such as placing you under arrest. My best wishes to you.

He added a 'PS': Keep your spirits up. I will do all I can at my end.[76]

Writing on the same day, 9 July, was another member of Sassoon's political support team. Middleton Murry's letter begins dramatically: 'Alea iacta est.' SS had crossed his Rubicon as surely as Julius Caesar two thousand years before. Murry anticipated Sassoon being arrested. He continued:

> I'm sure you'll never repent…The only real life, as I see it, consists in breaking people's hearts. Break them cleanly and they join together again; and you gain love instead of affection…I shall worry about you, having known you. I believe that our friendship may last. Lees-Smith, so far as I have judged him, is sound and good.[77]

From Edward Carpenter there was applause: 'Well done, good and faithful.' He offered to meet up in London if feasible and he told Sassoon to let him know if he could be 'of any use in the matter'.[78]

Harold Cox could find only one point of agreement: that most of those at home were callously complacent about the agonies of those at the front. Sassoon wrote back to him on 11 July:

> I can only say that I am willing to admit that I'm wrong when the results have proved it. I fail to see any prospect of a 'military decision' – or a German collapse. But I feel that Prussian autocracy is already doomed by the social upheaval in Europe.[79]

He was no doubt thinking particularly of the spring revolution in Russia but social instability was rife in the war zones – and there had been the mutiny in the French army. Sassoon told Cox:

> The only thing I am certain of is that nothing seems worth while except the truth of one's actions – whatever their result may be.

Cox batted back. He thought that Siegfried's negative view of the chances of Allied success was only true by the addition of the phrase 'in the near future'.

To cease fighting now would leave Germany in possession of 'a large part of France, the whole of Belgium, a large part of Russia and the whole of Serbia'. That would be 'a gigantic triumph for the German military party which would rivet their control over the people of Germany.' He was currently staying in Leigh, Kent and offered a meet-up for lunch or tea. Harold was family.[80]

Edward Marsh's 10 July response began warmly: 'My dear Siegfried, Thank you very much for telling me what you've done.' He went on: 'Of course I'm sorry about it, as you expect,' adding that as a non-combatant he had no right to blame. But he thought that Sassoon was 'intellectually wrong': British motives were 'not aggressive or acquisitive'. These had not changed since the start, he claimed; the Americans had now entered the war 'to safeguard liberty and democracy'; the Russians 'after being bitten with your view' had seen that they 'must go on fighting for the sake of their freedom'. [Actually, Alexander Kerensky seems to have launched his current offensive to try to strengthen his own domestic position.] On a personal level Marsh (after praising Sassoon's courage) urged him:

> But for God's sake stop there. I don't in the least know what 'They' are likely to say or do – but if you find you have a choice between acceptance and further revolt, accept. And don't proselytise Nothing that you do will really affect the situation; we have to win the war (you must see that) and it's best that we should do it without more waste and friction that are necessary.[81]

Up to 1915 Marsh had served Winston Churchill as private secretary, successively at Trade, the Home Office and the Admiralty. Churchill had been out of the Government since then but within days he would be restored and Marsh would resume his partnership. Sassoon's move was badly timed for him. Eddie was a believer in the war but also in SS. We may guess that his brain was buzzing on how to rescue Siegfried while distancing himself from the sentiments of his statement.

Sassoon could now no longer hold off from sharing with Robert Graves what he was doing. He sent Graves a copy of the statement on 10 July. This is recorded in SS's annotated copy of Graves's *Goodbye To All That*, in which Graves claims not to have seen the statement until the end of July.[82]

Robert Hanmer was in a War Hospital in Reading. Graves told him what was happening. This prompted a letter from Hanmer to Sassoon on 10 July:

> My dear old Sassons, What is this damned nonsense that you have refused to do any more soldiering? For Heaven's sake man don't be such a fool. Don't disgrace yourself and think of us before you do anything so mad.

> How do you propose to get out of the Army for the first thing? You will only have to join the ranks unless you become a Conscientious Objector, which pray Heaven you never will. Let me have a line soon.[83]

Arnold Bennett was dumbstruck: 'I was sorry to get your startling news.' He did not take issue except to say that it was his opinion that none of Sassoon's positions 'survive argument'. He said: 'For all that you have already done in the way of fighting, I as a civilian am very grateful, and as to the future my good wishes attend you.' After this stilted response, he sent a second letter (on 20 July), which was a carefully constructed and friendly critique ('I rely on you not to resent this epistle'). Without going into the rights and wrongs of the war, he considered that Sassoon could not have a sufficient understanding of the situation to make the declaration that he had signed:

> You are not going to tell me that you have studied it in all its main bearings and branches. A citizen is not justified in acting in such a way as will fundamentally thwart the desires of the majority as expressed by the accepted channels, unless he has with reasonable fulness acquainted himself with the facts of the case.[84]

There was, in Bennett's view, Sassoon's duty as a soldier, to which he had committed himself when he signed up: he did not have the right to opt out when he personally thought that the war 'ought to be over'. It should be mentioned that Bennett was a defender of free speech for peace activists. He was one of the signatories to a protest by Gilbert Murray, Professor of Greek at Oxford and political commentator, against the attack on the *Cambridge Magazine* editor by the 'Fight for Right' movement, an organisation of pro-total war moral jingoes. Murray was an Aristophanes authority, writing commentaries on the Athenian playwright's anti-war satire, including Lysistrata with its women's sex strike against war. The academic was in favour of this war, as he told C.K. Ogden in a separate letter. (Another of Murray's signatories was Thomas Hardy.) Bennett had read and much liked 'To Any Dead Officer', but he counselled Sassoon: 'The Army will ultimately lay it down that you are "daft". You aren't of course but that's how it will end. What is the matter with you is spiritual pride.'[85]

Bertrand Russell used his contacts in finding places to deposit piles of the Sassoon leaflets. These included Henderson's book shop at 66 Charing Cross Road, known as 'The Bomb Shop', not just because of its anarchist reputation but because that was its actual name. Francis Henderson, who was an author, promoted anyone, ancient or modern, of rebellious outlook. During the war his establishment was a hub of dissent. Here a school magazine turned up: a Repton history master supported peace by negotiation and stated his views in a school publication. The police of course kept tabs on Henderson's and swoops occurred. In October 1916 one such triggered questions in Parliament, including from Philip Morrell, about the seizure of *Two Short Plays: Patriotic and Unpatriotic* by Miles Malleson, an actor and playwright. Malleson, who joined the Army at the start of the war but was invalided home, was a Garsington visitor. In 'Black 'Ell' a young lieutenant who has won the DSO has become revolted by the killing and has decided that all soldiers, British and Germans equally, are victims. The character declares:

> I tell you it's all filthy, foul language and foul thinking and stinking bits of bodies all about…It's the whole world that's mad…I've done with it. Well, you can shoot me, because I'm not going back.[86]

The minister defended the confiscation:

> The book in question is, I am advised, a deliberate calumny on the British soldier. The visit to Mr Henderson's premises was ordered by the competent military authority.[87]

'Competent military authority' was the regular justification for action against anti-war material, as was 'calumny on the British soldier'. Invariably, the book, leaflet, or whatever, was directed against the Government and the authorities, not against the soldiers. For a few weeks Henderson's was an outlet for the Sassoon statement, probably with many copies entering circulation this way. Then a police raid removed the remaining stock.[88]

Another outlet was the offices of the No Conscription Fellowship. The police raided and seized a hundred copies. Ronald Clark in his biography of Bertrand Russell, wonders whether the NCF and other peace activist organisations had been infiltrated by moles.[89]

On 11 July, still waiting to hear what the Army was going to do, Sassoon wrote to Bertrand Russell:

> They are evidently 'keeping me in suspense' in the hope that I may become amenable to a chance of backing out of it. I can't go to any higher authority than my C.O. as they would take no notice. The only thing to do is to force them to take action, if it can be done without endangering the effectiveness of the show. But, as Murry writes to me – 'the only thing worth while is the honesty of one's actions.'[90]

In the late evening of that day another telegram arrived from Litherland from Sassoon's commanding officer. It read: 'Wire urgent how situated.' The Army was still not moving against him. But Sassoon knew that he was not going to be left alone for long.[91]

In the post was a letter from Joe Cottrill, who had read the statement:

> I admire you for your standing out and for having the courage of your convictions. But this war has shown what a lying underhanded swine the Bosche is – that no Peace now would be any use. He is still very strong, and would make the first attempt he could to pounce upon and eat up any small nation too weak to withstand him. War is hideous but I am afraid that we must go on – in the interests of our own preservation – till we are in a position to make peace which will gain us a certainty of the war not being resumed as soon as Germany thinks she is strong enough. I endorse all you say about the politicians. The exploiting of the poor more especially – the swines of profiteers – the hypocritical parsons and the callous complaisance with which those at Home regard the continuance of the agonies of other people.[92]

Cottrill, whose correspondence was regularly grim, mentioned the deaths of horses in battle, including his own, Polly. The quartermaster gloomily remarked: 'One dare not think in this war – if so we should go mad.' He concluded:

> I wonder what will happen to your Statement. I expect they will tell you to reconsider it – otherwise you will get a Court Martial for wilful defiance of military authority. I'm afraid the time is not yet ripe for this.

He wished him, 'Best of luck, old chap.'

On a busy letter day, Sassoon wrote to Edward Carpenter:

> If I am still at large in 10 days I'll try and see you. A man called Lees-Smith is trying to say something about my show in the House of Commons. He is supposed to be an honest chap. But, as you know, the only thing that matters is the honesty of one's actions – whether they be 'super-rational' or not. However plausible the arguments may be (that Prussian autocracy is still uncrushed etc) I have got beyond them somehow. The military people are still wondering what the h–l to do to me![93]

The next day a van from Matfield arrived with another telegram. Marked 6 pm and addressed to 2nd Lt S L Sassoon, it said: 'Report immediately Commanding 3rd Royal Welsh [sic].' This at last was the moment of truth.[94]

In his Isle of Wight recuperation home Robert Graves wrote a reply to a letter from Eddie Marsh, marking the midnight 12th July hour of composition. He remarked:

> About Sassons first. It's an awful thing – completely mad – that he's done. They all think he's mad: and they'd be prepared to hush it up if the Army Council don't get to hear of [the statement being stocked in Henderson's], but I don't think S.S. will let them hush it up…Personally I think he's quite right in his views but absolutely wrong in his action… You can be quite assured that I'm a sound militarist in action however much of a pacifist in thought. In theory, the War ought to stop tomorrow if not sooner. Actually, we'll have to go on while a rat or a dog remains to be enlisted. 'Better no world than a world ruled by Prussia!' (There speaks my old Danish grandmother!). This S.S. business has taken me at a very bad time, nervous breakdown…[95]

After receiving the latest telegram, Siegfried Sassoon headed during the late evening to London to stay overnight at the rooms of Robbie Ross at 40 Half Moon Street (Ross being away). He called on Bertrand Russell. The following day Russell wrote to Ottoline Morrell:

> S.S. came to see me last night. He posted his letter to his Colonel a week ago today. So far he has heard nothing, except an urgent telegram recalling him. He went up to Liverpool (where his regiment is) this morning – hating the prospect of painful interviews with people he is fond of, but quite resolute, and much happier inwardly than before he took the plunge. Yes, he is wonderfully brave – I admire his courage more than I can say.[96]

Siegfried Sassoon covers the journey to Liverpool in *Memoirs of An Infantry Officer*. The events are tweaked, with a London hotel for the journey-break rather than Ross's rooms, and with no mention of the meeting with Bertrand Russell. In the novel, after earlier help Sassoon is a solitary soul in his challenge. In fact, Russell was very much part of the action, with close communication between the two men. However, Sassoon's emotions at this time are well presented in *Memoirs of an Infantry Officer*, including the unreality of impromptu packing for a journey that might end in arrest. As usual, in place of SS's mother is the fictional Aunt Evelyn, who like his mother in reality, is not in his confidence about what is happening. Rebellion was men's business.

## Chapter 10

# Facing the Music

As Sassoon headed northwards, the press had news of 'Great Russian Success in Galicia'. The Russian military revival would prove delusional. A second revolution later in the year would lead to Russia's exit from the war. On Siegfried's train journey to Liverpool, he will probably have been too preoccupied with the prospects for him personally to ponder about Russia's military situation. *Memoirs of an Infantry Officer* records a moment of crisis:

> Alone in that first-class compartment, I shut my eyes and asked myself out loud what this thing was which I was doing; and my mutinous act suddenly seemed outrageous and incredible. For a few minutes I completely lost my nerve. But the express train was carrying me along; I couldn't stop it, any more than I could cancel my statement.[1]

A taxi took Sassoon from the station to the Litherland military camp. No one seemed to be about:

> For a few moments I stared wildly at the huts, conscious (though my brain was a blank) that there was some sort of climax in my stupefied recognition of realty. One final wrench, and all my obedient associations with [the Army] would be shattered.[2]

How did he fare? During the day he managed to scramble a letter to Bertrand Russell:

> No result so far except tolerant kindness, and extreme unwillingness to take action. They have consulted 'higher authority', whatever that may mean. I told them that the thing had gone beyond their control, or mine. I don't think they understand in the least what it's all about.[3]

Sassoon's rebellion was on track.

There is no account in *Siegfried's Journey*. We are left with the semi-fictional and commercialised tale of George Sherston, a sort of Bertie Wooster with a political conscience. The outline is there. The commander was temporarily absent. In charge was his deputy, a major. According to the memoir of Robert Graves, 'Colonel Jones-Williams was narrowly patriotic, had never been to France and could not be expected to take a sympathetic view, but the second-in-command Major Macartney-Filgate was humane.' The peace cause needed a collision between Sassoon and the Army: SS as martyr rather than SS being rescued. Sassoon was playing his part, against the grain though it was for him. He declined a friendly cigar. He steeled himself not to compromise his position. The major tried to coax him into backing down. His efforts were resisted. Sassoon was at particular pains to demonstrate that he was not 'dotty'. If he were diagnosed as shell-shocked, or otherwise mentally disturbed, it would wreck his principled revolt. *Memoirs of an Infantry Officer* has:

> I gazed fixedly at the floor and said, "Hadn't you better have me put under arrest at once?" – thereby causing [the major] additional discomfort. "I'd rather die than do such a thing," he exclaimed.[4]

It ended with a warm handshake and Sassoon being sent off to the Exchange Station Hotel in Liverpool to await further instructions. His relief, as he took tea, was intense:

> I had got over the worst part of the show, and now there was nothing to be done except stick to my statement for the M.P. to read it out in the House of Commons.[5]

What followed, as described in *Memoirs*, was a time of mental torture at and around the hotel through the weekend and into the next week. On Sunday night, 15 July, Siegfried composed a letter to Robert Graves. He told his friend that he had come to the battalion headquarters on the Friday and had walked into the Orderly Room, 'feeling like nothing on earth', though – with a touch of self-presentation to Robert – he imagined that he probably looked 'fairly self-possessed'. He had found 'Floods' (Major Macartney-Filgate) in charge since the commanding officer was away on holiday. Filgate, said SS, was 'nicer than anything you could imagine'. That had made him feel 'an utter brute'. He said that the Litherland authorities had 'consulted the General, who is consulting God'. Meanwhile he was staying at the hotel, having promised not to run away. He remarked: 'No doubt I shall in time persuade them to be nasty about it.' He thought that what he was doing would soon be very well known and that the Litherland chiefs did not understand this. He unburdened himself of his anguish: 'I hate the whole thing more than ever – and more than ever I know that I am right, and shall never repent of it.'

The letter has an interesting final paragraph:

> Things look better in Germany, but Lloyd George will probably say it is 'a plot'. These politicians seem incapable of behaving like human beings.

What was that about? On the day that Sassoon received his Army summons, there was a momentous event in the German Reichstag. The assembly carried by 212 votes to 126 a joint declaration by the socialist and centre parties demanding peace with no annexations (meaning that Germany would withdraw from all the territory that it had occupied) and with no indemnities (meaning no settlement price imposed by the Alles on Germany). The background was the emergence of a majority for democratic reform and a moderate peace.

Was it too good to be true? Not necessarily. There were yes-buts of course. Where did power really lie in Germany? German democracy was compromised by the Prussian franchise, a system favouring the rich. Generally, those who wanted to keep it were annexationists, while those who wanted reform were for a moderate peace. Now the reformers and moderate peace-makers had the upper hand in the Reichstag. There had not been enough sinking of British vessels to knock Britain out of the war. Britain was suffering food privations but not enough. The new majority decided that a peace statement should be made. The new Chancellor, George Michaelis, later claimed that he had deprived the resolution of significance by saying that he accepted the motion's principles 'as I understand them'. But the vote was the vote and it was taken very seriously. It provided a chance for the British Parliament to reciprocate in a people-to-people statement. In Germany desire for peace was growing. As Hans Gatzke puts it, the 'no annexations and no indemnities' slogan of the Russian Revolution 'held particular fascination for the poor and underfed masses behind the [German] Social Democrats.' Unrest was increasing, with 200 thousand metal and munitions workers striking in Berlin in April 1917 in protest about the shortage of food and fuel. An expert on the diplomatic history of the war, Holger Afflerbach comments that while the German attempt at compromise was 'ham-fisted' and the French wanted nothing less than outright victory, the British had 'room for manoeuvre to work for a political solution', which however they did not use. He notes that by 1917, 'the hardliners on both sides were now keeping each other in power and suppressing the forces of moderation.' The negotiation chance was slipping by. The peace activists in the British Parliament, including Bertie Lees-Smith, were hoping to use the brave move by Siegfried Sassoon to shake the British Government out of its rut. Germany's elected assembly had offered a road to peace. There were a host of unanswered questions but it was a start. Now the parliamentary peace-by-negotiation group was set to bid for accord between the Reichstag and the House of Commons.[6]

Siegfried Sassoon called his hotel days 'purgatorial limbo'. He took a train to Formby to tramp around the dunes, where he performed an action destined to be famous. He ripped his Military Cross ribbon from his tunic and tossed it into the water. Some accounts overegg this, with the actual medal whizzing into the waves. It did not, but the ribbon was a precious symbol. Sassoon illuminates this in a section of *Memoirs of an Infantry Officer* in which he banters about hospital visiting: being 'wishful to be wearing all possible medal-ribbons on pyjama jacket when the visitor is the sister of a fellow officer'. What SS did at Formby was drastic. However, committing the fabric to the Mersey estuary did not engage any cathartic relief. It floated away pointlessly. The desperate episode demonstrates Sassoon's wretchedness as he waited.[7]

In the late evening of the Tuesday, 17 July, Siegfried wrote to Ottoline Morrell. He had news of another visitor:

> I wish you were here to buck me up. I'm having the devil of a struggle with the impervious availability of my senior officers. It's very inconvenient being so popular…I came here on Friday and they talked to me like a father and refused to do anything, but asked me to stay at this hotel and think about it. Then they told me to go before a Medical Board at Chester where the H.Q. of the Western Command are. I refused because the Board had obviously been told by the local general to say that I am 'not quite myself'. And this evening the Colonel came hither and implored me for a ponderous and painful hour not to "do anything definite" for a few months. I begged him to let the thing take its course and bade him farewell with a wan smile. Of course he hasn't the slightest idea that anyone will ever hear about my protest. He asked me who I'd been persuaded by and I told him "by the people who argued against me, like he did". Which rather discouraged him, poor old dear! I hope and pray they'll send me to London to be dealt with; this sort of thing is absolutely heart-breaking. I shall probably remain here several days.[8]

Sassoon did not want kindness. He wanted a court-martial in a blaze of publicity, simultaneous with Bertie Lees-Smith and perhaps other MPs making his case in the House of Commons, while Bertrand Russell orchestrated the publicity. Litherland command evidently hoped that the affair would die away. SS presumed that his chiefs would get the message in due course that he was not for budging and that disciplinary proceedings would be engaged.

Why did Ottoline Morrell not come to Liverpool? 'I wish you were here' would perhaps normally have delivered her. But she was seriously ill. She had caught Julian's measles. She later wrote in her diary that she 'could not read or write and floated as a soul over the world.'[9]

News of Sassoon reached Uncle Hamo. Presumably it was a bombshell. He called on Robert Ross. He made notes on the information from the interview:

> Some weeks ago [Sassoon] got [?] in an abnormal state. He had applied for a post at Cambridge Training Corps: "He had not heard from Cambridge." He wrote to C.O. Liverpool saying that he would not obey orders nor go to the front. Also sent copy to Graves. Graves wrote to C.O. and got sympathetic letters. Must go to Medical Board. Graves no news on Tuesday 17th.[10]

In his correspondence with Litherland Graves tried to get Siegfried Sassoon's protest discounted as a product of battle stress. He suggested that Sassoon should have a medical board and be given indefinite leave. Ross wrote to Edmund Gosse about Graves's efforts:

> [Graves] received a most kind and sympathetic letter in reply saying that Siegfried would be ordered a Medical Board, and the best would be done to treat the whole thing as a medical case.[11]

The friendly attentions to Sassoon on the part of his senior officers suggest that Litherland would have gone for a medical board anyway. It would avoid a scandal featuring an officer who was very highly regarded in the Army. But Sassoon's cooperation would be needed and he was withholding it. The collision course was still on. Ross told Gosse that Sassoon was 'hurt with me because I am unsympathetic and did not give my blessing to his insane action.' The letter states: 'I have promise of powerful help, if necessary, at the War Office.' What might this mean? The date was 19 July. Two days earlier Winston Churchill, having been out in the cold since he took the rap for Gallipoli, had returned to the Government as Munitions Minister. Almost his first act was to reappoint as private secretary his previous ministerial aide and close friend Eddie Marsh, patron of poets, including Siegfried Sassoon. Marsh apparently had already been to the War Office to try to help Siegfried. But if Churchill was available as SS's rescuer, that would only work if he wanted to be rescued. And he did not. And Churchill might not be able to save him even so. This was a Conservative-dominated administration and there was Tory resentment that

Winston, the once Tory who had ratted on the party, had wriggled into Lloyd George's Coalition. Churchill's influence might not be enough.[12]

On the day after the Colonel's visit H.G. Wells was composing his reply to Sassoon. SS did not get to see it (in Wells's small, retina-challenging handwriting) until sometime later, when he would have trouble in deciphering it. H.G. wrote:

> I've thought on your statement for the last twenty-four hours. I'm very much in sympathy with your action. I agree the war is going on now through the sheer stupid inability of the responsible people to crystallise…the peace wishes that are now practically the same in the minds of [reasonable?] people everywhere…I hope you will keep me and others [informed?] about this statement of yours. It is a very striking act. I would like to find some way of backing you.[13]

Wednesday, 18 July brought a new turn of events. This was the appearance in person of Robert Graves, who had obtained permission to visit Sassoon, getting himself passed fit for home service. We are dependent on SS's Sherston memoir for the details of the day. The account in this may or may not be close to the actuality but the general outline is presumably factual. First, there was a rush of relief on Siegfried's part when he saw his friend. Then SS poured out his experience of being a rebel, quite against his upbringing but a rebellion that he was doggedly determined to see through. Graves was quiet, just listening. Then he spoke: 'I've come to tell you that you've got to drop this anti-war business.' That was a shock for Sassoon. His assumption had been that his poet chum had arrived to prepare for acting as 'Prisoner's Friend', the regular court-martial arrangement whereby a fellow soldier spoke up for the accused man. A prolonged and intense debate followed between Sassoon and Graves, partly conducted along the shore at Formby.

Graves agreed with Sassoon that the world had gone mad and that the soldiers were being sacrificed for the errors and insincerities of the politicians (though he disagreed with him about conscientious objectors, being sceptical of their motives). On what should or should not be done, there was a chasm between the two. Sassoon's attitude was: 'The War ought to be stopped and it [is] my duty to do my little bit to stop it.' Graves declared: 'The War [is] bound to go on until one side or the other collaps[es]; the Pacifists [are] only meddling with what they don't understand.' He told Sassoon that he had been 'wire-pulling' on his behalf, news that triggered angry sarcasm on Sassoon's part: with Graves's usual tact this would get him two years' hard labour for certain, 'and with any luck they'll decide to shoot me as a sort of deserter.' It was deadlock. Then Graves played an ace. He said to Sassoon that the Colonel had told him that if Sassoon continued to refuse to be medically boarded the Army would 'shut [him] up in a lunatic asylum for the rest of the War'. It was all arranged, said Graves: there would be no court-martial. He swore to the truth of this on an imaginary Bible. The story was a complete lie. It was an effective one. Sassoon's position collapsed. If the outcome was going to be a common lunatic asylum where he would have no publicity, he could not go on. Graves had won.[14]

As Siegfried Sassoon put it in *Memoirs of an Infantry Officer*, 'that was the end of my grand gesture.' Bertie Lees-Smith had not yet found a suitable moment in Parliament to raise Sassoon's case; no newspaper had yet published the statement. The rebellion was over. Graves reported to Litherland that Sassoon was backing down. A medical board was arranged.

The fixing was done next day, Thursday, 19 July. During this day Robert Graves wrote a letter to Bertrand Russell:

> Sassoon has been forced to accept a medical board and is being sent to a place in the country as suffering from nerves; which is certainly the case as anybody can see. The evidence supplied by various friends for the medical board is most conclusive. His opinions are still unchanged but there is nothing further for you to do with him for your cause. I blame you most strongly for having allowed him to do what he has done, knowing in what state of health he was. Now you can leave things alone until he's well enough again to think calmly about the War and how to end it.[15]

Graves was taking the result of the board as a foregone conclusion, namely Sassoon to be sent to a recuperation home as being mentally disturbed through battle stress. He was probably right about that. For a holder of the Military Cross, highly regarded by his superiors for his battlefield performance, to walk out of his service on the grounds that the war was no longer one of good purpose and that the soldiers were not appreciated at home, was potentially a severe embarrassment for the authorities. Bundling Sassoon off at the behest of a medical board to a mental convalescence institution would be a quietly discreet way of closing the affair down. The still recent mutiny in the French Army was a warning of what could happen.

The board came to Sassoon's hotel on the Friday. *Memoirs* mentions two stages to the proceedings:

> [Robert Graves] had a long interview with the doctors while I waited in an ante-room…[Graves] emerged, solemn and concerned, to usher me in…The Medical Board consisted of a Colonel, a Major, and a Captain.

> The Captain was a civilian in uniform, and a professional neurologist. The others were regular Army doctors, and I am inclined to think that their acquaintance with Army Forms exceeded their knowledge of neurology.

Robert Graves's memoir tells of him addressing the medical panel with tales of a traumatised Siegfried Sassoon hallucinating: 'visions of corpses strewn along on Piccadilly'. Sassoon and his statement team had worked hard in the composition to make his case in a rational and unexcited way. Now Graves was trashing Sassoon's mental credibility.[16]

Graves retired to the ante-room while Sassoon was examined by the doctors. Regular questions were asked: Did he object on religious grounds to fighting? (Answer: No); 'Do you consider yourself qualified to decide when the war should stop?'

His attitude to the Germans was raised:

> 'Your friend tells us that you were very good at bombing. Don't you still dislike the Germans? I have forgotten how I answered that conundrum. It didn't matter what I said, so long as I behaved politely.[17]

That was the key. So long as Sassoon was cooperating with the Army authorities, it did not matter what his opinions were. He could comfortably be classed, as he put it in *Memoirs*, as 'a harmless lunatic'. *Memoirs* gives the result of the proceedings as: 'It was decided that I was suffering from shell-shock.'[18]

There is a record in Sassoon's Army file of PROCEEDINGS OF A MEDICAL BOARD assembled at Exchange Hotel, Liverpool on July 20th 1917 by order of Western Command. The soldier's 'disability' to be examined is stated to be 'Mental breakdown'. The preliminary statement is:

> His mental condition is abnormal. His conversation is disconnected and somewhat irrational. In addition to this his family history is neuropathic. He is suffering from a nervous breakdown and we do not consider him responsible for his actions. This officer may be examined by Army Board.

The conclusion was that the disability was contracted under circumstances over which the soldier had no control, as a result of 'active service acting on a nervous temperament'.[19]

Siegfried Sassoon wrote to Edward Dent in laid-back fashion on 25 July: 'The people at Liverpool insisted on treating me as an amiable idiot, which was a little annoying. My Medical Board agreed that my poems in the C[ambridge]

M[agazine] showed strong pro-German tendencies.' A letter to Edward Carpenter was similarly phrased:

> I was forced to appear at [a medical board] by a threat of incarceration in a lunatic asylum and it consisted of 2 elephantine R.A.M.C Colonels and a very sensible nerve specialist, who had difficulty in dissuading them from treating me as (a) insane (b) a pro-German.'[20]

He was threatened, he said, with being sent to 'a proper lunatic place'. This was Graves's story, not anything that was said at the board.

What happened to Sassoon now? *Memoirs of an Infantry Officer* puts it thus: 'The Colonel willingly allowed the Captain to suggest that they couldn't do better than send me to Slateford Hospital.' This was the *Memoirs* pseudonym for Craiglockhart War Hospital, a convalescent home for military officer neurasthenics near Edinburgh.[21]

At the moment when Siegfried Sassoon stood his campaign down, it was showing signs of bearing fruit. The statement was in circulation. On the day after Sassoon's medical board, Irene Cooper Willis, Secretary of the Women's International League, which promoted the cause of negotiation of a permanent peace, wrote to Sassoon:

> My Executive has asked me to write and express their admiration of the statement which you have sent to your Commanding Officer, and their thanks to you for taking such a courageous step. We should very much like to have news from you if anything happens in consequence of your having issued it.[22]

Willis, later a barrister, was in the process of writing her book of national psychological analysis, *England's Holy War*, on how the Liberals abandoned their principles of pacifism and backed the war as a crusade.

Arrangements were made that on the Monday (23 July), Siegfried Sassoon should be escorted by Robert Graves to Craiglockhart. Actually, as Sassoon put it in his letter to Edward Dent: 'of course he missed the train and I came alone!'

A letter was sent on the date of the medical board by Bertrand Russell to women's suffragist and peace campaigner Helena Swanwick, who had written to her colleague Catherine Marshall about Siegfried Sassoon. Russell told Swanwick:

> ...[Sassoon] has been aware from the first that the authorities would attribute his action entirely to shell shock. We have to meet that view by

> pointing out the sobriety of his statement, together with the fact that he was not going to be sent back to France…I cannot speak highly enough of him. He is altogether splendid, physically, mentally and spiritually. He has shown amazing courage by his defiance. There is nothing in the faintest degree hysterical or unbalanced in his attitude, which is the inevitable development of the thoughts and feelings expressed in his poems. The sheer impulse of humanity is the basis of his action…[23]

Russell was unaware that Sassoon's stand had collapsed. The following day Robert Graves's letter reached him. He sent it to Ottoline Morrell:

> Enclosed from Graves was brought me from the Bomb Shop. It was just what was to be expected on the part of the authorities but I had thought better of Graves. Could you make him see that he is not acting the part of real friendship tho' he thinks he is?[24]

Graves had visited Garsington a number of times while he was at Oxford. His letter to Russell had the opposite effect to that which he intended. It speeded up bringing the case of Siegfried Sassoon to the attention of Parliament. Russell reported to Ottoline:

> I have told Lees-Smith, who heard from S.S. this morning. S.S. remains absolutely unshaken. We have to see there is "scandal" and no "hushing up". Lees-Smith is raising the matter in the House.[25]

It was of course wishful thinking on Russell's part that Sassoon was 'unshaken'.

Lees-Smith took the Russell prompt and without waiting any longer handed in a parliamentary question about Sassoon, to be answered by the War Office minister. Meanwhile it is worth noting that Ottoline Morrell was Bertrand Russell's choice of confidant during these events. The impression is sometimes given that with her intensities and passions and ostentations, Ottoline was not a serious thinker. In fact, she was, and she was a closely informed follower of politics.

Robert Graves's *Goodbye To All That* is as dubiously trustworthy as it is brilliantly diverting. The author gives the impression that, at not quite twenty-two, he pulled strings in (very) high places to rescue Siegfried Sassoon. He states that he got a canoeing chum, who was private secretary to a government minister, to intervene with the War Office to persuade them to give Sassoon a medical board instead of a court-martial. The account is preposterous on multiple grounds. The minister was not (as stated in the Sassoon biographies, which follow the Graves grandstanding) Minister of Labour. William Bridgeman, a Conservative (a future Home Secretary) had the modest position at this time of Parliamentary Under-Secretary to the Minister of Labour. Graves's friend was Evan Morgan, Welsh poet and author. Graves did write to Morgan (a letter of characteristic swagger). According to *Goodbye to All That*, 'Evan's Minister persuaded the War Office not to press the matter as a disciplinary case but to give Siegfried a medical board. Evan had done his part well.' This is nonsense, not least because the letter's date does not fit the story. It was Graves's lie about the authorities planning to incarcerate Sassoon in a common lunatic asylum and the consequent dropping by him of his demonstration that averted the court-martial.[26]

Bridgeman was anyway not the sort of minister to have any sympathy with a rebellious war dissenter. He kept a diary. This is silent between February 1917 and February 1918 but entries elsewhere show hostility to those not with the war crusade. He called Sir John Simon who resigned as Home Secretary over conscription 'most unpatriotic'. He approved (in June 1916) of what he called 'The New Labour Movement' (meaning the nationalist pro-conscription wing of Labour) and its programme 'to fight the I[ndependent L[abour] P[arty and] the Pacifists'. It is hard to see that Bridgeman would have any goodwill whatsoever towards a military officer who declared against British war purposes and refused to go on fighting.[27]

Graves's letter to Evan Morgan was written *after* the conclusion of the Medical Board. He wrote:

> You have I expect heard about the poet Siegfried Sassoon being exploited by the pacifists Bertrand Russell and Lees-Smith when in a state of (now certified and official) nervous breakdown after being wounded in some marvellously brave fighting in France…After enormous struggles I've smoothed things down and got him certified suffering from nerves, etc, by a Medical Board and told the pacifists that they've been thwarted…Well you belong to the Trades Union of poets and so you must see what you can do in connexion [with] counter-propaganda bureau to stop his 'defiance letter', copies of which he has sent to B. Russell and to Henderson's 'Bomb Shop' going any further. Everything is being hushed up. James Hope the M.P. (Treasurer of the Household) has been working on behalf of a quiet solution to the business…Any scandal would spoil all our efforts.[28]

It sounds from Robert Graves's letter that he is at the heart of government. This may be taken as fantasy to impress his friend. Nor, one suspects, need time be taken in wondering about the enigmatic James Hope, whose connection with

Sassoon and/or Graves, whatever it was, is irretrievable. The jeering tone about 'the pacifists' is that of a young man who was hospitably received at Garsington Manor by Ottoline Morrell and her 'pacifist' friends. This was the disagreeable side to Graves. The gulf between Graves and Sassoon was vast. There was a shared cynicism about the war, but Graves was helping the authorities to squash what could be an 'ace' for the peace cause, as Bertrand Russell's biographer puts it: 'an officer whose courage and intellect were equally beyond dispute was risking court-martial and disgrace in order to attack the continuation of the war.'[29]

Who did save Siegfried Sassoon? 'Saved' may not be the right word since Sassoon wanted the court-martial. The Sassoon biographers (and other writers) have generally gone with Robert Graves as hero of the hour. Graves's memoir runs two contradictory versions of how he sprang his friend from a court-martial. The influence-in-high-places saviour narrative is refuted by the timing. What about the other rescue account: that it was Graves's persuasion of the medical board that averted a court-martial? At Litherland at the time in question was Julian Dadd. Writing to Sassoon twelve years later, Dadd recalled Graves being 'master of the situation…his ability and tact were wonderful.' There is no doubt that Graves did make a strong declaration of Sassoon's bravery and efficiency, while maintaining that he was unhinged at the time of his writing the statement. But it is difficult to think that had there been no Robert Graves the board's decision would have been different. Sassoon's commanders had tried hard to persuade him to take a board instead of being disciplined. When he did agree to this, the outcome was what his chiefs had wanted all along: committal to a specialist military hospital. The Graves version of Siegfried Sassoon's story is, one may think, patronising and insulting to him. In fact, as Sassoon stressed throughout, he was in possession of his senses and trying to stop the slaughter and to save countless lives. Graves's self-promotion has robbed Sassoon of the credit that is surely due to him.[30]

Robert Graves was not the only claimed rescuer of Siegfried Sassoon. A bid for that palm was put in by Winston Churchill, who told a friend of SS, Miriam Lane, at a lunch in the 1950s, that he saved the poet from possible execution for mutiny. Churchill had a habit of getting rather carried away in his mealtime conversation, especially when he was talking to women. To be sentenced to death by court-martial, Sassoon would have had to be returned to the active service zone. As previously mentioned, Sir Douglas Haig in 1916 had been blocked by Prime Minister Asquith from having war dissenters shot. One cannot imagine that Lloyd George would have changed that policy. Churchill, who was appointed Munitions Minister on the day that Graves visited Sassoon, can hardly, one may think, have been behind the Army's decision not to court-martial him. But with WSC, who knows? It is quite possible that, always a meddler, Churchill did get involved in smoothing the arrangements for Sassoon's placing at Craiglockhart. At his side was Eddie Marsh, and Winston loved poetry, including Sassoon's.[31]

In the matter of the military top brass and Siegfried Sassoon, there is the highly pertinent circumstance of his war record, which was regarded by his superiors as exemplary. Executing him would, one may think, have been preposterously foolish. Of course, successive governments did make some spectacular blunders during this war, including the shooting of some of the Irish rebels, which started a chain of events that eventually would break the union. But Sassoon was surely at no serious risk of being put before a firing-squad. However, if he had stuck to his non-cooperation, he would have stood a real chance of being imprisoned in a civilian jail.

An event two months later showed the consequences that could lie in store for opponents of the war. The chief organiser of the Union of Democratic Control, Edmund Dene Morel, was jailed on a charge of 'inciting' a friend to send his pamphlet 'Tsardom's Part in the War' to the pacifist writer Romain Rolland in neutral Switzerland. Under the Defence of the Realm Act it was illegal to send controversial literature regarding the war to enemy or neutral countries. The UDC's peace by negotiation campaign (including pointing out, as in Sassoon's statement, the changes in British war aims) was looking to the authorities dangerously persuasive. The view in the Foreign Office, as an official had put it in October 1916, was that Morel ought to be 'safely lodged in gaol'. That wish was fulfilled. Charles Trevelyan wrote to his wife on 4 September 1917:

> I am just going off to see my friend imprisoned. We are now living in a world where we know the injustice of power....We have hitherto been essentially on the side of the government classes. Now we are essentially opposed to the present system.[32]

E. D. Morel got six months. He was a powerfully built 44-year-old but prison permanently broke his health. Bertrand Russell, on meeting him when he came out, was shocked to see that his hair had turned white. Pentonville conditions were tough: sewing mailbags in a dust-filled room; weaving rope; carrying heavy jute slabs. Food was meagre (at a time of food shortage) and malnutrition resulted. The cells were bitterly cold. Such was the fate that could have come the way of Siegfried Sassoon. The following year Bertrand Russell himself would be sent to prison for six months for a newspaper article. Thanks to his brother being an earl, high-place connections intervened to grant him 'First Division' status (an extreme rarity). Had Sassoon had gone to jail there would have been no such amelioration. He would have had to cope psychologically with permanent surveillance. At Aylesbury (women's) prison the spy-hole in the door of every cell had an eye painted round it, complete with brow, lash and pupil staring at the prisoner. This was part of the lingering regime of breaking prisoners' spirits. Winston Churchill (Home Secretary 1910-1911) and other recent ministers had done much to turn things around but there was a long way still to go and the war was throwing reform backwards. Sassoon's nature was to be highly active, physically and mentally. Prison would have been a different type of endurance challenge to that of Western Front.[33]

E.D. Morel was of French birth. His foreignness told against him (even though the French were allies). For Siegfried Sassoon, the likely prejudice against a bearer of a first name that was not just foreign but Germanic, needs no spelling out. On the Western Front no one cared about such things. The home front was a different matter. On 31 October 1917 Parliament heard Commander Josiah Wedgwood, who had served in Flanders and at Gallipoli (being wounded) – and who was a Garsington visitor – speaking on the subject of Morel: 'It is a real national disgrace that we have put Mr E.D. Morel into prison.' Siegfried Sassoon might have been a fellow jailbird. Bertrand Russell had warned him what his protest could mean. But had Sassoon persisted with his stand, there could have been uproar in the House of Commons and condemnation in the press, that one of the bravest soldiers in the British Army, a holder of the Military Cross, recommended for further honour, had been jailed for voicing what was the feeling of many in the Army. Out of that fury, the Government policy of rejecting negotiation opportunities in favour of war to the utmost end and the 'knock-out blow' which Lloyd George boasted was going to be delivered, might have faced serious question. We cannot know. It did not arise because Robert Graves travelled to Liverpool and told Sassoon a clever lie.[34]

*Sherston's Progress*, the sequel to *Memoirs of an Infantry Officer*, opens with Siegfried Sassoon's arrival at Craiglockhart. Siegfried feels gloomy foreboding. A consolation is a doctor called Rivers. On 25 July SS wrote to Edward Dent from the hospital:

> I have been sent here for a bit. Do you know Dr Rivers (of St John's)? He is enquiring into my mental aberrations. I like him very much so far.[35]

He wrote to Roderick Meiklejohn a week later:

> The only 'treatment' I have is to talk to a doctor about the war for an hour every two days. Luckily he is a very fine chap, W.H.R. Rivers – of St John's Cambridge.[36]

The field of Dr Rivers encompassed anthropology, ethnology, psychiatry and neurology. His specialism was shell-shock. His new patient would in time become a good friend. But Siegfried Sassoon was not a happy resident of Craiglockhart. He had lost the role that he intended for himself. His memoir, with its humorous self-deprecation, speaks of 'the ripe man of martyrdom', but it was not a joke. It was serious and political and thought out, and it had backers in Parliament. Sassoon was meant to be linking in now to moves in the House of Commons. But his side of the operation was gone.[37]

Siegfried had an ally in his family. This was the husband of the daughter of his Uncle Hamo. Herbert Farjeon, who would have a considerable career in theatre, was a conscientious objector. Bertie was waiting for the result of his appeal against being called up. An undated letter of July 1917 to Farjeon's mother has survived. He had just seen Robert Ross at Half Moon Street, who passed on what he had learned from Siegfried Sassoon about his intentions regarding the protest:

> He said that he went to see Lees-Smith (a pacifist), in order that if the opportunity arose, he might be able to put a question in the House, and to give pacifist papers a chance of commenting on his action. This was the dominant note in the letter to me: that his protest wasn't intended as a purely personal protest, but that he wanted it noised abroad. Mr Ross however thinks (though what Siegfried wants is the only thing that counts) that things had better be left as they are, that he will probably get a discharge from the Army on medical grounds in time, that "one man can do so little" (though he agrees with every word of Siegfried's protest) and that a man with a Christian name such as "Siegfried" is particularly not the man to do good by a protest of this kind.[38]

Farjeon's attitude regarding self-sacrifice in the interests of trying to get the war stopped was the same as Sassoon's. His letter to his mother includes an exchange that he had with Ross:

> 'And what will you do if your appeal fails?'
> 'Go to prison', I said.

Farjeon thought that Ross's attitude to life was 'pitiful'. He himself was with Russell, Ottoline, Murry, Lees-Smith and the peace-by-negotiation advocates in Parliament. He thought that Sassoon, far from being exploited, had thought the matter out for himself, knowing the self-sacrifice that it would involve and that he was prepared for it, as he was in his own situation.

The version of Sassoon and Craiglockhart that Ross gave Farjeon was the Graves-as-hero one: Sassoon had been arrested; the Colonel was very angry and intended to court-martial him; by good fortune the Colonel had fallen ill; his deputy had taken over; it was mainly due to Graves's efforts that Siegfried was given a medical board and declared to be of unsound mind. Ross told Farjeon that at the War Hospital, according to Graves, Sassoon was 'calm and contented'. Farjeon doubted this. He thought that Sassoon had been badly wronged: 'confined to an asylum, unable to make any headway, without hope of getting any justice'. He felt 'very angry' about 'those who think, like Ross, that respectability is a better god than truth to one's ideals.' He thought that Ross had been 'not quite faithful to Sassoon'. He said that he would try to see Lees-Smith. He wondered whether Siegfried was maintaining his protest:

> If he is trying to make a stir, if he is still anxious to, the weapon that has been used against him is not a fair weapon.

Siegfried Sassoon did not have shell-shock. He had none of the symptoms – no tremors, no paralysis. He was at the sanitorium (an ex-hydro, dominated by a sweeping marble staircase) as a political consequence of what he had done. The assessment sheet on Sassoon by W.H.R. Rivers is interesting regarding his patient's views:

> He discusses his recent actions and their motives in a perfectly intelligent and rational way, and there is no evidence of any excitement or depression… At the present time he lays special stress on the hopelessness of any decision in the War as it is now being conducted, but he left out any reference to this aspect of his opinions in the statement which he sent to his commanding officer. His view differs from that of the ordinary pacifist in that he would no longer object to the continuance of the War if he saw any reasonable prospect of a rapid decision.[39]

As we have seen, Siegfried Sassoon did think that the deadlock on the Western Front was a hopeless situation – and that the expending of vast numbers of lives in futile attempts to break it was objectionable. The difference in focus between his views as expressed in his statement and in the hospital may have been to accommodate himself to the military doctor. He did not recant on his statement.

Did Sassoon at Craiglockhart receive mail from the general public? It is unlikely that much could have reached him since the public did not know exactly where he was. *Sherston's Progress* mentions an anonymous postcard: 'Men like you who are willing to shake the bloody hand of the Kaiser are not worthy to call themselves Britons.' One may guess that this was from someone in the neighbourhood who had learned of his arrival. (Had it been from England the word 'English' would have been more likely than 'Britons'.) The writer followed the popular misconception that it was the Kaiser who directed German policy.[40]

## Chapter 11

# The Fusilier and the Green Benches

At this juncture in the story of Siegfried Sassoon and his move to try to end the war we need to take a look at the group in the House of Commons of MPs who were set to champion his cause and hoped that he would give their campaign a lift, perhaps even a decisive one with the right sort of publicity. The parliamentary group had launched its second House of Commons debate the previous year. Leading off, during the proceedings of the government's latest request for credits to finance the war, was Liberal Arthur Ponsonby, with a protest at statesmen standing on ceremony:

> While Europe is bleeding, and the death toll continues to increase, we must not allow the etiquette and formalities of stale diplomatic tradition to stand in the way of our taking the lead, definitely and boldly, in conducting the nations back to sanity and through sanity to peace.[1]

Siegfried Sassoon would have agreed with that. Later in the debate another Liberal, David Mason (not a member of the group as such but an ally) told MPs of a bronze statue of Christ in the Andes made out of Chilean and Argentinean cannon. He reflected on this monument:

> It is set there to commemorate the fact that these two countries rather than go to war, preferred to refer their differences to arbitration and to a conference such as we desire.

He warned against leaving 'a crushed and beaten Germany with a rankling spirit of revenge'. There was a lesson from the past, he said:

> If we study history we find that Napoleon tried [permanently to crush] Prussia but failed. She rose up again and eventually took her revenge on France in 1870.

This is one of the peace group's predictions of what would be the Nazi sweep across Europe, with which the First World War Hansards are studded. Mason would live to see his Coventry constituency's fourteenth century cathedral flattened in 1940 by German bombers. The arguments of the peace group about the manner in which the war of 1914 ought to be settled would, as we shall see, be voiced by Siegfried Sassoon next year both in his private writings and on public platforms.

The parliamentary side of the Siegfried Sassoon protest was waiting for Bertie Lees-Smith to find an opportunity in the House of Commons. When Sassoon told the Northampton MP of the medical board and its decision, Lees-Smith must have realised that this meant the collapse of the joint strategy, posited as it was on the assumption of a court-martial or something like that. Lees-Smith decided however to persevere. SS was too good an asset to the peace-by-negotiation campaign to abandon. He had already put down his question. The Parliamentary Under-Secretary for War, Ian Macpherson, a Liberal lawyer, became aware of this on Saturday, 21 July, as he later informed the Commons. At 36, the MP for Ross and Cromarty was probably happier to be on the Government bench than in the trenches. MPs without a war-significant job would not be exempt from conscription until the next year.[2]

The first reference on the floor of the House to Siegfried Sassoon was not by Lees-Smith but another Liberal MP of the peace-by-negotiation group. It was 26 July, three days after Sassoon's admission to Craiglockhart. The Member was Leonard Outhwaite, who sat for Hanley in the Potteries. It was the day on which Ramsay MacDonald in effect moved the Reichstag peace resolution in the House of Commons. His motion had to be squeezed into humdrum procedure as an amendment to the Consolidated Fund Bill, a multi-day financial debate which allowed for a wide range of subjects to be raised, sometimes with votes. MacDonald proposed that:

> ....this House declares that this [Reichstag] statement expresses the principles for which this country has stood throughout and calls upon the Government, in conjunction with the Allies, to re-state their peace terms accordingly.

In the ensuing debate Bertie Lees-Smith talked about Russia:

> Mr Kerensky has most solemnly pledged to the Russian people and to the Russian soldiers that he will not call upon them to continue to fight unless the Allies publicly announce that they abandon all projects for colonies and conquests and economic war.

He asked the Government:

> Are you going to announce it?

The Government were not. Leonard Outhwaite's speech was a long one, characteristically pugnacious and, as often, angrily interrupted. He told MPs:

> A young officer of one of the most famous regiments, asked by me a few days ago on the terrace of this House, "do you know anything about the views of the men in the trenches?" said, "They are all revolutionary in spirit, but they do not want to lay down their rifles afterwards until they have dealt with the politicians who have kept them in the trenches." You may in the end find yourselves in conflict with the men in the trenches.[3]

The 'young officer' must, we may think, be Siegfried Sassoon. The identification can be no more than inference from the circumstances and the timing, but it would be a remarkable coincidence for it to be anyone else. The words quoted by Outhwaite do not sound like Sassoon, but the MP will have paraphrased to fit his regular thesis of a revolutionary spirit of opposition to the war being in the air. He saw revolution everywhere. In his speech he claimed that his constituency was revolutionary in its indignation about the refusal of the Government to look at a peaceful settlement. Arthur Ponsonby was doubtful about Outhwaite's style, writing to Charles Trevelyan in the previous November: 'Outhwaite overdoes it.' Siegfried Sassoon's diary is silent at this time and he was selective anyway about what he chose to write about. That was even more true with his later-years memoirs, each book being designed for the market of its day. In the voluminous Sassoon records there are big gaps. Hansard's faithful log of the wartime Parliament (extraordinarily neglected by historians) fortuitously, it may be thought, lights up one of these. The meeting on the terrace of the House of Commons, with its pleasant view of the river below, between the forthright Tasmanian-born MP and the rebel poet in his Royal Welch Fusiliers uniform, must be left to the reader's imagination. But it probably did happen.[4]

It was a typically noisy Outhwaite occasion. The MP rounded on a Conservative who was heckling him:

> You sit here in safety while our men are slaughtered by hundreds of thousands in the trenches.

Endorsement of the Reichstag declaration went down by 19 votes (including Lees-Smith, Philip Morrell and Richard Lambert) to 148. The peace resolution mustered (including tellers) just sixteen Liberals and the ILP peace-supporting five (including Philip Snowden). Instead of a potent peace demonstration, knock-out blow was confirmed. The Irish Nationalists, who sometimes augmented the war dissenter vote, were not to be seen. Disillusioned with the Government and losing their hold on Ireland to the rising Sinn Fein, they were currently absenting themselves from Westminster. The vote was disappointing to the peace cause but the *Daily Chronicle* commented that:

> It must be said that the pacifists made excellent use of their opportunity today. Their appeal avowedly is to the people over the heads of the statesmen.[5]

The benches of the House of Commons were a darker green than those of today's House, which is close to a replica of the chamber that was destroyed by German bombs on the night of 10-11 May 1941 in the second war with Germany that the First World War parliamentary peace-by-negotiation group repeatedly warned would happen if the present war ended in Germany being crushed rather than by a mutually agreed settlement.

Next day, Friday, 27 July 1917, the day of Siegfried Sassoon's medical board, his statement appeared in a newspaper. It was not one with a large circulation. *The Bradford Pioneer* was an ILP paper. Its publication of Sassoon was a start in bringing his declaration to the public. *The Pionee*r had:

> FINISHED WITH THE WAR
> A Soldier's Declaration [Text follows.]
> This statement was made to his commanding officer by Second-Lieutenant S.L. Sassoon, 3rd Battalion Royal Welsh [sic] Fusiliers, as explaining his grounds for refusing to serve further in the Army. He enlisted on August 3rd 1914, showed distinguished valour in France, was badly wounded, and would have been kept on Home Service if he had stayed in the Army.[6]

The report is included in Robert Graves's *Goodbye to All That*. Graves adds 'recommended for D.S.O.' The book states incorrectly that Sassoon's sending him the page of the paper is how he learned of Sassoon's statement.[7]

Word now buzzed on the dissenting grapevine. Next day Sassoon's statement was on the front page of Sylvia Pankhurst's *Workers' Dreadnought* (which consistently argued for peace by negotiation). This was the first London publication of the statement. Scotland Yard was alerted and Pankhurst's offices were raided, with a hundred copies of the leaflet seized.[8]

By the time Bertie Lees-Smith found his debate moment in the House of Commons, it must have been apparent that the pacifists' bird had flown. Siegfried Sassoon had been sent to a sanatorium as being sick in the head and was not resisting that. Lees-Smith went ahead regardless. Robert Graves had failed to shut down hearing of Sassoon's protest. 30 July was another day of the Consolidated Fund Bill. During this there was a mini-debate on the breaking up of meetings in favour of peace-by-negotiation and against conscription by gangs of soldiers and sailors. Here was Lees-Smith's chance to speak about Siegfried Sassoon.

The background was the recent Labour and Socialist Convention at the Coliseum Theatre, Leeds, on 3 June 1917, at which 1,150 delegates assembled to hail the Russian spring revolution. The watchword was 'Follow Russia'. A Provisional Committee of a Workers' and Soldiers' Council was set up. The plan was to give to ordinary soldiers a say on what they were fighting for. It was resolved also to set up local Workers' and Soldiers' Councils ('British soviets'). The Leeds Convention voted for universal suffrage, a free press, free speech, political prisoner amnesty and the end of conscription, as well as peace by negotiation.[9]

The meeting to set up the London and Home Counties Workers' and Soldiers' Council was scheduled for the Brotherhood Church in Southgate Road, Islington, with Labour MP William Anderson in the chair. Anderson was a Garsington Manor visitor. He was young and a rising star in the Labour Party, moderate and pragmatic, and with personal charm. Anderson might eventually have become Labour Leader, perhaps even Prime Minister, had he not been one of the victims of the 1918-1920 influenza pandemic, a product of the war, which is reckoned to have caused 50 million or more deaths worldwide. The Islington meeting gathered on Saturday, 28 July. What happened was still reverberating. One of the participants was Bertrand Russell. There is the famous account in Russell's *Autobiography* of the meeting's destruction by a semi-military gang. Leaflets had been circulated in the nearby public houses warning of a nest of collaborators with the Germans, who were signalling where to drop bombs. The hit squad consisted of Canadian and Australian soldiers and a mixed band of others, led by an officer, and including women. All except the officers, according to Russell, were 'more or less drunk'. He described how, 'two of the drunken viragos began to attack me with their boards full of nails.' He was saved by a young woman there for the meeting who interposed herself between him and his assailants. The *Times* reported that two or three hundred men and women singing 'Rule, Britannia', 'swept aside the small guard...Some of the delegates were injured.'[10]

Canadian troops were prominent in accounts of the breaking up of peace activist meetings. Arthur Ponsonby's diary records his home being surrounded by Canadian troops, creeping round the house and firing guns. Shulbrede Priory was an isolated building in the Sussex/Surrey border woods. It is difficult to see what military purpose the exercise can have had other than to intimidate an anti-war MP. Ponsonby remarked to his journal:

> How intensely futile it seems that these splendid men who ought to be occupied in a hundred different remunerative ways should be engaged in this tragic farce which has only one object, one purpose, one aim and one lasting consequence – death and destruction. [11]

He knew about the Western Front from his brother John, who was a general there. He was not condescending when he called the Canadian soldiers 'splendid'.

Sylvia Pankhurst has an insight into soldiers breaking up meetings in her memoirs. A khaki group was sitting on the front row of one of her London events. At this a speaker for peace by negotiation was Helena Swanwick. The military men were taking their cue from their officer in singing nonsense choruses to drown out Helena. Seeing that her colleague was not coping, Sylvia intervened. She won the men over. She knew how their families were struggling in the war.[12]

The use of dominion troops to wreck anti-conscription and peace advocacy meetings was widespread. How systematically organised it was is not known. There has been no study. The authorities allowed the patriot mobs and the khaki squads to wreck dissenter meetings. In the case of the one at Southgate Road, they made sure that there would be a riot. Basil Thompson of the police special branch asked the *Daily Express* to publish the address in advance.[13]

The protests about the destruction of the London meeting were led by Shoreditch Liberal MP Henry Chancellor, a paint manufacturer. Chancellor's anti-conscription meetings in London parks were regularly disrupted. He said that the gang at Southgate Road was 'led by Canadian and Australian troops accompanied by an officer, contrary to Army Regulations No. 451' (which prohibited soldiers in uniform from attending political meetings):

> One soldier told a lady I know that they had orders to break up the meeting; another that he had been instructed to bruise the men and to tear the clothes off the women. When one woman was being attacked and a policeman was appealed to by a lady to interfere, he smiled in her face and allowed the attack to go on.[14]

Speaking with his familiar West Country burr, Chancellor made an appeal:

> I ask that...the force of the Army of liberty and the Navy of liberty, shall be used for the purposes for which they claim they are fighting, namely liberty abroad, and not to destroy it at home.

The MP linked the suppression of meetings to curtailment of the press, which included the (temporary) closure of *The Globe* for revealing dissension within the Government, and more recently the Government ban on the foreign circulation of the *Nation*.

The complaints about the failure of the police to protect the Islington meeting were replied to by the Home Secretary, Sir George Cave, a Conservative. Cave said that between 100 and 150 policemen were present, some of them in plain clothes: the police had done their utmost to protect the building and those in it. He called the allegation of instructions to break up the meeting 'a libel on the Army'. The response has the look of whitewash, explicitly contradicted as it was by a number of eye-witness reports. Bertrand Russell wryly recalled that when he was being assaulted, the police on being informed that he was an eminent philosopher, merely shrugged but did move in on being told that he was the brother of an earl. Cave would later become Lord Chancellor, 'the least distinguished occupant of the Woolsack in his era' in the view of Roy Jenkins.[15]

For Lees-Smith, the debate perfectly fitted his Siegfried Sassoon move. The Northampton MP gave the Commons some background detail regarding Sassoon's statement and his letter to his commanding officer. Then he read out Sassoon's declaration. The time of day was not the best, a few minutes before 7 p.m., the parliamentary dinner hour, when the chamber tended to be depleted. This was a regular experience for peace campaigners. Still, Lees-Smith did have some listeners. Importantly, they included the compilers of the Hansard record and the reporters in the press gallery. L-S told MPs of the diagnosis that Sassoon was shell-shocked. He said:

> I read this letter because I think that it contains no indication whatever of having been written by a man suffering from any kind of nervous shock. The fact is that the decision of the medical board is not based upon health, but upon very easily understood reasons of policy.

The MP explained why he had put down his question:

> In order to have the case put in as official form as possible, I put down the question whether he did create this breach of discipline, and I asked whether disciplinary action had been taken. I knew he had been told that he would have to come before a medical board and I knew he had refused to go.[16]

The question was never taken on the floor of the House.

Lees-Smith did not speak about politics or Sassoon's charges that Britain's war was now being fought for dishonourable purposes, though his group did make the same arguments as Sassoon at other times. He talked about discrimination in the Army. On the one hand there was the treatment of Siegfried Sassoon.

On the other, soldiers were 'permitted month after month to break up meetings held by those whose opinions are opposed to those of the Government': there were photographs of soldiers inside halls smashing up proceedings. The War Office had 'never lifted a finger' to stop them. An MP shouted: 'It has encouraged them.' Lees-Smith had suffered himself. Several months earlier, speaking for a peace-by-negotiation candidate at a by-election at Stockton-on-Tees, he had trouble from a gang of sailors, who climbed onto the platform and harangued the audience. One promised 'something hot [for Lees-Smith] when he is finished'. During the candidate's speech there was singing of the National Anthem and, said a local newspaper, 'at intervals disorder so great that he could not proceed'. Even if the khaki and bluecoat gangs were not the creation of governmental or military agencies, the authorities evidently knew what was happening and looked the other way. There were various departments to this. The offices of the *Cambridge Magazine* were vandalised.[17]

The MP condemned 'using soldiers as a pawn in the political game'. The meeting-breakers, he said, misrepresented the feeling of the Army. He issued a challenge:

> If the Under-Secretary would give the necessary leave for twelve hours, the organisers of this very meeting could bring up to London in two hours, as he knows very well, whole battalions of soldiers in their support...A brigade could have been brought up within two hours, with 95 percent of the soldiers in that brigade ready to support the initiators of this meeting. What is the use of the Home Secretary saying that there are no soldiers on that side?

This went to the heart of the issue of democracy and the troops who were doing the fighting. The campaign for soldiers' democratic councils might a hundred years on seem pie-in-the-sky, a fanciful, even absurd notion. In fact, in 1917 it was a very real issue. Britain, according to its original stated aims, had entered the war in 1914 to repel the German invasion of Belgium and France, not to conquer Germany, or even to reduce Germany to submission. A year later the war was mutating into a very different set of purposes. Johnnie Ponsonby, the previously mentioned active service general, told his MP brother Arthur in November 1915 that the majority of Britain's soldiers were in favour of a negotiated peace: he said that he 'hated all the extremist talk of smashing Germany and going to Berlin'. The 'extremist talk' had become the orthodoxy, backed not by the fighting men at the battle front but by those in the safety of the home front. With the fall of Asquith, the policy of fighting to the knock-out blow was confirmed. The Leeds Convention sought to give the rank-and-file soldiers a voice. The vast numbers who had signed up in 1914 and 1915 had not done so to fight a prolonged war to the bitter end to land a knock-out blow on Germany. Nor was it to enable Britain, France and Italy to add to their colonial portfolios.[18]

Lees-Smith brought the debate back to the statement of Siegfried Sassoon:

> The letter of a young officer is worth reams of articles in newspapers, and it is worth hundreds of soldiers got together in order to break up a meeting without knowing what the meeting is about. That is why it is necessary to prevent the action of this young officer being stifled and discredited by the absurd doctrine that it has been due to the effects of nervous shock.[19]

The ministerial reply was given by Ian Macpherson:

> ...I thought that [Lees-Smith] with his well-known humanitarian feelings thought that the War Office or the military authorities in the Western Command were going to treat this man as if he had committed a breach of military discipline. I called the attention of the Director-General of Personal Services to this case. [The Directorate of Personal Services was a board of senior military officers (with a staff), which dealt with various Army matters including discipline and courts-martial.] Here is a case where the War Office would at once court-martial this man for writing this letter as a breach of discipline, but they have not done so, and there must be some other reason.[20]

Here, Philip Snowden shouted: 'There is.'

Macpherson pressed on quickly, getting on the record what was to be the official line:

> The proper reason is that the military authorities saw that there must be something very wrong in the case of such an extremely gallant young officer who had done excellent work, and who had shown, by getting the Distinguished Service Order, that he was no mean soldier. He comes home, and when it is found that a man of this character has written a letter of this sort to his fellow officers, they conclude that there must be something radically wrong, and instead of taking disciplinary action they take the natural course of asking him to appear before a medical board. I do not think even my hon. Friends opposite would go so far as to say that a medical board, knowing the man to be guilty of a breach of discipline,

> would say that this man was suffering from shell shock in order not to assist the political attitude of my hon. Friend and his colleagues.[21]

The phrase 'my hon. Friends opposite' reminds that the anti-war Liberals (Liberals being Macpherson's own party) were on the Opposition side of the chamber. The minister is here with some candour admitting that if Sassoon were not declared to be mentally disturbed, the peace-by-negotiation cause would be boosted by his statement. A point of interest in the minister's statement is the reference to Sassoon having won a DSO. This seems to imply (since Macpherson's information was from the Army authorities) that the recommendation had been going through.

The debate moved on but Siegfried Sassoon's statement was on the record. Next day would bring the press coverage.

Was Siegfried Sassoon's statement representative of widespread feeling in the Army? There is interesting evidence on this. Robert Graves, back with the 3rd Battalion, wrote to SS on 31 July 1917:

> ...Well, you are notorious throughout England now you silly old thing! Everyone here who's been to France agrees with your point of view...[22]

After the war Siegfried Sassoon became close friends with his battalion's medical officer, Dr James Dunn, who compiled the chronicle *The War the Infantry Knew*. Dunn was well placed to assess Army attitudes. In 1927 he wrote to Sassoon:

> A note in my diary might interest you in retrospect:
> August 6th 1917: "Sassoon's outburst has led to his being sent to a shell shock hospital; but a great many are saying the same thing."[23]

In the RWF history Dunn is one of the contributors. The 6 August 1917 section is probably composed by him:

> Sassoon's quixotic outburst has been drenched in a "shell shock" retreat. He will be among the degenerates, drinkers, malingerers, and common mental cases, as well as the overstrained. It is an astute official means of denying our cold-blooded, cold-footed, superior persons the martyr they are too precious to find from their own unruly ranks. Sassoon gave a moral flavour to a gibe everywhere current at the front for a couple of years, that a lot of individuals in cushy jobs don't care how long the War lasts....For one in the Army with an interest in the prolongation of the War there are now hundreds of "indispensables" at home in well paid war-jobs...

> [Their] affluence [has] made it hard for the serving-men's families and exasperated the serving-men…There is great unrest, and an intensity of feeling and determination that make certain the coming of great political and social disturbance after the War; the early phase many precede the end of the War.[24]

This may explain Leonard Outhwaite's interpretation of his recent conversation with (presumably) Siegfried Sassoon that, 'The men in the trenches are all revolutionary in spirit.' Dunn's view of coming social and industrial upheaval at home were certainly correct. The chapter headings of Simon Webb's book, *1919: Britain's Year of Revolution* include: Mutiny in the Armed Forces; Tanks on the Streets; The Triple Alliance [of trade unions] Flexes its Muscles, Purging the Police; Warships in the Mersey. Social turbulence was already bubbling up in 1917.[25]

The subject of 'the profiteers' tends to be treated as a discrete sub-topic of the war. The correspondence and diaries of Siegfried Sassoon and his military circle, James Dunn, Joe Cottrill and others, persons with much insight, make it clear that profiteering was integral to the continuation of the war in its later years. Total war had become a system, in which large numbers of people, safe from personal risk, had an embedded interest in many ways, economic, political, personal, in the continuation of the contest. Thus it was that negotiation opportunities came and went – and H.H. Asquith, who might have ended the war, was ousted from power, to the dismay of liberal values adherents, including the Morrells at Garsington. The vested interests in the prolongation of the hostilities, as we see from Siegfried's Sassoon's various writings, included the general staff, on whose guzzling and comforts he poeticised so acerbically.

Britain's leading newspaper was the *Times*. The major organ of the establishment always gave extended coverage to the proceedings of Parliament. Did it have Lees-Smith's reading of the Sassoon statement.? It did, verbatim. The *Times* comes well out of this. Its position was one of full-blooded support for fight-to-the-finish but there was no snipping out of a powerful declaration heard by Parliament of the contrary case. The paper treated its readers as grown-ups: no censorship of the speech. It should be mentioned that the *Times* did not, like so many – indeed most – papers, run the line that Britain had entered the war to defend Belgium. For The *Times*, that was a side-issue: Britain was in the war to fulfil its commitment of honour to France, and to uphold the interests of the British Empire.[26]

Robert Graves's letter to Sassoon included a hope that, 'old Gosse won't think better of celebrating his protégé in the Edinburgh Review.' His expectation that

Edmund Gosse would see the Sassoon statement in one of papers was correct. Gosse wrote to Siegfried's Uncle Hamo on 31 July:

> You see the distressing disclosures in all the papers today. I enclose the *Times*, as it gives the best report. It is most deplorable, because it will fill poor Siegfried with insensate vanity. Vanity, indeed, is a great source of the whole trouble. Now of course he becomes the hero and the martyr of everything that is most unwholesome and vicious in current politics. I really cannot say to you how miserable I feel that his crazy words of defiance should be circulated to all the world in tens of thousands. And what makes it worst is to know that his own self-conceit will be gratified to the summit of exultation.[27]

One who was not depressed was a person of indecipherable signature who was associated with Liverpool Repertory Theatre and had apparently got to know Siegfried Sassoon in Liverpool. He wrote to wish Siegfried well. He hoped to see 'little by little the universal recognition of principles that you have championed in the days of their unpopularity'.[28]

Siegfried Sassoon was not in all the papers. Many studiously avoided any mention of him in their coverage of the debate on broken up meetings. Still, what Gosse said is revealing. Sassoon as the persecuted martyr for the cause of peace, the man on everyone's lips, was what the peace-by-negotiation cause was looking for. The problem for the parliamentary peace groupers was that their protagonist had left the stage.

The final paragraph of the Gosse to Hamo letter has a retrospectively ominous significance: 'I wonder what is happening in Flanders. The silence of Haig is very mysterious.' This day saw the opening of the Battle of Passchendaele, which would last until November, with less than five miles of ground gained and a further 70 thousand British dead added to the total, the special horror being the watery terrain, with soldiers drowning on the battlefield. On the first day two poets fell, both 29, both hit by shells in the attack on Pilcken Ridge, which involved the Royal Welch Fusiliers. The Welsh-speaking Ellis Evans, whose bardic name was Hedd Wynn, was posthumously awarded the Bard's Chair at the 1917 National Eisteddfod, the occasion of the 'Empty Chair'. The Irish poet Francis Ledwidge was reported by a chaplain as having been 'blown to bits' while drinking tea.[29]

The *Times*'s sister paper in the Northcliffe stable, the big-selling *Daily Mail*, covered Siegfried Sassoon's declaration. It was indirect speech rather than verbatim, but it was there. Sassoon somewhat later sent a *Mail* cutting to Edward Carpenter. His letter is intriguing:

> The ballads amuse me greatly. Of course I don't mind your printing the one about me, and the name will do all right. The court-martial might be altered to "Medical Board"...

The *Mail*'s coverage of the debate on meeting-breakers is under 'M.P.s AND PACIFISTS: RIOT QUESTIONS IN THE COMMONS'. Its Sassoon column is beneath 'AN OFFICER'S LETTER: SUFFERING FROM SHOCK'. Lees-Smith's claim of support in the Army for a Soldiers' and Workers' Council gets: 'A BOAST AND THE FACTS', concentrating on the War Minister's scepticism. Even with some adverse or unhelpful editorial spin, Lees-Smith's group and its allies will have been pleased to see their point of view on the war getting much more coverage than usual.[30]

It is no surprise that Sassoon's statement appears in full and is prominently presented in the *Daily News*, Britain's leading Liberal newspaper. The *News* had:

> OFFICER'S LETTER: SERIOUS STATEMENT IN THE HOUSE

The paper's parliamentary correspondent was Philip Wilson, a former Liberal MP. Wilson uses indirect speech for the statement but the full content is there. He called Sassoon, quoting Lees-Smith, 'this gallant officer, a man of unusual mental power and exceptional determination of character'.[31]

The coverage brought a letter to Siegfried Sassoon a couple of weeks later from two admirers, who signed as Cecile Walton Robertson (Edinburgh) and Dorothy Seward (Cambridge):

> We find it obvious from your poems that your present attitude of mind is the result of a perfectly clear evolution of thought and certainly not the result of any physical shock from which you may suffer.[32]

Robertson was a distinguished illustrator and sculptor (associated with the Symbolist movement). If this letter is any way representative of public reaction to reports of the exchanges in Parliament regarding Siegfried Sassoon's protest, the Government's presentation of a valiant soldier now writing strange things as a result of shell-shock, was not washing. It is one of a number of indicators that had Sassoon stuck to his campaign, he could have done some damage to the credibility of the Government's position on the war.

The other big Liberal newspaper published in London was the *Daily Chronicle* (which was close to Lloyd George). The *Chronicle* covered the raising of Sassoon's case in Parliament in a newsy sort of way. The *Manchester Guardian*, as might be expected from a radical and critical newspaper (it circulated chiefly in the north of England, arriving in London at midday), had the full Sassoon statement. The headline was: 'AN OFFICER'S PROTEST'. Edited by C.P. Scott (who after opposition at the start of the war to British entry, had fallen into line), the *Guardian* was the most obvious of the major papers in which to look for dissent.[33]

Most of the provincial press avoided Siegfried Sassoon's declaration. There is little or no reference to it in accounts of the debate in Parliament about meeting wrecking by soldiers. The *Liverpool Daily Post* and the *Birmingham Daily Post* had an identical garbling of the debate, with no mention by name of Sassoon, presumably these papers using the same news source. Just a handful of provincial papers reported on Sassoon. However, the *Aberdeen Evening Gazette* had the whole statement and some background on the Sassoon family. The *Birmingham Gazette* stated that Sassoon 'wrote a letter to his commanding officer' and it quoted a snippet of the statement. It called the Sassoons 'that numerous and wealthy clan'. There were small bits of the declaration in the *Burton Evening Gazette*, the *Southampton Echo* and the *Dundee Advertiser*. The fragments amounted to not much. But still there was the detailed coverage by four or five big-selling London newspapers plus the major reporting in Manchester and Aberdeen. As Edmund Gosse's letter indicates, the news of Sassoon spread.[34]

The publications that campaigned for peace by negotiation of course backed Siegfried Sassoon with enthusiasm. The ILP's *Labour Leader* carried the full statement, adding:

> Lieutenant Sassoon is not only a distinguished soldier but the brilliant author of a striking volume of poems. What will be posterity's verdict upon those who have sought to prove him mad?[35]

We cannot know what the outcome would have been if the publicity for Siegfried Sassoon's statement had gone with the soldier continuing his challenge to the war and as a result being put before a court-martial. Readers of big press papers saw what in many cases was quite unfamiliar to them. The press was drenched day-in-day-out in justification and glorification of the war. The Government's agencies did all they could to suppress dissent. Censorship, the Defence of the Realm Act, and soldiers breaking up peace meetings, ensured that most people never read the case against unnecessarily prolonging the war. Might that have changed if Sassoon's case, as he had intended, had gone before a court-martial? It is a question worth consideration.

Did Siegfried Sassoon feel any pangs over letting down his statement support team by taking the medical board? We need to visit Sassoon's *Sherston's Progress* account of his arrival at Craiglockhart. This is concerned with his impressions of the sanatorium and the start of being a patient of Dr Rivers. There is no wondering how Bertie Lees-Smith and his colleagues were feeling, with their hopes knocked back by his abandonment of the campaign. In Sassoon's thoughts, the parliamentarians were fading. The man of his moment was Dr Rivers. He was almost jerked back into his political self when he read about the debate of 30 July. But he tells readers of SP: 'There, I think [the protest] may safely be allowed to remain at rest.' In the tone of self-mockery that flavours these Woosterish memoirs, he remarks: 'I needed a holiday from that sort of thing: the intensity of my individual effort to influence the Allied Governments had abated.' It would be unfair to call Sassoon a flibbertigibbet. There would be more politics from him next year. The protest was over but not the principles. And his preparation for martyrdom had been the real thing. Nor did he change his views on the war. In his many deep conversations with Rivers, the doctor's pro-war attitude made no impression on him.[36]

Siegfried Sassoon's attitude to Craiglockhart was one of lofty disdain. Several days after his arrival he wrote to Robbie Ross:

> The are 160 Officers here, most of them half-dotty. No doubt I'll be able to get some splendid details for future use.[37]

The letter is written on hospital notepaper. Sassoon has written above CRAIGLOCKHART WAR HOSPITAL "Dottyville". With the joke he distances himself from the mental frailty of the residents. Later he wrote to Uncle Hamo:

> I am very sorry if I have caused you worry and annoyance by my recent actions. Of course you don't agree with me; but I hope you won't join the people who wriggle out of the situation by saying I'm dotty. I am having a pretty decent time here...[38]

It was of supreme importance to Sassoon that he should not be considered to be mentally compromised. On 1 August he wrote to Roderick Meiklejohn:

> I am perfectly free, and there is no pretence made of anything wrong with my health...Anyone who says I'm "not responsible for my actions" is a sanguinary liar.'[39]

Did any other soldier go public with a denunciation of the war while still in service? An Australian parallel may be found. A soldier tried to issue a statement with arguments closely similar to those of Siegfried Sassoon. He was in the

Australian Imperial Force (AIF). He was Private Edward James Ryan from the mining town of Broken Hill. Ryan was twice wounded in France. In August 1916 he was in London at Denmark Hill Hospital (a Sassoon coincidence), diagnosed with shell shock. He later convalesced at Perham Down camp in Wiltshire. From there on 18 October, he wrote to Ramsay MacDonald, then the best-known peace-by-negotiation proponent in the British Parliament, a letter condemning the war and urging negotiations. Ryan told MacDonald something of the soldier experience of the Somme ('The Abbatoirs'), far removed from the propaganda pictures of Anzacs coming out of the firing-line 'bright and cheery and hooraying'. Ryan said: 'Every man I have spoken to is absolutely sick of the whole business... To every man its frightfulness was beyond their imagination.' He gave JRM the sort of details that Siegfried Sassoon would have recognised. His impression was that England still had 'her old ideal of Conquer'. Conquest was the English motivation that Siegfried Sassoon's statement asserted was driving British war policy. He urged:

> Now Mr MacDonald, I hope you will do everything in your power to bring about a Peace and save this slaughter of Human Lives.[40]

He chose the wrong politician. Ramsay MacDonald may have replied but he did not use Ryan's letter. The ex-Labour Leader was a pariah because of his opposition to conscription and his promotion of peace-by-negotiation and perhaps this had an effect on him because he became ultra-cautious, anxious at every turn to prove his patriotism, to the exasperation sometimes of his anti-war colleagues. Had Ryan written to his fellow Australian Leonard Outhwaite, we may say almost certainly that it would have resulted in a speech in Parliament, with quotation. Ryan was court-martialled three times for 'desertion', the third time having been arrested at Le Havre for having been away for 14 days. He ended his (written) statement to the court:

> I enlisted to fight for a Peace without conquerors or conquered...nothing to justify another war, either as a war of revenge by the Conquered or a war of Glory and Patriotic land-grabbing by the Conquerors.[41]

This sentiment was precisely that of Siegfried Sassoon and the peace-by-negotiation group in the British House of Commons, the MPs issuing their regular warning that if the war ended in the triumph of either side, there would certainly be another one. Ted Ryan was sentenced to death. No Australian soldier faced a firing-squad for the reason that all Australian death sentences were commuted – in Ryan's case to 5 years' penal servitude. The following year the sentence was suspended and he was released. If Siegfried Sassoon had been sentenced to death, there would have been no automatic commutation. Over 300 British soldiers were 'shot at dawn'. The differences however between the situations of Sassoon and Ryan were very considerable. Ryan was a private soldier while Sassoon was an officer. Hardly any officers were executed. And Sassoon had a cousin who was private secretary to Sir Douglas Haig. He was also a decorated hero, who was highly esteemed militarily. But he could well have been sent to prison had he maintained his defiance. And Ted Ryan's death sentence is a reminder that tangling with the Army about the war was dangerous indeed.[42]

As events fell out, the British Army and the British Government were not too much embarrassed by Siegfried Sassoon's declaration against the war. It was managed. Robert Graves's persuasion of Sassoon to accept a medical board made all the difference. SS was a talking-point for a while but the position of the authorities on the war was not seriously damaged. They remained however vigilant against dissent. Sassoon wrote to Roderick Meiklejohn on 14 August:

> The Edinburgh bookshops don't sell *The Old Huntsman* – I suppose they are too respectable. Rob Nicholls is displayed everywhere in large numbers. (I am not jealous!)[43]

Lieutenant Robert Nichols's *Ardours and Endurances* had been published in June and it had already gone into a second edition. Nichols is given the largest space in *The Muse in Arms*. Editor Osborn saw his verses as showing that: 'the last sacrifice is but the price that is due for the beauty of England inwrought inextricably in [a soldier's] being.' The Nichols lines that he quotes in this respect are pure 1914-1915:

> ...The wet, lit lane and the yellow-hammer,
> The orchard and the chaffinch song,
> Only to the Brave belong;
> And he shall lose their joy for ay,
> If their price he cannot pay.[44]

If this sort of offering was keeping Siegfried Sassoon's poetry out of the Edinburgh bookshops, he had good reason, one may say, to feel aggrieved. Nichols was an upper-class socialite, with a shrill ring when he did his (frequent) readings, contrasting with Siegfried Sassoon's mumbling diffidence when he was pressed to perform. Though he joined the Royal Field Artillery in 1914, Nichols was in action for only three weeks (in the summer of 1916). He was invalided home with shell-shock, actually suffering from syphilis (being deprived of his commission on that account), as he confided to Robert Graves. He did not go out again. He worked for British propaganda. Sassoon later met him and seems to have got on with him, to the extent that Nicholls came to Weirleigh for a fortnight's stay. Nicholls was an establishment favourite. His poetry shared with Sassoon's the realism of battle, but there is not the same dimension of horror. Furthermore, Nichols exhibited some bloodthirsty Germanophobia. His 1916 'The Assault' ends:

Ha! Ha! Bunched figures waiting.
Revolver levelled: quick!
Flick! Flick!
Red as blood.
Germans. Germans!
Good! Oh good!
Cool madness.[45]

Siegfried Sassoon will have been correct in thinking that for bookshops, Nicholls's poetry was 'respectable', a safer marketing choice than his own. It includes 'Sonnet: Our Dead', which is right in line with morale boosting in the face of slaughter: 'They are not gone from us…They flame in every star…they chant on every wind…' This was poetry to please Sybil Brassey.[46]

Here, close chronicling of Siegfried Sassoon must conclude. The soldier poet's famous time at Craiglockhart, with Doctor Rivers, Wilfred Owen, and others, is a story to which justice has been done, both in history and in Pat Barker's well researched *Regeneration* novel (the first of her trilogy), which brilliantly recreates sanatorium conversations. Siegfried Sassoon's political protest against the war, which is the subject of this particular account, was over, though its reverberations would continue. At this point it seems not inappropriate to quote the comment on the outcome of the Sassoon Statement by Caroline Playne in her astute (1933) analysis of British Home Front attitudes and behaviour during the last two years of the First World War:

> The attention of people at home should have been awakened by Mr Lees-Smith's inquiry in the House, and the questions posed by the brilliant young soldier on behalf of fellow-soldiers. The whole affair when noticed at all only met with reprobation, mass obsession having deflected the ability of judgment. It was the great majority who were mad![47]

## Chapter 12

# 'Murder'

Though Siegfried Sassoon's rebellion was over, his views remained firm, as he made sure that he told people. In his third week at Craiglockhart he was writing to Robert Graves. The two used to fantasise in France about places they would go to together after the war. Sassoon now said, 'We go to New Zealand and Polynesia aprés la guerre. Rivers gives noble accounts of both regions.' He hoped that Robert had got hold of the daring novel *The Loom of Youth* by new author Alec Waugh. He disliked the big type of his own book: 'only fit for latrine work – like its author'. His self-regard had taken a knock. Life at the sanatorium was not so unpleasant, but it was not what Sassoon wanted. What he thought about great matters had not changed. He told Graves: 'My opinions remain four square.'[1]

The chief drawback for Sassoon about Craiglockhart was having to share a room. He got out quite a lot however, playing all the local golf courses. His continuing verse production included:

> Love drove me to rebel,
> Love drives me back to grope with them through hell.[2]

Hell was Passchendaele. 'Love' was for his men there, of whose sufferings he got plenty of word one way and another. He wanted to return.

One bond was weakening. In this war Sassoon's special friendship up to now had been with Robert Graves. In 'Two Fusiliers', Graves wrote:

> Show me the two so closely bound
> As we, by the wet bond of blood...[3]

The closeness still existed, and there was still warmth in the correspondence, and the two occasionally met, but Graves's intervention over Sassoon's protest put a wedge between the Two Fusiliers. On 31 July 1917, Graves wrote to Sassoon about his action:

> ...Those that don't know you think it was not quite a gentlemanly course to take; the quixotic English-sportsman class especially.[4]

Graves seemed to agree: Sassoon had let down the regiment. On 12 October Graves made a trip to Edinburgh, where he played golf with Sassoon and Wilfred Owen, the three war poets and a doctor who had been torpedoed on *The Transylvania* making up a remarkable foursome on Baberton's links, three miles from Craiglockhart. Sassoon and Graves dined later in Edinburgh. A week later Sassoon concluded a letter to Graves:

> O Robert, whatever will happen to end the war? It's all very well for you to talk about "good form" and "acting like a gentleman". To me that's a very estimable form of suicidal stupidity and credulity. You admit that the people who sacrifice the troops are callous b-----rs, and the same thing is happening in all countries (except some of Russia). If you had real courage you wouldn't acquiesce as you do.[5]

Graves came back with, 'I should hate to think that I'm a coward.' He backtracked somewhat but he still saw Sassoon as 'turning round in the middle of the war, after having made a deliberate contract'. He told Siegfried that he should be ready 'for pride's sake to finish your contract whatever it costs you, yet all the time denouncing the principles you are being compelled to further.' For Graves, battalion loyalty came first, though he was in agreement with Sassoon in wishing that, 'our people could state definite peace terms.' Graves's poetic approach was changing. He was tiring of battlefield realism. 'Don't send me any more corpse poems,' he told Sassoon: SS should regard the war as 'a nightmare' from which he would wake when it was over; he should be making plans for after the war. Sassoon could have pointed out that the war dead would not wake 'to jolly mornings' (Graves's phrase), nor did lost limbs return. The war was continuing. Siegfried had done something to try to stop it. The friendship of the poets was on the slide. A signal was Graves's decision to change the dedication in his third book, *Fairies and Fusiliers*, from Sassoon to the Royal Welch Fusiliers.[6]

Siegfried Sassoon did aim to return to the Army. He did not want it to be in a non-combatant role. He wrote to Edward Dent on 24 November: 'I have now received an assurance from the W.O. that no obstacles will be put in the way of my resuming my place in the sausage-machine.' He left Craiglockhart two days later, having been passed fit for General Service, the first stage towards a return to the Western Front.

Reports from France were of the appalling time the Royal Welch Fusiliers were having. On 16 October Joe Cottrill wrote to Siegfried Sassoon in despair:

> I got your letter last week when we were in HELL. [Polygon Wood]...It is the same men all the time. If you don't get killed on Monday you can

> go over the top again on Tuesday and so on till you get outed. The only people in the Army who yell about the war being prosecuted till 'Germany is brought to her knees' etc, etc, are the people in nice safe-cushy jobs miles behind the lines – They are the people who pack the leave boats...Buck up and go to Parliament. Surely they cannot keep you against your will.[7]

Here in capitals was the repeating word of 1917. The letter is a remarkable turnaround by the quartermaster. In July Cottrill had disagreed with Sassoon's statement. Several months of Passchendaele had changed the Army veteran's mind. He now wanted Siegfried to go to Westminster and work with MPs to get his protest going again. But SS was off politics. He wanted to be back in the trenches. He was distant from Lady Ottoline when she came to Edinburgh, playing golf rather than seeing her off, and leaving her distraught. Ottoline's would-be soulmate was slipping away. Siegfried told her that nightmares about the war confirmed his intention to return to his comrades.

There was one issue that the poetry of Siegfried Sassoon that was published during the war did not address. That was the treatment of prisoners. He did write a poem about it. On 12 November 1917, he sent C.K. Ogden the draft of 'Atrocities', with an accompanying letter. He wondered whether Ogden had heard Canadians and Australians 'airing their exploits in the murder line'. He knew of some atrocities. He told Ogden that the other day at Craiglockhart an officer of a Scottish regiment, 'one of the many "lead-swinging" cases here', was regaling him with stories of how his men put bombs in prisoners' pockets and then pushed them into shell-holes full of water. This sort of thing, he remarked, was not an atrocity on the British side. But it was 'an indictment of war': war brought out a certain kind of behaviour in some people.[8]

'Atrocities' was not published until after the war:

> You told me in your drunken-boasting mode,
> How once you butchered prisoners. That was good!
> I'm sure you felt no pity while they stood
> Patient and cowed and scared, as prisoners should.

How did you do them in? Come, don't be shy:

> You know how I love to hear how Germans die,
> Downstairs in dug-outs. 'Camerad!' they cry;
> Then squeal like stoats when bombs begin to fly.[9]

Siegfried Sassoon knew that such a poem was hardly likely to get into even Ogden's *Cambridge Magazine*. Notable in the original draft of the poem is the word 'murder' about the killing of German prisoners. As we have seen, Sassoon had used the word 'murder' in 'The General', later replacing 'murdered them' with 'did for them'. Publication of Sassoon's 'Atrocities' poem would have been a shocking challenge to the official presentation that, while the Germans committed war crimes, the British war was clean. The last surviving British Western Front veteran, Harry Patch, who was at Passchendaele, used Sassoon's word about the whole war: 'War is organized murder and nothing else.'[10]

On the subject of war crimes, Niall Ferguson's *The Pity of War* quotes the war memoir *A Private in the Guards* by Stephen Graham, which claims that, 'the opinion cultivated in the Army regarding Germans was that they were a sort of vermin like plague-rats that had to be exterminated.' Siegfried Sassoon's bayonet-lecturing Colonel Ronald Campbell turns up in Ferguson's discussion, with a quotation cited from Philip Gibbs's *Now It Can Be Told*, of the bayonet showman telling his trainees: 'You may meet a German who says "Mercy! I have ten children!" Kill him! He might have ten more.' Protocol regarding prisoners was murky and sometimes fudged. On occasion prisoners were shot while trying to escape; sometimes prevention of escape provided a pretext for butchering; sometimes when soldiers surrendered, they were shot down as if the battle was still on. In the 'war of attrition', it can be no surprise if blind eyes were turned to the killing of captives. Robert Graves remarks in *Goodbye to All That* on 'the interval between the surrender of prisoners and their arrival (or non-arrival) at headquarters': 'nearly every instructor in the mess could quote specific instances of prisoners having been murdered on the way back.' Such was the war, but its presentation on the home front was one of an ethically proper British Army battling gamely against atrocity-committing Germans. Siegfried Sassoon's 'Atrocities' poem was – or could have been – a significant challenge to the presentation of the war as good versus evil, one which made peace negotiations less likely.[11]

In December 1917 Siegfried Sassoon heard that Arthur Balfour, ex-Prime Minister and currently Foreign Secretary, had shown interest in his prospective new collection of war poems. It would come out on 27 June 1918, entitled *Counter-Attack*. Sassoon wrote to Roderick Meiklejohn:

> I should have expected Mr B. to dislike anything so direct and plain spoken. They ought to let me state our war aims in verse.[12]

SS here echoes the repeated pleas of the House of Commons peace-by-negotiation group that the Government should state precisely (rather than in vague emotive rhetoric) what its terms were for making peace: if both sides did that a settlement would have a better prospect of being reached.

Siegfried Sassoon hailed the famous 'Lansdowne Letter' in the *Daily Telegraph* on 29 November 1917, in which the Marquess of Lansdowne, who had been Foreign Secretary in the Conservative government which signed the Entente Cordiale between Britain and France, called for peace negotiations to save civilisation from ruin. Sassoon wrote to Ottoline Morrell on 4 December 1917, 'The Lansdowne affair has given us all a feeling of hope, hasn't it?' Support for Lansdowne's letter was fairly general in the front-line Army. It went with the expressed agreement in the fighting ranks of the Army with the sentiments of Siegfried Sassoon's declaration in July 1917. Ex-Home Secretary Sir John Simon reported widespread support for Lansdowne in France in 1917; so did Lord Newton, a Foreign Office minister.[13]

As 1917 drew to an end, Siegfried Sassoon was back at the RWF depot at Litherland. A letter to Roderick Meiklejohn casts some light on his frame of mind half a year after his aborted protest. On Christmas Eve Sassoon and three others of his battalion were dining at the house of Colonel Jones-Williams. It was an evening of merry seasonal festivity, including the old (and now dangerous-seeming) lark of having threepenny bits (the 12-sided pre-decimal coin) hidden inside the Christmas pudding, producing squeals of excitement when they were bitten on. Sassoon's diary details have cracker-pulling, the giggling daughters of the Colonel, and a card game called 'loo'. 'Peace on earth and three cheers for the Morning Post [a right-wing newspaper which later merged with *The Daily Telegraph*]', he remarked sardonically. He ended the entry:

> A scene of German domesticity, but very kind-hearted. I wish I were like that, and could see my fellow men as anything but guzzling, gabbling grotesques.[14]

At surface level Sassoon was rehabilitated with the establishment and its war. Running deep was scorn and indignation about what he saw as the unfairness and hypocrisy of the great national crusade.

In January 1918 Sassoon could have had no way of knowing that in London he was under investigation at the War Office. A Mr S. Sullivan of Birmingham, on a train to Preston, stumbled on one of the statement leaflets in the luggage rack of a compartment. He alerted the authorities and the sheet made its way to the War Office. It did the rounds of W.O. officials, who duly scribbled their observations on a circulating document, including (19 January):

> Lt Sassoon was undoubtedly the author but when it was written he was a lunatic (vide medical board). It seems that it is possible that some pacifists are circulating Sassoons [sic] insane effort.[15]

No action was taken.In the spring of 1918, the travels of Siegfried Sassoon's battalion took him to Palestine. He was in Gaza and Ramallah. On 11 December 1917 the British General Allenby had captured Jerusalem from the Turks, causing the British jingo press to evoke medieval English crusades. On 2 November 1917 the so-called Balfour Declaration had been issued, a letter from British Foreign Secretary Arthur Balfour to Lord Rothschild, a leading British Zionist. It said that British Ministers 'view with favour the establishment in Palestine of a national home for the Jewish people.' Balfour was a genuine supporter of the cause, but the Declaration provided moral cover for British post-Ottoman ambitions in the Near East. In a *Herald* article Arthur Ponsonby (who six years later would be Under-Secretary at the Foreign Office in the first Labour government) called Balfour 'an incorrigible dilettante', lacking 'the critical responsibility which must rest on the shoulders of the Foreign Secretary'. British endorsement of Zionism would, it was hoped, spur American and Russian Jewish zeal for the war, though Russia was by then on the way out of it. The final version included the qualification of nothing being done to prejudice the rights of non-Jewish communities in Palestine but here and elsewhere dragon's teeth were being sown. What was happening in 1918 underlines what war consequences might have been averted had Siegfried Sassoon's declaration of July 1917 succeeded in shaking up the block on peace-making at the British end of things.[16]

Of course, there were numerous outcomes of the war which were already developing before 1917, including in the Near and Middle East, a part of the world that Siegfried Sassoon was briefly getting to know. These included Arabia as a British target, as British influence in eastern Arabia expanded through patronage of the nationalist Arab revolt against the Turks. The British Government agreement of December 1915 with Sheikh Ibn Saud, in later times ruler of what became Saudi Arabia, made for purposes of war advantage, did much to assist Ibn Saud and his promotion of the anti-modern and anti-tolerance doctrine of Wahhabism. The long-term consequence would be the growing strength of an aggressive and polarising form of Islam later in the twentieth century and into the twenty-first. Sassoon's springtime voyages made him muse on *Arabia Deserta*, the Victorian travel book of 1888 by English traveller and poet Charles Montagu Doughty. In early April there was an officer sweepstake on where the battalion would end up. The most dreaded destination, Sassoon felt sure, was the Western Front.[17]

A court-martial in Britain, at Stockton-on-Tees on 5 April 1918, needs to be mentioned here. Lieutenant Max Plowman, journalist and poet, had taken a commission in the RAMC in 1914. He had twice been wounded. He had been at Craiglockhart, a patient of Dr Rivers, though he did not overlap with

Siegfried Sassoon. In January 1918 Plowman asked to resign his commission and as a result faced the court-martial. He made a statement to it, later published in *The Tribunal*, the magazine of conscientious objectors and their supporters:

> I am resigning my commission because I now believe that "national responsibility" is an insufficient excuse for committing acts in the name of the nation, which no sane person would be guilty of as an individual... The designed and intentional killing of any person against whose personal character you can make no charge, is I consider murder of the worst possible kind; such murder betrays the calculated and deliberate perversion of reason, and is therefore immoral to the last degree.[18]

The officer had written to his adjutant: 'For some time past it has been becoming increasingly apparent to me that for reasons of conscientious objection I was unfitted to hold my commission.' His objection was based on his Christianity. Max Plowman was the 'out-and-out' conscientious objector that Siegfried Sassoon was not. His statement was not political in the way that Sassoon's was; and he went through the proper channels in trying to get out of the Army, rather than making a demonstration. Still, his resignation request did amount to a rejection of the war by a serving officer. He was not imprisoned. He was dismissed from the Army, but subsequently called up as a rank-and-file soldier, the outcome that Robert Hanmer had predicted for Siegfried Sassoon. He contested this. He could have done non-military work classified as of war value but he contested this too. The matter was unresolved when the war ended.[19]

In early May, Siegfried Sassoon was back in France, at a rest camp outside Marseilles; then he headed north, giving lectures on the way. By late May, he could hear the guns. Familiar things now popped up, including Colonel Campbell with his Spirit of the Bayonet lecture. Standing on a farm-waggon in a field, Campbell told his audience that, 'Every Bosche you fellows kill is a point scored to our side...shortens the war by one minute.' Now, as Sassoon wrote in his diary, the touring Colonel's show 'only disgusted' him as 'the spirit of Militarism incarnate'.[20]

In early June came a moment of emotional crisis. Sassoon recorded it in his diary:

> ...I am nothing but what the Brigadier calls 'a potential killer of Germans' ['Huns' added]. O God, why must I do it? I'm not. I am only here to look after some men.[21]

The bite of satire stayed with Siegfried Sassoon. Around mid-June there is a notebook piece entitled 'Supreme Sacrifice'. Sassoon, as the diary portrays, is coming down a communication trench and having to squash himself against its chalky side to make way for two Canadians who are carrying a dead body slung along a pole, this apparently being the Canadian method of transporting their corpses away from the front line, with the hands tied together at the wrists; similarly with the ankles. The transportation duo hail another corpse-carrying pair: 'What's the weight of your pig?' The diarist comments:

> What splendid common sense! And how jolly the War is! But I wish they'd put a sand-bag over the face.[22]

Here is the Sassoon sting in the tail.

Much was happening in mid-1918. There had been Russia's second revolution in the previous November; Russia was out of the war. On the British home front, at a Wansbeck, Northumberland by-election on 28 May, an independent candidate, a Ruskin College-educated working miner, standing on a Labour and peace-by-negotiation platform, sensationally took 47.5 per cent of the vote, almost beating the Government candidate. This followed a successful pre-poll meeting at the Miners' Hall, Ashington, addressed by Charles Trevelyan of the parliamentary peace group, speaking for the candidate, Ebenezer (Eb) Edwards. The Government was shaken. William Straker, the Northumberland Miners' Leader, writing in *UDC* magazine, declared that the election had shown that 'the working man is tired of the insane struggle for military victory.' Governmental news management could not cover up the fact that the Northumberland coalfield had come close to sending a miner to Westminster with the message that it was time for an honourable negotiated peace. If Siegfried Sassoon saw the Wansbeck result (he probably did not) he was no doubt delighted, albeit sorrowful that Edwards did not quite make it to Westminster to proclaim the message of his July 1917 statement.[23]

The chance for the peace movement to build on Wansbeck never arose because the war picture was radically changing. 1918 was militarily quite unlike the previous two years. No longer was the Western Front virtually static. It was on the move for the first time since late 1914. The spring of 1918 saw the German Ludendorff Offensive, with Paris again threatened. The Germans tried for a decisive breakthrough before the Americans could swing the war in the Allies' favour. The situation was still grave in June when Siegfried Sassoon, now promoted to acting captain, was back on the Western Front. On 2 June the Germans took 4,500 prisoners on the Marne and on 6 June there was an emergency meeting of company officers where Sassoon was based. On 12 June his diary records:

> After lunch today I glanced at *The Times* – killed in action – Lt. C.N. Dobell, R.W.F. Little Colin who was with me at Mametz Wood. 'It can't be true; it can't be true,' I thought. But it's there in print. Fool-poems in the *Spectator* about 'our unforgotten dead'. 'We must live more nobly, remembering those who fell,' etc. Will *that* comfort *Colin* and his girl? *He* wanted life; fox-hunting, and marriage, and peace-soldiering. Now he's lost it all; aged 21.[24]

A poem entitled 'Colin' follows. It ends:

> Is there any more to say?
> Colin's name's been printed in The Times,
> 'Killed in Action'. He can't read my rhymes.

At Habarcq, 11 kilometres from Arras, on 18 June, Sassoon composed 'I Stood with The Dead':

> I stood with the Dead, so forsaken and still;
> When dawn was grey I stood with the Dead.
> And my slow heart said, 'You must kill, you must kill:
> 'Soldier, soldier, morning is red.'
>
> On the shapes of the slain in their crumpled disgrace
> I stared for a while through the thin cold rain…
> 'O lad that I loved, there is rain on your face,
> And your eyes are blurred and sick like the pain.'
>
> I stood with the Dead…They were dead; they were dead;
> My heart and my head beat a march of dismay:
> And gusts of the wind came dulled by the guns.
> 'Fall in!' I shouted: 'Fall in for your pay!'[25]

Dawn was breaking in the early hours of 13 July as Siegfried Sassoon was returning from a night expedition into No Man's Land, throwing Mills bombs in the direction of a German machine-gun. Reckless as ever, he took off his steel helmet and stood up to view the German line. He was hit in the head. Blood gushed. The injury was later described as a 'glancing wound over the right parietal of the skull'. The strike was an inch or two from killing him. It was Siegfried's second close-call with death, again the result of lack of elementary caution. The hit was 'friendly fire'. A British sergeant had mistaken him for an advancing German. Other suggestions about the origin of the bullet have been advanced, including the perhaps inevitable conspiracy theory of the high command out to get Sassoon – a nonsensical idea since he was a valuable asset to the Army. On 18 July Sassoon left the Western Front for the last time, on his way to recuperation in Britain. In his normally pseudonymous Sherston memoirs he put in the actual name of the errant sergeant: Wickham. Was this because the man nearly killed him? Or was it because Wickham's blunder very likely saved Mad Jack's life by getting him back to Blighty? In *Sherston's Progress*, Sassoon blames both himself and Wickham (a decorated soldier whom he highly praises). He says, with admitted 'understatement', that he (SS) was 'well out of it'.[26]

On the day Siegfried Sassoon's military career ended, a bruising review of *Counter-Attack and Other Poems* appeared in the *Nation*. It shocked Bloomsbury because of its authorship. (It was unsigned but everyone knew who it was.) The writer was Middleton Murry. The reviewer slammed Sassoon's war verses as not poetry but 'the incoherent cry of a man in torment…ugly and painful… It rasps at the cords of nature.' The critique is developed at some length. Murry had been asked to do the review by Ottoline Morrell. She can hardly have anticipated that.[27]

Was it fair? Certainly, the selection was bold. *Counter-Attack*, with an extract from Barbusse in French as its preface, included 'The Rear Guard', 'The Effect', 'Base Details', 'The General', 'Editorial Impressions' and 'To Any Dead Officer'. And there was 'Suicide in the Trenches':

> I knew a simple soldier boy
> Who grinned at life with empty joy,
> Slept soundly through the lonesome dark,
> And whistled early with the lark.
>
> In winter trenches, cowed and glum,
> With crumps and lice and lack of rum,
> He put a bullet through his brain,
> No one spoke of him again.
>
> You smug-faced crowds with kindling eye
> Who cheer when soldier lads march by,
> Sneak home and pray you'll never know
> The hell where youth and laughter go.[28]

There is the smack of campaign rhetoric about *Counter-Attack*. Does that make it not true art? So said Murry. The charge seems a perversely purist definition of poetry. May we see a motivation deriving from grievance? Murry had expended time and energy on Sassoon's rebellion. That campaign depended on SS resisting pressure and blandishments. He had about-turned by going before a medical board and accepting Craiglockhart; now he was back in the fighting line; yet his production of anti-war poetry was continuing. Murry seems to have been riled by what he saw as hypocrisy: with Sassoon's poetry career advancing and the war being in no way inconvenienced by him.

There was no support for Murry from the others who had worked on the statement. Bertrand Russell wrote to the *Nation* rebutting him. So did Philip Morrell. Ottoline was furious with Murry. Did JMM have any moral high ground? One has to say that he did not. He took a salary at the War Office during a war of which he disapproved. Other reviews of *Counter-Attack* were favourable. Max Plowman in the *Labour Leader* wrote:

> Mr Sassoon has delivered the finest counter-attack in the war by making a breach in the sinister ranks of official reticence and unofficial ignorance and self-complacency. *He has told the truth about the war.* …Judged from the official dispatches and those disgusting accounts given by correspondents to the yellow journals, war is most like a comic game of chess which White is always winning. A soldier on leave commonly thinks it his duty to play the gallant hero, and make light of his job. More often he wants to forget it for the time being, besides he has too much care for his people to come to them presenting nightmares. So he unwittingly joins the conspiracy of silence. Mr Sassoon's book is phenomenal because it breaks that conspiracy. France has Henri Barbusse's account of "Le Feu", but so far as I know this is the first time a truthful picture of the war has been given to Englishmen. I do not know the war as described in the *Daily Mail*, but this book vividly recalls what I saw on the Somme in 1916.[29]

He quotes from the title poem of *Counter-Attack*:

> A yawning soldier knelt across the bank,
> Staring across the morning blear with fog;
> He wondered when the Allemands would get busy;
> And then, of course, they started with five-nines [99.999% reliability shells]
> Traversing, sure as fate, and never a dud.
> Mute in the clamour of shells he watched them burst,
> Spouting dark earth and wire with gusts from hell,

While posturing giants dissolved in drifts of smoke.
He crouched and flinched, dizzy with galloping fear,
Sick for escape – loathing the strangled horror
And butchered, frantic gestures of the dead.

The end of the poem encapsulates the message of futility:

...Down, and down, and down, he sank and drowned,
Bleeding to death. The counter-attack had failed.[30]

The literary journals were encouragingly favourable.

This account will not follow Siegfried Sassoon's recuperation in England, but a letter of 24 July to Robert Graves from the American Red Cross Hospital for Officers at Lancaster Gate, West London, includes some verse that needs to be visited:

I'd timed my death in action to the minute –
(The Nation with my deathly verses in it) –
The day told off – 13 – (the month July) –
The picture planned – O threshold of the dark!
And then, the quivering songster failed to die.
Because the bloody Bullet missed its mark.

The poem moves through dense stanzas packed with allusions (including to the pop-songs on the interminable hospital gramophone). One line jumps out:

Someday my brain will go BANG.[31]

It is apt.

The general expectation in the mid-1918 months was that the war had at least one more year to run, perhaps two. But the month that returned Siegfried Sassoon to England marked a turning- point. By 17 July the German offensive on the Marne had been halted. Thereafter the movement was the other way, with the Germans falling back. There was a breakthrough by the British at Amiens on 8 August, called by Erich Ludendorff 'the blackest day of the German army'. It signalled the start of a withdrawal of the German army back to the Hindenburg Line.

Over in London in the House of Commons on 8 August 1918 MPs were preparing for the summer break. On this day the peace-by-negotiation group staged what would be its final debate. Did Siegfried Sassoon give much thought to the group who had taken up his cause the year before? We know that he stayed in touch with Bertie Lees-Smith. Soon he would be working with another peace group member Philip Snowden. In September 1918 a pen picture by Harry Jones of the *Daily Chronicle* appeared in *UDC* magazine. The article confirms 'the second bench below the gangway on the Opposition side of the House of Commons' as the home of the group. The journalist's assessment was that:

> It is a small group and conveys to the onlooker a sense of isolation. But though small, it is not futile. It has elements of real power and is sustained in a hostile environment by that inward strength that springs from intense moral conviction.[32]

Bertie Lees-Smith draws approving comment:

> A man who is steadily building up a Parliamentary reputation. His industry and talents are assisted by a very youthful appearance, an attractive manner, and a direct, clear-cut oratorical style.

Leonard Outhwaite gets a mention as 'very pertinacious in debate' and an asker of 'awkward queries', upsetting 'the band of Jingoes seated immediately beneath him'.

In the debate Arthur Ponsonby declared that:

> The prolongation of war now means the loss of hundreds of thousands of lives and I do not believe that the sacrifice of valuable lives can be justified in any way simply for triumph through military victory.[33]

During the evening, as debates ranged across an assortment of subjects, Andrew Bonar Law interrupted Commons proceedings with news from the Western Front. An attack had been launched that morning by a combined British, Australian, Canadian and French force, on a front of 20 kilometres. The report was of complete success by 3 o'clock in the afternoon: 100 guns captured and 7,000 prisoners 'already in the cages'. An advance of up to seven miles had made in front of Amiens. 'Its strategic importance will be obvious to everyone,' Law declared. Erich Ludendorff's day of despair was under way. Amiens of course was well known to Siegfried Sassoon. Here he had marvelled at the dazzling glass in the cathedral. Here he had conceived the idea of his poem 'Died of Wounds', having listened to the delirious young soldier groaning about a wood that he and his comrades would never be able to capture. Now that stalemate was gone. Amiens was being left behind as the Allies swept on. The *Times* had:

'THE NEW OFFENSIVE...GREAT ALLIED ATTACK...A BRILLIANT SUCCESS'. After all the make-believe routs of the Germans, this at last seemed to be the real thing.[34]

When Leonard Outhwaite managed to be called, just before the adjournment, he had difficulty because of the excitement on the fringe of the chamber. At one point the Deputy Speaker had to intervene to quieten the noise. The advance had set tongues loose. The last speaker was Philip Morrell. He had very little time but he managed to declare that while the peace group was 'a very small minority in this House', it spoke for 'a very large number of people in this country'. He hoped that it would have more opportunity of bringing before the House the great issues of peace and war. But the day's events at Amiens, though it could not then be realised, would mean that both the war and this Parliament would soon be over.

Before we leave the House of Commons peace-by-negotiation group it is worth visiting Parliament on the day before the 8 August 1918 final peace debate. Prime Minister Lloyd George on this day made one of his infrequent visits to the Commons. He brought bad news for the peace-promoting group. He made it clear that there would be no place for Germany in any League of Nations as far as the British government was concerned. Germany must be soundly beaten rather than negotiated with. 'A power which can enforce its decrees' was required. Germany must not be left with its Army intact. There would be in effect a League of Victors. The Lloyd George speech brought a startling revelation. He 'let the cat out of the bag', as Arthur Ponsonby put it, on the actual British reason for supporting France in the war. His words caused some MPs to sit up. The Prime Minister said: 'We had a compact with France that if she were wantonly attacked, the United Kingdom would go to her support.' This produced a shout of 'We did not know that!' from James Hogge, a forthright Scottish Liberal. There was supposed to have been *no* pre-arrangement with France. A military understanding – a sort of gentleman's agreement with France – had been strongly suspected since 1911 but this had always been denied. The regular government line was that the reason for British entry into the war was Belgium. 'So the truth is avowed at last!' wrote E.D. Morel in *Labour Leader*.[35]

Where does this leave Siegfried Sassoon and his campaign? It may be argued that it supports him. Sassoon continues to get a poor press politically. The latest book on the soldier poets, Michael Korda's stimulating *Muse of Fire*, calls Sassoon's 1917 statement 'in many ways curiously wrong-headed'. He follows the Sassoon biographers in his put-down of Sassoon's views on British foreign policy. But arguably, Sassoon and the parliamentary peace-by-negotiation group got it right. In the early months of the war each belligerent state produced a 'colour book': a collection of diplomatic documents regarding the coming of the war. There were the German White Book, the Russian Orange Book, the British Blue Book, the Austro-Hungarian Red Book, and others. Each of course put its own country in a good light and its enemies in a bad one. Of some controversy in Britain was the English translation when it appeared of the Belgian Grey Book. In 1914 the British decision for military assistance to France was taken at a cabinet meeting between 11 a.m. and 2 p.m. on 2 August, two days before British entry into the war. The Belgian government's Grey Book stated that the German demand for passage through Belgium was presented at Brussels at 7 p.m. on 2 August: some hours therefore *after* the British government had in effect determined that Britain would be in the war. The crucial sentence in the Belgian book was omitted from the English translation, which was provided in a British Government White Paper. On 19 July 1916 in the House of Commons Leonard Outhwaite raised the omission with Lord Robert Cecil, Parliamentary Under-Secretary to the Foreign Office. Cecil said that it was presumably 'due to inadvertence'.[36]

Amiens was the beginning of the end. Now the Americans were bringing their forces seriously to the battle. Austria-Hungary was stricken by starvation and mass desertions. A public appeal by the Kaiser to President Wilson on 16 September for peace terms was rejected. On 30 September Germany's ally Bulgaria surrendered. In Germany there was a cascade of events. On 3 October the Kaiser appointed as Chancellor the Liberal Prince Max who in 1916 had been encouraged by the support for peace by negotiation of Lord Brassey. Then came a further tumble of events: another change of Chancellor, the abdication of the Kaiser (9 November), and the 11 November Armistice.[37]

During the final months of the war the authorities looked for civil service work for Siegfried Sassoon. On 3 October, his diary has: 'Long interview with Winston Churchill at Metropole in the morning'. At this requisitioned hotel, close to Whitehall, Churchill had his Munitions Ministry headquarters. It was not the first attempt to put Sassoon into Munitions administration. He wrote to Edward Carpenter on 15 August: 'I have been offered "a job in town in Munitions" by an influential Person. Of course it is unthinkable.' That was probably Eddie Marsh. Churchill knew plenty about Sassoon. His wife Clementine had been a Lancaster Gate visitor of Siegfried (persistent apparently). The interview was set up by Marsh. Winston Churchill was creative in his appointments. As Home Secretary, he had brought into his civil service team a (then) Labour MP. Sassoon's being a favourite, if wayward, protégé of Marsh, prompted another bold WSC move. It is impossible to see how SS could have accepted a post carrying responsibility for the manufacture and delivery of the engines of misery whose consequences he deplored in his poetry.[38]

Siegfried Sassoon will no doubt have been amazed to discover that the Minister of Munitions knew several of the poems of his *Counter-Attack* by heart. He was expecting a brief meeting. It was anything but brief. Winston's manner was, as SS recalled, 'leisurely, informal and friendly'. (He told Siegfried that *Counter-Attack* had narrowly escaped being suppressed by the censor.) Siegfried took an immediate liking to Churchill, losing his initial shyness. It is not so surprising. The two men had much in common. Both had served on the Western Front, both ambivalent about whether they wanted to be there, Winston gladly seizing an early opportunity to return to politics. Both loved writing. Both were accomplished horse-riders; both were keen golfers. Sassoon was a poet; Churchill adored poetry. Both were opponents of the establishment: in Churchill's case turning the Home Office upside down in 1910-1911, as he challenged engrained conservative attitudes and launched major prison reform. After the war Sassoon became a prison visitor at Pentonville. Did Winston tell him about his own interviewing of prisoners there when he was Home Secretary? The list of matches goes on. And Churchill had empathy with gay men. SS enjoyed later recreating the interview, describing Churchill 'pacing the room with a big cigar in the corner of his mouth…From time to time he advanced on me, head thrust well forward and hands clasped behind his back, to deliver the culminating phrases of some resounding period.' Sassoon was surprised that the minister wanted to hear his viewpoint on war. But Churchill, man of so many parts, had had his 'pacifist' period, in 1908 and 1909, when he was all for peace-making and strongly against excessive military expenditure. Among WSC's favourite poetry was the lament in A.E. Housman's *Shropshire Lad*:

> On the roads of earth go by,
> Dear to friends and food for powder,
> Soldiers marching, all to die.

Now Churchill was expounding on the beneficence of war's by-products: inventions, social progress, and so on. Siegfried Sassoon was inwardly completely at variance with this theme, but plainly there was personal chemistry between the two men. Waiting in an ante-room for his turn was a restless Admiral Lord Fisher. Churchill knew that but he was in no hurry to finish with Sassoon. There was a job for Siegfried if he wanted it. The minister told him to think it over. It was never going to be, but the session evidently made a deep impression on both men. By the time Sassoon wrote the occasion up in *Siegfried's Journey*, Churchill was Prime Minister, waging a war that had his full support.[39]

## Chapter 13

# Mill Town Electioneer

The Army rank-and-file became more politically attuned during 1918. The diary of Sir Douglas Haig has a revealing entry for 27 February. He had been lunching with Sir Aylmer Hunter-Weston, a Coalition Conservative MP serving as an officer on the Western Front. Some MPs were over from Westminster. Hunter-Weston told Haig that some of his men had spoken to the MPs. They had asked them if they were Labour MPs:

> The men then expatiated on the horrors of the war, and said they wanted to know for what they were fighting.[1]

The front line rank-and-file soldiers – many of them at least – were sick of the war and they wanted to get out of it. Labour's newly declared war aims offered hope of a peace settlement. Labour policy on the war was getting around the Army. At home by mid-1918 mainstream Labour support for war to the finish showed signs of cracking. The party's annual conference in London in late June voted that the wartime party truce should not be renewed. This development came hot on the heels of the big vote for a peace-by-negotiation Labour candidate in the Northumberland by-election. Siegfried Sassoon's poetry was hailed by peace-makers. SS exclaimed in a letter on 4 August 1918: 'The *Clarion* and the *Labour Leader* have produced columns of eulogy!! [of *Counter-Attack*].' Sassoon's poetry had made the jump from literary circles to political ones.[2]

With the Armistice, Labour's policy on the war became a matter of the terms of the peace settlement to be hammered out next year. Siegfried Sassoon was at Garsington on Armistice morning, 11 November. It is perhaps worth mentioning (since it has apparently been forgotten) that the killing would have continued through the morning and into the early afternoon but for the enlightenment of the British representative at the 5 a.m. signing of the Armistice, Admiral Wemyss, who overrode the wishes of Lloyd George, who wanted 2.30 p.m. for the cessation of hostilities, so that he could announce when the House of Commons met at its usual time, that the war had ended a few minutes earlier. Admiral Wemyss instead specified 11 a.m., with its eleventh hour of the eleventh day of the eleventh month poetic ring. Even so, 863 British and Empire lives were lost on the final morning, as the snipers proceeded with their business regardless. Thanks to Wemyss, when Siegfried Sassoon arrived in London later in the day, the cease-fire was into its eighth hour. The celebrations were well developed. Sassoon's diary has:

> I got to London about 6.30 and found masses of people in streets and congested Tubes, all waving flags and making fools of themselves – an outburst of mob patriotism. It was a wretched wet night, and very mild. It is a loathsome ending to the loathsome tragedy of the last four years.[3]

The mafficking, documented in many a memoir, would last three nights. It was a prolonged explosion of joy. There was Victory, actually achieved after every Government organ for over four years had pronounced that this was the be-all-and-end-all: good against evil; the war to end wars. Siegfried Sassoon's allies in the House of Commons had warned that an Allied triumphalist victory would in due course bring a full-scale renewal of the horror. Twenty years on they would be proved right, but for the moment there was peace in Britain. The near-revolutionary ripples in parts of the country in 1919 would soon be taking shape, but for now it was the rapture of victory over the Huns. Sassoon's diary reports that he and a like-minded friend annoyed the group with whom they were dining on Armistice night. He wrote:

> They were all very excited and silly and shallow. I hated them and their good dinner and their sympathy with the mob flag-waving.[4]

The diners smiled on the frolics in the streets. Siegfried and his friend were seen as mean-spiritedly grumpy. These two however were far from being the only ones who viewed the rampaging celebrations with distaste. Harry Patch, last survivor of the fighting Tommies, would write in his 2007 memoir: 'For me, 11 November is just show business...nothing but a show of military force. The day I lost my pals, 22 September 1917, is my Remembrance Day.' Patch and Sassoon had much in common: brave soldiers and anti-militarists, who cared most about their fallen comrades.[5]

The day after the Armistice Siegfried Sassoon wrote in his diary verses which he called 'The Patriot':

> He waved his flag when the War began;
> A staunch and thriving English man.
> And now, when fighting's finished,
> He buys the Union Jack again...

...I see him marching with the crowd,
Cheering for Victory, flushed and proud,
Because the danger's ended![6]

Presumably The Patriot did not fight. Siegfried Sassoon, like Harry Patch, did fight. Now they were among those who declined to join in the flag-waving Victory frenzy.

The announcement of a General Election to be held in December offered opportunities for the Labour Party. The existing Parliamentary Labour Party of 40 or so MPs was a working-class niche, owing most of its seats to a pre-war unspoken electoral arrangement with the Liberals, who stepped aside in certain constituencies. That was all out of the window now. The Liberal Party was split between the followers of Lloyd George and those of Asquith. Its identity was damaged by its having largely abandoned its old principles of civil liberty and international peace-making. Lloyd George was bidding to continue his Coalition. For Labour, the defining moment came at the party's mid-November conference when Bernard Shaw, present as a Fabian delegate, won thunderous applause when he declared that the Prime Minister, asking Labour to stay in, should be told 'Nothing doing'. That marked the end of the Labour leadership's subservience to the Government's patronage. Had it happened earlier, the movement could perhaps have been mobilised behind the campaign for a negotiated peace. Like Siegfred Sassoon and the question of what if his 1917 political initiative had not been scuppered by Robert Graves, that must remain unanswered. The Government found that Labour, which it had humoured and utilised, was in the end out of its control. In the coming election the Labour Party would be fully separate from the Liberals and contesting many more seats than previously. Its class base was broadened, with many disillusioned middle-class Liberals finding a new home in it. In this process, Siegfried Sassoon, popular in the Labour Party, found approaches being made to him.[7]

The first Labour approach to Siegfried Sassoon came from the Hampstead constituency in September 1918, when the war was still very much on and a 'Khaki [General] Election' (as in 1900 during the Boer War) was anticipated – because the artificial extensions of the December 1910 Parliament had run out of toleration. Sassoon wrote to Ottoline Morrell:

> I have received an invitation from the Hampstead Labour Party to stand as their Labour Candidate! I wrote a non-committal reply asking for their programme. Do you think there is anything in the idea? I had quite made up my mind that it would be ages before I'd gathered sufficient experience – and knowledge of facts – to be able to do anything like that; and the idea

> of an election is odious to me. But I gather that 'Hampstead' is a safe Tory seat, so it would be long odds against success. Anyhow I should be glad to know what you and Philip think about it. It need not have any effect on my activities as a steel-worker! I can't imagine who put them on to me. I wonder if your brother Henry could advise me about it. O what a funny world it is for a dithering poet![8]

Siegfried Sassoon as a steel worker'? It was a real idea. Siegfried's Army service had drawn him closer to the lives of working men. He wanted to extend the experience. He was trying to act on an idea of Edward Carpenter of a job in a Sheffield steel works. Carpenter said that he could find him one in a 'democratically enlightened' place. SS was resisting the moves by the authority to place him in the civil service. He wrote to Carpenter on 3 September: 'I'm quite determined not to be bluffed into an arm-chair job.' The steel worker project was impracticable. A Sassoon letter of 8 October told Carpenter that, 'All sorts of obstacles have been put in the way of my Sheffield scheme. If I were discharged from the Army it would be possible, but this is not to be done.' Sassoon's Army record states that, 'This officer was ordered to the Ministry of Labour on X/7 [7 October 1918].'[9]

Was it Bertie Lees-Smith who put Hampstead Labour Party onto Sassoon? L-S was a resident of Hampstead. He had lost out for reselection as Liberal candidate at Northampton to his fellow Northampton Liberal MP Charles McCurdy, a man of noisy patriotic righteousness. McCurdy, a barrister, scorned Lees-Smith's peace promotion in 1917, quoting Wordsworth: 'No parleying now...It is Victory or Death.' Like many, Lees-Smith was in transition to the Labour Party. At Hampstead, in the General Election there was a National Party candidate. This Conservative breakaway group wanted to clamp down on 'alien enemies'. There was a whiff about this of proto-fascism. Back in September, with the war still on, it could perhaps have been thought that for Labour to have a candidate who was a decorated war hero would boost its patriotic credentials. Sassoon had kept in touch with Lees-Smith. The MP would have his contact details to supply to his local neighbour, the secretary of Hampstead constituency Labour Party.[10]

The summer and autumn were ugly on the home front. In the course of a July 1918 diary entry written in hospital in France, Siegfried Sassoon mused: 'I'll stay in France just to spite those blighters who yell about "our alien enemies" in Trafalgar Square.' There was a growing vigilante campaign to intern foreigners. Feelings had been whipped up after the sinking by a German submarine of the Liverpool-bound Canadian hospital ship *Llandovery Castle*, with over 200 dead. The Government humoured the xenophobia with a bill to extend powers to revoke certificates of naturalisation. One of the speakers in the parliamentary debate was Sir John Butcher of the National Party, which sat on the bench in front of that usually occupied by the peace-by-negotiation group. Butcher took a swipe at its members (who were absent on this day), calling them 'noisy and mischievous pro-Germans'. On 24 August the National Party's Leader, General Page-Croft, held a monster demonstration in Hyde Park, with five platforms, his message being that, 'we want to say to the Prime Minister that it is the will of the nation that the rich enemy aliens' great circle in this country with their friends in the House of Commons should no longer be tolerated.'

The political struggle was increasingly resolving itself into stop-the-war versus knock-out-blow. The middle ground of diplomacy and defining war aims as an arm of war was looking increasingly hopeless. The Women's International League, which as we have seen supported Siegfried Sassoon's protest, was now taking an unequivocal stop-the-war position. If the men would not do something to end the madness, the women would. On 11 July in Parliament General Page-Croft drew the attention of Home Secretary Sir George Cave to a Women's International League peace rally scheduled for Hyde Park three days later, with Helena Swanwick as a speaker. He asked whether the minister was aware that the W.I.L:

> advises women to abstain from war work and from giving any sort of material, intellectual or moral support whatever to the war; and whether he would take action to end such action?

Cave replied that he had decided, in the interest of public order, to prohibit the W.I.L. demonstration. Page-Croft came back:

> Has the attention of the right hon. Gentleman been called to those words in the programme of the Women's International League which appear to be seditious? Might not a raid take place at the offices of the Women's International League?

This brought in peace group sympathiser Joseph King, a Somerset Liberal:

> Is the right hon. Gentleman not aware that he has already raided the Women's International League, quite unsuccessfully, several times?[11]

Those like Page-Croft, leader of the 'Intern Them All' campaign, would have liked to see the parliamentary 'pacifists' rounded up along with aliens who were still loose.

Vigilantism had become viciously toxic during 1918. At a Clapham by-election in June 1918 vigilante candidate Captain Henry Hamilton Beamish proclaimed his Vigilante Society's demand that for the duration of the war all aliens should have to wear a badge of their nationality on the lapel of their coats. Beamish was virulently anti-Semitic. In a straight fight with the Government candidate, he took 42% of the vote. Another London by-election marked by vigilante campaigning was East Finsbury, which polled on 16 July, the day after Siegfried Sassoon's diary entry mentioning the yelling about 'our alien enemies'. The contest was rowdy and violent. There were two vigilante candidates, both with squads of heavies. Between them they took 40% of the vote. This sort of climate would, one imagines, have been very uncomfortable for Siegfried Sassoon in view of his recent history. The home front could be menacing for those seen as 'enemy aliens' or not onside with the war. In June 1918 the Scottish socialist journal *Forward* reported on the singer/comedian Harry Lauder's current show in Glasgow. Lauder was declaring to his audiences:

> KILL EVERY GERMAN. We are fighting the whole German nation, and the man in the street is just as bad as the Kaiser is, and there will be no peace until we kill them all. (Applause.)[12]

The Government had recently sent Lauder to the United States to promote the war. There were plenty in Glasgow who wanted peace with the Germans but Lauder's violent Germanophobia chimed with some. Had Siegfried Sassoon accepted the Hampstead invitation, he would have run the risk of being targeted both for his peace stance and as someone with a German name. Also, his family was part-Jewish and some of the anti-'enemy alien' sentiment was anti-Semitic. And Sassoon's wider family was proverbially rich, fitting the profile in vigilante characterisation of rich alien undesirables. SS may not have taken in the likely hazards for him at Hampstead in a wartime election. A postscript to his letter to Ottoline indicates that he viewed the election humorously but naively:

> Vote for Sassoon. The Labour Hope of Hampstead. Shade of King Edward VII!! [13]

Presumably the late King would have been shocked by a Sassoon standing for Labour. But these days there was an uglier side to elections than traditional class issues.

A feature of the vigilante campaigning was the call for a boycott of German trade after the war as punishment for U-Boat attacks on Allied merchant shipping. Siegfried Sassoon took this as his subject in a poem entitled 'Trade Boycott'. It appeared in the *Cambridge Magazine* on 14 September 1918:

> General Currycombe (half pay)
> Toddles round, and day by day
> Swears he'll boycott (if he can)
> German merchants to a man.[14]

With the sudden ending of the war, the General Election would now take place in peace. Polling day was set for 14 December. For the first time all the constituencies would vote on the same day. With time needed to gather in the votes from far and wide, the results would not be declared until a fortnight later. For the first time some women would be voting. Siegfried Sassoon now had another approach from the Labour Party to join its election cause.

In Philip Snowden's Blackburn constituency, the Coalition put up a Victoria Cross holder. Percy Dean of the Royal Naval Volunteer Reserve had won his medal at the famous Zeebrugge engagement (22-23 April 1918) for his rescue, as commander of a motor-boat, of over a hundred officers and men from the sea under heavy close fire. It was exceptional heroism, deserving of the honour, but Dean does not seem to have been particularly interested in politics. He appears to have been paraded to scoop in the patriotic vote. Another motor-boat commander at Zeebrugge who was noticed was Cedric Outhwaite, son of Leonard Outhwaite. Cedric sank a German destroyer, for which he was awarded a DSC. News of this produced what a journalist observer called 'a distinct change in attitude' in the House of Commons towards Outhwaite senior on the part of the jingoes of the National Party who sat in front of him.[15]

The Snowden-Sassoon go-between was Max Plowman, of whom Sassoon had heard (and whom he admired) but whom he did not know personally. Plowman wrote to Sassoon on 22 November:

> Dear Sir,
> Will you speak for Philip Snowden at Blackburn?

He went on:

> Pardon my abruptness, but if such a thing appeals to you I have reason to believe your action would be singularly appreciated. The government have put up a Commander Dean V.C. to oppose Snowden, hoping to unseat a sincere and honest opponent by what I regard as the political exploitation of a man's bravery. I believe you could stop that rot. I make the proposal

> to you simply because it is one that would appeal to me were I in the position to do it, quite irrespective of Snowden's politics and simply out of appreciation for his personal character.[16]

Plowman was helping women's rights activist Emmeline Pethick-Lawrence, the Labour candidate for Manchester Rushholme. Blackburn was a two-Member seat, each elector having two votes. Sassoon agreed to Plowman's request. It was remarkably and characteristically brave. As well as Siegfried's personal diffidence, there was his complete inexperience of the public stage. He had followed Philip Snowden's career. He states in his memoir that: 'I had felt grateful to Snowden for his anti-war attitude in Parliament, and had been angered by the abuse thrown at him.' Would SS be out of his depth? He knew from articles in the *Nation* how complex politics was. Plowman wrote to thank Sassoon warmly for his acceptance telegram, telling him that '[Snowden] will be exceedingly pleased to see you.' Snowden himself wrote to Sassoon to express his 'great satisfaction': he would make the necessary arrangements for him; he himself would be based at Blackburn's Mellors Hotel.[17]

Snowden's home address was Golders Green. During the war he commuted by tube to Westminster. On 13 February 1918 he told the House of Commons:

> When I came down to the House this afternoon the train was filled with men with one leg, with broken legs, without arms, and in other ways crippled.[18]

In the nine months between then and the end of the war there had been many more casualties. The fallen included Wilfred Owen, who died in northern France one week before the Armistice. Owen had been helped with his poetry by Siegfried Sassoon at Craiglockhart, including with his defining masterpieces 'Dulce et Decorum Est' and 'Anthem for Doomed Youth' – SS thought of 'anthem' and 'doomed'. Unimpressed at first with Owen (Wilfred's 'grammar school accent' did not help), Sassoon had grown to admire him more and more. Now the war was at last over. The manifesto of Philip Snowden's Labour Party called for a peace of reconciliation in order to avoid the resumption of world war within a generation. A fair and secure peace was a major plank of Snowden's Blackburn platform. Siegfried Sassoon was now set to join his campaign. He wrote to Ottoline Morrell on 29 November:

> I am writing to let you know that I've promised to go to Blackburn on Dec 11th and 'speak' for Snowden, who has a V.C. stunt candidate against him. I have no idea what I shall say when I get there, but I couldn't refuse

> when they asked me. Will you send me a letter of safe advice as to what attitude to adopt? Of course I admire Snowden's courage and integrity very much, or I'd not be going there. What an excite for me! Are you pleased? [19]

This was dubbed 'The Coupon Election' because the Government decided which candidate would get its nod in each constituency. Blackburn's two 'coupons' went to a Lloyd George Liberal, Sir Henry Norman, former junior minister and recently Liaison Officer (carrying the rank of Major) of the Ministry of Munitions to the French Minister of Inventions; and Percy Dean, the decorated Conservative. Dean had his military backstory but Norman also has some biographical interest. He had been part-educated in Germany; in 1910 he was Philip Snowden's (successful) running-rate at Blackburn; then there was his wartime career. On how to approach electioneering, it is no surprise that Siegfried Sassoon sought Ottoline Morrell's advice. She had been with Philip through three General Election campaigns, including December 1910 at Burnley, another Lancashire mill town.

Loose pages enclosed in a Sassoon notebook of this time show him working out the line he was going to take on the election platforms in Blackburn. The phrase 'comic turn' appears. It would be no good his marching onto the stage as though a seasoned practitioner of political cut-and-thrust. Humorous self-deprecation from a newcomer was safer ground. We see him working this out with 'Fancy self as a speaker'. 'Gag' is heavily underlined. 'Keep cheers for candidate,' he warns himself. However, he would work into his performance some serious points.[20]

Prepared arguments are a mixture of personal and political. Regarding Snowden: 'He has the interests [of his electors] at heart; he keeps his promises; he has maintained his dignity.' 'S. and soldiers' is a reminder to emphasise that Snowden, though opposed to the war, had looked after his soldier constituents and their families. The single word 'Hardy' indicates one speech direction. On politics, the jottings have: '…Liberty of peoples and of individuals to choose representatives; live at peace with one another; close door of the mind against violent methods; liberty of thought – religion and in social and industrial affairs; pensions and allowances.' 'Conscription' means Labour's campaign to end it. There are notes on the campaign to expect from the other side: 'Revenge'; 'Make the Germans pay'.[21]

The second sheet has the point that Sassoon is 'speaking <u>for</u> the soldiers at the front'. There is a passage attacking the glamorisation of war:

> Exposure of war – sham glory, chivalry – Heroism and self-sacrifice come out in other ways than wallowing in mud and blood – heroism does not outweigh the horror and degradation.

It continues:

> ...We fight clean – we fight with a laugh, as the boys fought Fritz. We aim at construction, not destruction – cooperation and amalgamation of classes, not war between classes. We fight with our hearts as well as our heads – and when we fight with our tongues we fight clean – not with lies and half-truths and slander...The old ordeal is over. The new one is to come. We are fighting for the faith of those who died...We must remember what they died for...[22]

There is also:

> Let us keep before our minds the thought of serving the world...the positive desire to nourish life in the world rather than to minister to death. War develops in almost all a certain hysteria of destruction, self-destruction among the more generous but still destruction. We have to stand out against this hysteria and realise, and make others realise, that life, not death (however heroic) is the source of all good.[23]

The notebook includes newspaper clippings. One of these looks at the prospective settlement of the war:

> ...What we want is not punishment for the past, but security for the future...For it is essential that the new order shall start on the basis of mutual confidence and mutual cooperation between all nations...Our duty is not to gratify feelings, whether of justice or revenge, but to build a new world in which our children may be safe and free.[24]

Siegfried Sassoon had already set out in verse his opposition to policy driven by revenge. In the *Herald* of 16 November 1918, he had a poem entitled 'Reconciliation':

> When you are standing at your hero's grave,
> Or near some homeless village where he died,
> Remember, through your heart's rekindling pride,
> The German soldiers who were loyal and brave.

> Men fought like beasts; and hideous things were done;
> And you have nourished hatred, harsh and blind.
> But in that Golgotha perhaps you'll find.

Snowden wrote Sassoon a further letter on 30 November:

> I should be willing to leave it to you to say what you feel moved to say. You would not be expected to make a long speech. You will find the audiences very good and very sympathetic…It is a purely industrial town and the Labour questions will be an important issue. But I emphasise also the need for a clean, non-vindictive peace which will establish permanent good international relations. I will have a talk with you before the meetings.[25]

Sassoon recalled Philip Snowden in *Siegfried's Journey*: 'My heart went out towards this man of bleakly uncompromising convictions, crippled with lameness, and fighting a losing battle against a frenzied intolerance whose catchwords were 'Hang the Kaiser' and 'Make the Germans Pay'. 54 years old, Snowden used two sticks, having been paralysed from the waist down by a cycling accident in his 20s. He was reviled in nationalist circles as the Arch-Pacifist. In Parliament his moral conviction and the brimstone of his oratory rather fascinated some Tory MPs, even compelling some reluctant admiration. In Blackburn he was sustained by his team, including his wife Ethel, a younger woman of oratorical flair and political accomplishment. Ethel was on the Executive Committee of the Women's International League. Her glamorous vivaciousness contrasted with the dour earnestness of her husband.[26]

Siegfried arrived at Blackburn on Tuesday, 10 December (having hunted in the Home Counties the day before). He records in his diary being met by 'a friendly man in seedy clothes' who told him that he had come to escort him to Princes Theatre where Philip Snowden was at that moment speaking. The world into which Sassoon now plunged himself came as 'Hell of a shock', as his diary notes. He reaches in his account for familiar Army parlance: 'Wind up'. This environment was all new and he did not know whether he was up to its challenges. He walked with the man a few hundred yards through some narrow streets. It was already dark. His escort took him into the theatre by a back entrance. He was given somewhere to sit behind the stage. He could hear Snowden speaking. He was struck by the loudness of his voice. Snowden was an arresting speaker in these days before microphones. This was a women's meeting. It was a big one. The theatre was full to capacity with about one-thousand-five-hundred. The moment of truth for Siegfried had come. He stepped onto the stage to face the audience. He was warmly greeted. He did not yet have to speak because Snowden had not finished. Sassoon sat to the side of him, feeling 'very shy and nervous'. And that was that for his first public appearance. After ten minutes he was beckoned off the stage and bundled into a cab by a woman. The next destination was a meeting at a school. He discovered that this was a hostile meeting. 'A sallow young man' was in mid-speech. Then it was Siegfried's turn. He got to his feet and addressed the audience for ten minutes. In the middle Snowden arrived. SS's journal records that he was listened to attentively. The audience was not sympathetic but still the Sassoon self-verdict was 'Quite a success'. The ice had been broken. Then it was back to the theatre and the women. Now he gave 'a hell of a speech punctuated with laughter and cheers'. They were 'a jolly lot and seemed to enjoy it.' The day ended with cocoa with Philip Snowden and his wife and others at their hotel. He got back to his room at The Bull about 11.15 with a good feeling of having gained the confidence he needed. The entry concludes: 'Snowden and his wife are good people. I am thankful I came here.'[27]

The Blackburn contest was covered by the *Daily Dispatch*, a big-selling newspaper serving the Greater Manchester area and beyond. It fervently backed Norman and Dean and was correspondently hostile to Philip Snowden. It could not resist reporting a statistic that Snowden was using. That was that during the war he had raised 1,653 separate matters in Parliament and that his questions and speeches occupied 357 columns of Hansard. But the paper's tone was jeering:

> BLACKBURN LAUGHS AT SNOWDEN
> A Beautiful World – Had his Dream Come True.[28]

This presumably refers to Snowden's argument that had his group been listened to, many lives would have been saved and that society would be in a better shape. The newspaper did not send reporters to Snowden's meetings. It used hearsay. One Coalition speech which it reported casts valuable light on the arguments in the contest:

> It is being rumoured in the town that a vote for Snowden would mean that the rich will have to pay for the war, and that a vote for Norman or Dean would mean that the workers will have to foot the bill. The fact is that if the electors support the Coalition candidates it will mean that Germany will have to pay for the war.[29]

Social unfairness stemming from the war was the lead argument on the Labour side in the Blackburn election. Siegfried Sassoon, having heard much about wartime working-class deprivation in Lancashire (while the profiteers prospered) from quartermaster Captain Cottrill, no doubt found plenty in Philip Snowden's oratory that he could recognise. The Coalition was deflecting from the issue of fair wealth distribution by insisting that if Germany was properly squeezed (as they maintained it deserved to be) *everyone* in Britain would do well, as money flowed in from there. This thrust was replicated nationally. Lloyd George had started his campaign with reassurances to Liberals that he was still one of them. When the reception of the Coalition's pitch was underwhelming, it reset its message: with 'Hang the Kaiser' and 'Make Germany Pay' now leading the slogans. Sassoon was disgusted, as were many. The result of the post-war economic war against the Germans would be severe malnutrition in Germany, as the blockade continued. Irene Cooper Willis's (early post-war) *England's Holy War* mentions an admission in the House of Commons by Winston Churchill as War Minister on 3 March 1919 that, 'Germany is very near starvation.' It should be stressed that Churchill had not been one of those who wanted to 'skin Germany alive'. He was for magnanimity, as was Siegfried Sassoon.[30]

Sassoon was enjoying himself in Blackburn. His early nerves were gone. He quoted Walt Whitman and Thomas Hardy ('In our heart of hearts believing'). He received a friendly reception each time he spoke. He had the company of the trade unionist Margaret Bondfield. In 1923 Bondfield would knock Charles McCurdy – baiter of Lees-Smith – out of his Northampton seat. In 1929 she would become the first woman cabinet minister. Also at the Blackburn election was Richard Lambert, with whom SS will have been able to compare notes as a fellow Garsington visitor. Lambert, having retired from Parliament (he became Librarian of the Athenaeum Club), was going round the country supporting former peace-by-negotiation group members. The gatherings of the Snowden team over cocoa at the end of each campaigning day were 'happy family', with the tall Siegfried as the 'big brother'. It should be mentioned that at some point Sassoon received a telegram appealing to him to go to Scarborough to help Osbert Sitwell, standing as a Liberal against a Coalition Conservative. 'Impossible as he is opposing a Labour man,' wrote SS in his diary.[31]

The Irish community in Blackburn was strongly with Snowden. A newspaper advertisement for a Snowden meeting at the Overlookers' Hall on the evening of Thursday, 12 December, promoted by the United Irish League of Great Britain, lists the speakers as MR PHILIP SNOWDEN, MRS SNOWDEN, CAPT SASSOON, M.C., MR R.C. LAMBERT. It urges: 'Irish Men and Women, rally round the Friend of Ireland.' The venue is a reminder that Blackburn was a town of textile mills. 'Overlookers' were responsible for the working of the frames. The mills echoed to deafening noise. The hours were long and exhausting. These were the people for whom Snowden aimed to win a better life. Siegfried Sassoon recalled hearing the workers go by his hotel early in the morning. The cobbled streets rattled to the clatter of their clogs. The electors of the parliamentary constituency of Blackburn were on their way to work, unaware that, 'a new adherent to the Labour movement had arrived among them.'[32]

Campaigning was in the afternoons and evenings. In the mornings Sassoon investigated the area, taking tramcars. Everywhere he found 'a horizonless unity of grimy houses and dismal gas-smelling streets'. It was the same in nearby Burnley and Accrington. There seemed to Siegfried no prospect of a better world until this conurbation had been demolished and rebuilt.[33]

Sassoon's education about the lives of workers and their families in industrial Britain marked a continuation of the broadening of his mind from his conventional upper middle-class attitudes. Closeness to working-class soldiers had already had a big effect on SS. Blackburn continued the process.

Sassoon's diary entry for Friday, 13 December, the day before polling day, well captures his campaigning experience:

> 11.30 p.m. Have just got in. I shall look back on these days as a time filled with happy striving, pleasing thrills of nervousness, jolly comradeship, and rather bewildering success. Got down to the Theatre as the parson (Peck) was finishing. Toddled on to the stage – (loud cheers). P.S. had spoken there earlier – (one of his best efforts, they said). I did my usual comic turn before Mrs S. spoke (very friendly for half an hour). The meeting was rather terrific, with its excitement and enthusiasm. These simple people, who believe in P.S. are very moving. I think he is worthy of them.[34]

'Comic turn' is perhaps a pointer. Siegfried now realised that he had talent as a funny man.

This week was a watershed for Sassoon:

> These days are undoubtedly the beginning of a new phase of my life – I am being inflamed to an ardour which cannot fail me. I have made a strong appeal to these Blackburn people, but I must justify my words by deeds. A great vista has opened to me, and I have escaped – for ever – these reactionary and self-indulgent influences to which I was bred and educated. I have offered myself to the people and they have accepted me. Will I be worthy of their trust? Who knows? [35]

SS's diary for Polling Day, 14 December, reports the town being very quiet, with no hostile demonstrations except from a few children. There was a big meeting in the evening at Princes Theatre. Snowden made 'a good speech but rather spoiled it', Sassoon thought, by 'a bitter reference' to the poster of his opponents, 'Vote for the Two Britishers'. At the post-meeting cocoa Snowden said he deeply regretted having brought up the poster. Sassoon observed in his diary: 'He has been goaded beyond endurance by the malignant hostility of his enemies.' Ethel Snowden, in Sassoon's view 'spoke well, and with great effect, but also overdid it a bit.' He himself spoke for 10 minutes. He thought that his speech was: 'far the best and most effective speech I have made – I felt absolute confidence and never hesitated for a word. Blackburn has won my heart, and I think I've won theirs.'[36]

On Saturday evening at his hotel, as the polls were closing, Siegfried Sassoon wrote to Ottoline Morrell:

> I am rather tired of elections, but it has been a splendid experience, and I believe I've helped a bit. My remarks against Conscription and so on have gone down well. I have spoken at 12 meetings. The biggest was last night – about 2500. The people who support S. are most impressive. I have been driving round with him today, (in a ramshackle old Ford Car), and the people make me very glad I came to help him. The Coalition people described me as 'a stage-soldier who's never been near the war, but had been got down by the Pacifists! Something like this appeared in the Daily Despatch, so I have rolled up in all his meetings in uniform; but nothing has been said about that.[37]

The *Daily Dispatch* piece in question appeared on 12 December, under 'Stage Soldiers: Chocolate Variety of the Snowdenites'. The paper informed its readers that:

> One of the hearers of the uniformed youth after he had made slips about seven days' leave instead of fourteen, and had given a few more indications that his facts were not sound, asked him a few fraternal questions, such as his division, etc, which threw the searchlight of exposure full on him. He was a soldier, tis true, but one of a few days making. The soldier who has never seen fire beyond the butts, is one of the type the pacifist crowd is using for stage-dressing.[38]

How would the soldiers from Blackburn vote? It was reported in one of the papers (as SS recalled) that 'Captain Sassoon remarked that the soldiers on active service had "not a dog's chance of registering their vote at the election".' Generally, Sassoon's speeches were little reported. On the matter of the soldier vote, with the rank-and-file apparently having been in favour of peace by negotiation, in contrast with the Home Front which backed fight-to-the finish, and with Labour now that the war was over being seen as the best prospect for soldiers of early demobilisation, it is likely that the military vote would have helped Snowden if it had managed to be substantially counted.[39]

Shortly before polling day the *Daily Dispatch* carried a cartoon: *Saturday's weather forecast – Blizzard at Blackburn: Philip Snowed-on.* We see PS battling through a welter of ballot papers all apparently marked with a cross by the name of either Dean or Norman. On the Sunday following polling day, the *Observer* had a more sober assessment of the Blackburn trends, which was also discouraging to the Snowden cause:

> Mr Snowden, though sure of the Irish vote in Blackburn and backed by trade unionists, lost ground in the last few days, and the feeling among his supporters was that he was fighting a forlorn hope.[40]

Philip Snowden knew that. Psephologically, he was a sharp analyst. He was the number cruncher who had been Labour's Treasury spokesman before the war and throughout it. (Even with its pro and anti-war wings, the Labour Party, unlike the Liberal Party, had not fractured.) Sassoon reckoned that Snowden knew to within several hundred votes what the Blackburn result was going to be.

Nearly all adult males were now eligible to vote (before the war it had been only two-thirds). And there were the over-thirties women. The female age voting rule had a conservative effect. While politically radical younger women were excluded from the franchise, conservative matrons were able to place their crosses. Conscientious objectors were punished by losing their votes in this election (making a nonsense of the conscience clause in the conscription legislation). One way and another the voting roll of December 1918 was skewed.

The Blackburn result was: Norman 41.4% (elected); Dean 38.9% (elected); Snowden 19.7%. Snowden had no running mate, making for distorted percentages, but still it was a rout, a two-to-one defeat in a seat that he had previously held comfortably. Philip paid the price for his opposition to the war, as did the other former peace-by-negotiation group members (those who stood again). Their best result was that of Fred Jowett, who came close to holding on at Bradford, where some read in the *Bradford Pioneer* the first publication of Siegfried Sassoon's statement.[41]

What happened at the election to Siegfried Sassoon's peace-making ally of 1917 Bertie Lees-Smith? The ex-Northampton MP with his seat disappeared in the boundary revisions, opted to contest the Don Valley division in Yorkshire's West Riding. In this constituency the Government 'coupon' went to James Walton of the National Democratic Party, a right-wing breakaway from Labour, which continued to support the Lloyd George Coalition. Lees-Smith stood as a Liberal but he was already semi-detached from the Liberal Party in the move away from the Liberals at this time by radical progressives. He was described in the local press as the Radical candidate. In the campaign the question arose, as it did nationally, of making Germany pay. Lees-Smith chose his words very carefully. A local newspaper reported a Lees-Smith speech:

> We stand at the end of the queue, and you know what happens to the people at the end of the queue. When Belgium, France, Poland, Serbia, Montenegro, Italy and all other invaded districts have been repaired, and their peoples compensated, we shall take what is left. Can anybody tell me what there will be left after all these people have had justice? If you can get indemnities from Germany, all well and good but I am not going to allow talk about hypothetical indemnities from Germany to divert my attention from the wealth that I know exists, the wealth that will have to be conscripted.[42]

The newspaper approved:

> Mr Lees-Smith is a practical politician, and that is why he does not yield, for the sake of winning votes, to the temptation to talk at large about the booty that is coming from Germany.

Actually, the talk of squeezing Germany hard for reparations was playing well across the country and would deliver a landslide victory for the Lloyd George Coalition, though the 'booty' was not there: Germany was on its knees and heading for starvation. Lees-Smith knew that reparations were popular. Rather than directly oppose them, he scorned them as impractical (which they were). His election line on paying for the war was the same as that of Philip Snowden and Siegfried Sassoon in Blackburn. He wanted the money of the profiteers who had done very well out of the war (as Quartermaster Cottrill told Siegfried Sassoon) to be conscripted for the nation. Like Snowden and Sassoon, Lees-Smith wanted a fairer distribution of the national wealth. As we see from Lees-Smith's use of the imagery of shoppers at the market stalls, he had a folksy touch. So did Siegfried Sassoon, as he was discovering. But SS did not yet have the seasoned political skills of Lees-Smith. He would have to acquire these if he wanted to go seriously into the political game.

Lees-Smith came a respectable second, beating Labour, in the three-corner contest, with almost 30 percent of the vote. The runaway winner was the NDP Coalition candidate. James Walton's tenure would be relatively short. He would be heavily beaten by Labour at the next General Election, in 1922. Lees-Smith joined the Labour Party and won Keighley in 1922. He lost it in 1923, but won it back in 1924. He was Postmaster-General and then President of the Board of Education in the cabinet in Ramsay MacDonald's second Labour Government. He lost his seat in 1929, but won it back in 1935. In the Second World War he strongly supported Winston Churchill's government. He died in December 1941.[43]

An important aspect of Siegfried Sassoon's electioneering experience at Blackburn deserves a moment of consideration. That was women in politics. As we have seen, Sassoon was present at a number of women's political meetings. That will have been daunting for him, coming as he did from a male world, one reflected in his poetry. But he acclimatised and seems to have got on well enough. And there were his female co-workers on the Labour campaign team, including a future cabinet minister. Just as Blackburn broadened Sassoon socially in terms of class so it did in respect of gender and politics. He seems especially to have admired and appreciated Ethel Snowden as a platform orator (even if he did think that she overdid the theatricals). Here was Siegfried finding a perspective on politics and women. Even before the 1918 General Election, SS's anti-war campaigning had brought political women into his life. There was Irene Cooper Willis, Secretary of the Women's International League, backing him when he faced likely court-martial; there was Catherine Marshall, parliamentary coordinator of anti-war groups, helping to publicise his statement; there was the radical feminist Sylvia Pankhurst organising the first London newspaper publication of his statement.

The First World War is notoriously fraught with misapprehension of one sort and another. A major component of war mythology has to be that this conflict was good for promoting women's social and political advancement. Of course, there *were* spin-off benefits for women along the way, but they tended to be very transient. The females who entered the worlds of professional work to fill the gaps caused by the departure of Siegfried Sassoon's comrades to the the trenches, were removed in short order when the men returned. One example of the reversal process is the suppression by the men of women's football, which thrived, on major grounds before large crowds, towards the end of the war and in the early years after it. Women footballers would not have the chance again until later in the century. It needs to be remembered that many of the women at Sassoon's Blackburn meetings will not have been able to vote, either because they were under 30, or because they were not property-qualified. In the years before the First World War, society had been seeing rapid change, political and social. A female suffrage bill was passed by Parliament by a large majority on Second Reading in 1910 (the 'Conciliation Bill'), only to be blocked by the Government, which refused it further time. What if there had been no British war in 1914?

We may imagine that there would have been female parliamentary voting by 1918 on better terms than under the poor (for women) 1918 Representation of the People Act., since the electoral imbalance resulting from the prolonged slaughter of males would not have been a shaping factor. What of Siegfried Sassoon had there been no war? How might his literary career have progressed? What might he by now have been doing? These are among the many tantalising but unanswerable hypothetical questions of this story.

In the post-war world, Sassoon would stay in the memory of the Snowdens. In his 1934 *Autobiography*, Philip, while admitting that Sassoon was 'no orator', recorded that he 'became immensely popular during the contest through his transparent honesty and sincerity.' He wrote to Sassoon in an unidentified year:

> Dear Friend
> I send the enclosed appreciative review in case you have not seen it. We hope you are keeping well and are hoping to see you soon.
> Yours sincerely
> Philip Snowden.[44]

The reunion, which Siegfried wanted too, never happened. In 1924 Snowden would be Labour's first Chancellor of the Exchequer. That Government would be short-lived but he would return to the Exchequer in 1929. In the period between he shadowed the Conservative Chancellor Winston Churchill. Visitors to Snowden's house in those years would observe if they happened to enter his study, that the room was dominated by a big picture of Ethel on the mantelpiece and that next to it was one of Siegfried Sassoon.[45]

Sassoon was serious about his involvement with the Labour movement. In order to improve his understanding of political theory, he began a course at Oxford University. He left when he was offered the (new) post of Literary Editor at the *Herald*, now back to being the *Daily Herald*. In two years there he developed his own style of editing – with a light touch.

In February 1919 Siegfried Sassoon visited Glasgow to report on the near-revolutionary industrial rioting. He was sent by H.W. Massingham, who wanted material for *The Nation*. The work was largely done for Sassoon by John Langdon-Davies, poet, Labour activist and former conscientious objector, who had local contacts. In Glasgow a woman let SS know at a socialist meeting that, while his support was appreciated, he would never understand them because he had not imbibed 'Marx with his mother's milk'. There are different accounts of this encounter. Sassoon's memoir states that the individual was friendly and warm-hearted. As at Blackburn, SS did a district tour. The slums of Cowcaddens made a profound impression on him: 'These courts and alleys were cliff-like and cavernous, chilling me to the bone. The few unfortunates who scowled at us from doorways looked outlawed and brutalized.'[46]

Siegfried Sassoon was now a gentleman revolutionary: corduroy jacket and bright red tie. His deep political identification with the workers is shown by an incident that he describes in *Siegfried's Journey*. In mid-January 1919 he was one of a dozen guests at a dinner-party hosted by Edward Marsh ('titled blokes and blokesses' SS called them). News had broken of the murder of Karl Liebknecht and Rosa Luxemburg, leaders of the Spartacist revolutionary uprising in Berlin. Eddie said that no one would miss them and there was agreement from those around him. Siegfried's tact snapped. He exploded: 'I wish I were half as brave as Leibknecht!' He relates that, 'Judging by Eddie's scared expression, my demeanour must have been a bit volcanic.' Leibknecht had been a hero of British opponents of the war. In the Reichstag, with one other Social Democrat, he voted against war credits, on 2 December 1914 and on 19 March 1915.[47] No one in the British House of Commons voted against war credits.

But Sassoon lived a life of compartments. While being a man of Labour and the workers, he hunted with his upper-class chums in the Home Counties. He was elected to two clubs after the war. One was the Reform. The other was the 1917, founded in its eponymous year (seen by some as the real start of the twentieth century). Here men and women of politics and the arts mixed with soldiers on leave, planning a new world. It was Philip Snowden who proposed SS for membership. Siegfried had a disquieting moment on his first appearance. He was feeling comfortable enough. His 'tousled unshaven condition' would be 'evidence of my exertions as a Socialist', as he recalled. He overheard a young man asking another whether he knew anything about him. The answer was: 'Not much but I've heard he spends a hundred a year on scent.' Quickly leaving, Siegfried sped to Lady Ottoline at Garsington.[48]

Sassoon's Army file records his retirement on 20 February 1919: 'To be placed on the retired list on account of ill-health caused by wounds, and to be granted the rank of Captain.' Siegfried's military life was over. He wrote a poem in March 1919 to mark his exit. 'Aftermath' shows that Sassoon stood by the politics of his July 1917 revolt:

*Have you forgotten yet?...*
For the world's events have rumbled on since those gagged days,
Like traffic checked while at the crossing of city-ways...
Do you remember the dark months you held the sector at Mametz –
The nights you watched and wired and dug and piled sandbags on the parapets?
Do you remember the rats; and the stench

Of corpses rotting in front of the front-line trench –
And dawn coming, dirty-white, and chill with a hopeless rain?
Do you ever stop and ask, 'Is it all going to happen again?...'
*Have you forgotten yet?...*
*Look up, and swear by the green of the spring that you'll never forget.*[49]

This was Siegfried Sassoon's alternative version of 'Lest we forget'. During the war his allies in the House of Commons had counselled what would be the outcome of a victory in which Germany was humiliated. That had happened. Here was Sassoon's 1919 warning to watch out for the return of the horrors of Mametz Wood and the rest.

Punitive vengeance was confirmed with the terms of the Versailles settlement. Arthur Ponsonby, having seen them, exclaimed to his diary:

> Annexations, dismemberment, robbery and ruin. No faint pretence of justice or generosity. This is the culmination of all the massacres and horrors.[50]

Siegfried Sassoon's employer of these days, the *Daily Herald*, carried a cartoon entitled PEACE AND FUTURE CANNON FODDER. As Lloyd George, Wilson, Clemenceau and Orlando emerge from conference, the French Prime Minister says, 'Curious! I seem to hear a child weeping!' On the left, by a pillar, we see a sobbing infant, over whose head are the words '1940 class'. Here, eerily precise with the date, was the warning delivered so many times by the wartime peace-by-negotiation group in the British House of Commons with whom Siegfried Sassoon in July 1917 made his bold alliance to try to stop the slaughter cycle in its tracks.[51]

# Chapter 14

# The Peace That Got Away?

What mark did Siegfried Sassoon's July 1917 protest make? In the short term, as we have seen, there was a brief stir, then it quickly faded. With Sassoon aborting his campaign early when Robert Graves intervened with his false story about the lunatic asylum, it was easy for the authorities to contain the affair. Had Sassoon kept going (had there been no Robert Graves), history, not just that of the Sassoon event but more widely, might have been very different. Sassoon's declaration has had only passing attention. The reputation of Sassoon the poet endures, SS being seen as second in rank in the British 'War Poets' behind his protégé Wilfred Owen, and with his greater fame being as a memoirist. The British Army First World War poets have their place in literature. But Sassoon's action in 1917 as a political move does not receive serious consideration.

A quarter of a century ago, the promotion of a big publication seemed to some (including this writer) as perhaps at last being about to give a run to the political message of Siegfried Sassoon and his allies. Niall Ferguson's *The Pity of War*, with a poppy aboard its cover, looked bracingly revisionist. Were the peace activists in the World War One Parliament, and their friends like Siegfried Sassoon, Ottoline Morrell and Bertrand Russell, after three quarters of a century of historians failing to notice them, at last going to have their day in the sun? It was not to be. *Pity*'s thrust was that Britain's imperial interests would have been better suited by staying out of the war. The brief coverage of Siegfried Sassoon is of a shell-shocked soldier in the clutches of exploitative peace-mongers. The author tells us that Sassoon's protest 'delighted a small clique of pacifists', the impression being that those who thought like him were faddists on the margins, a minor nuisance, not voices requiring attention from mainstream history.[1]

The years around the millennium brought positive promotion of Britain's role in the First World War, the most influential book being Gary Sheffield's *Forgotten Victory*, with its thesis that the wailing over the toll of the Somme and Passchendaele has been excessive: that these were a learning curve in the process by which Britain and its Allies ultimately defeated Germany, a vital outcome because of the nature of the German regime. The author argues that the Somme was 'an essential precondition to success in the last two years of the war'. A particular target is the War Poets, including Siegfried Sassoon, and the way these have been used in the teaching of history. Sheffield complains that 'a small and unrepresentative group of junior officers' are 'the most frequently quoted figures of 1914-1918'. He puts the war poets with the musical *Oh! What a Lovely War*, which has as its finale a scene from the Barbusse novel in which soldiers, baaing like sheep, follow their officer in a crazy offensive and are mown down; and books like Alan Clarke's 1961 *The Donkeys*, about bloodthirsty, blundering British generals: these, *Forgotten Victory* claims, distort the history of the war.[2]

2013 saw the publication of Nigel Biggar's *In Defence of War*, another swipe at the supposed pacifist-leaning history establishment. Biggar seizes on a comment by Siegfried Sassoon in *Siegfried's Journey*:

> In the light of subsequent events it is difficult to believe that a Peace negotiated in 1917 would have been permanent. I share the general opinion that nothing on earth would have prevented a recurrence of Teutonic aggressiveness.[3]

This looks damaging for the Siegfried Sassoon declaration and its supporters. Through the interwar period Sassoon had not wavered from what he wrote. Then, as the Second World War passed through its concluding agonies, he made this apparent admission that he had been wrong. For Biggar, the admission confirmed his view that 'There is no evidence that Britain could have secured satisfactory peace terms before November 1918.' Game, set and match then to the rebuttal of Sassoon's protest? Not so. The time and context of Sassoon's memoir must be weighed. 1945 revealed the special nature of the crimes against humanity of the Nazis but it took some time for it to sink in that there was something different about the Nazis from what had gone before in Germany: that this was fascism, not the old 'Teutonic' or 'Prussian' militarism. The Nazis were a product of how the First World War ended. It may be argued that Sassoon of 1917 was right and that Sassoon of 1945 was following a common misconception of that time.[4]

Might Siegfried Sassoon's protest have nudged things in the direction of peace making? If it had done so, the circumstances, one may think, could have carried things forward. There had been the peace resolution in the Reichstag. There were the indications that Sassoon's points in his statement were in line with widespread feeling in the British Army, which was far different from the war-to-the-bitter-end sentiments on the home front. In mid-1917 Russia was partway to democracy and adopting liberal principles after its spring revolution.

There were the plans for an international socialist conference to bring the two sides of the war together in a common peace-making purpose. The peace-by-negotiation aspiration featured in the joyous excitement of the June 1917 Leeds Convention, which looked to the building of a kinder and fairer world. Of course, plentiful cold water may be poured: Germany had a lot of acquired territory out of which it had to be negotiated. The chances were probably against peace. But it was by no means impossible. The yearning on both sides for a settlement was considerable.[5]

It is worth considering what was at stake in those summer months of 1917 when Siegfried Sassoon made his move. The war ended in November 1918. But did it? In many senses it did not. The turmoil and misery that was loosed on the world in 1914 and which expanded as the war's extent spread and its purposes mutated, would go on in wide areas until 1923. It has been calculated that in the three or so years after the official end of the war more people died as a result of it – the figure four million has been given – than during its progress. The war triggered multiple civil conflicts and revolutions, ethnic cleansing, starvation and disease. We noted Sassoon's satirical poem about the projected trade war against Germany to follow the end of the shooting one. That happened. There were the terrible health consequences from the blockade of Germany long after the Armistice. Further, the remains of the disintegrating empires blockaded each other, including the newly created state of Czechoslovakia stopping food supplies to Austria. There were the refugee consequences, with displaced groups on the move – to places where there was no food. Even on the victorious side there was civil strife, as in Italy where there were conflicts over the new borders. Italy was on the road to fascism, as was Germany. One way and another the world was in a deep mess.[6]

And there were the longer term still consequences of the war, as two of the amalgam states created out of the way the war ended, Czechoslovakia and Yugoslavia, ultimately failed to work, the uncoupling being peaceful with the former but in the case of the latter involving civil wars and massacre. And on it goes in the twenty-first century. Russia's present-day direction is, one may argue, a long-term consequence of the snuffing out of the liberal democracy that dared briefly to flicker there in 1917, until the lack of interest on the part of the Allies in the peace moves in Russia (which were followed intently by Siegfried Sassoon's allies in the British House of Commons), caused the bright hopes to be doused by a second and very different revolution. That was yet to come. There was all to play for in July 1917. Could the war have been stopped? Undeniably, the chances were overwhelmingly against any end other than one of the two super-alliances beating the other. A huge problem was that the constituents of the alliances each had their own aims and aspirations and therefore reasons for keeping the war going. And there were all the numerous factors of groups and individuals with vested interests in the war, like the profiteers. Rightly, Hans Afflerbach calls the First World War 'a political crisis without a solution'. And yet we must surely argue that Siegfried Sassoon was right to make what was in effect his bid for peace by mutual negotiation. Perhaps the window was only slightly ajar, but what if Siegfried's train ride had set running consequences which had led to its being thrown properly open? That question can never be answered because Sassoon was thwarted by false information from Robert Graves. But it is a real one.[7]

# Abbreviations

| | |
|---|---|
| BL: | British Library |
| NA: | National Archives |
| IWM: | Imperial War Museum Archives |
| NAM: | National Army Museum Archives |
| Bodleian: | Bodleian Library, University of Oxford |
| Brotherton: | Brotherton Library, University of Leeds |
| CUL: | Cambridge University Library. |
| KCL: | King's College Library, University of Cambridge |
| Newcastle: | Philip Robinson Library, University of Newcastle |
| Carlisle: | Cumbria Archives Centre |
| Sheffield: | Sheffield City Archives |
| Shrewsbury: | Shropshire Archives |
| Shulbrede: | Shulbrede Archives, Shulbrede Priory |
| HRHRC: | Harry Ransom Humanities Research Center, University of Texas at Austin |
| Carbondale: | Morris Library, Special Collections Research Center, University of Southern Illinois, Carbondale |
| McMaster: | McMaster University, Hamilton, Ontario |
| Tulsa: | University of Tulsa, McFarlin Library |
| Hansard: | House of Commons Parliamentary Debates, Fifth Series (numbered by volumes and columns) |
| D1: | *Siegfried Sassoon Diaries, 1915–1918*, edited by Rupert Hart-Davis (his first volume of Sassoon diaries) |
| CP: | Siegfried Sassoon, *Collected Poems* |
| TWP: | Siegfried Sassoon, *The War Poems* |
| Counter-Attack: | Siegfried Sassoon, *Counter-Attack and Other Poems* |
| TOH: | Siegfried Sassoon, *The Old Huntsman and Other Poems* |
| MIO: | Siegfried Sassoon, *Memoirs of an Infantry Officer* |
| SP: | Siegfried Sassoon, *Sherston's Progress* |
| OC: | Siegfried Sassoon, *The Old Century and Seven More Years* |
| WOY: | Siegfried Sassoon, *The Weald of Youth* |
| SJ: | Siegfried Sassoon, *Siegfried's Journey* |
| GTAT: | Robert Graves, *Goodbye to All That* |
| RR: | Dudley Ward (editor), *Regimental Records of the Royal Welch Fusiliers* |
| JMW: | Jean Moorcroft Wilson, *Siegfried Sassoon* |
| OG: | Ottoline At Garsington: *Memoirs of Lady Ottoline Morrell*, edited by Robert Gathorne-Hardy |
| RWF: | Royal Welch Fusiliers |

# Acknowledgements

Thanks are owed to very many people in respect of this book.

Special gratitude must go to the archive staff of Cambridge University Library for their patient and friendly help regarding the diaries and other papers of Siegfried Sassoon. I thank particularly John Wells, Senior Archivist in the Department of Archives and Modern Manuscripts.

London's Imperial War Museum archives were as always, a rich storehouse, not without some surprises. I thank its staff for their kind help, especially Jane Rosen, Research Support Librarian, Imperial War Museums.

I must thank the staff of the British Library for some most valuable archive assistance, particularly regarding the papers of Lady Ottoline Morrell. Special gratitude is also due to Adrian Goodman, grandson of Philip and Ottoline Morrell, for his interest and help regarding Lady Ottoline's diaries and the Garsington Manor Visitors' Book.

Thanks are due to Kate and Ian Russell for allowing me to consult the diary of Arthur Ponsonby (Catherine's grandfather) and their kind assistance.

This book could not have been produced without the assistance of archivists and librarians in many places in Britain, the United States and Canada. In mentioning Stephen Ennis, Betty Brumbalow Director at the Harry Ransom Humanities Research Centre, University of Texas, along with his colleagues Elizabeth Garver, Reference and Research Services Librarian, and Kayleigh Voss, Aaron Lisec, Research Specialist at the Special Collections Research Center at Morris Library, Southern Illinois University, Abigail Dairaghi of the Deparment of Special Collections and University Archives at McFarlin Library, University of Tulsa, Gillian Dunks, Librarian at McMaster University Archives, Tom Davies, Assistant Archivist at King's College, Cambridge, Rebecca Higgins, Collections Assistant, Special Collections and Galleries, Leeds University Library, and Alison Mussell, Archives Assistant at Shropshire Archives, I thank also those whose names I do not have, with apologies for omissions.

I must particularly mention the kindness and generosity of Annette Campbell-White, author of *Beyond Market Value: A Memoir of Book Collecting and the World of Venture Capital*, owner of the original draft of Siegfried Sassoon's poem 'Atrocities' and a letter relating to this, for letting me have sight of these and for use of them in this book.

Lastly but not least, I thank my editor Lester Crook and Pen & Sword production editor Harriet Fielding and her colleagues for their excellent work.

# Notes

**Chapter 1**

1. Keith Robbins, *The First World War*, 16; *Times*, 15 January 1916.
2. CP, 13-14.
3. *Times*, 15 January 1916.
4. OG, 90-91.
5. OG, 91.
6. BL: Ottoline Morrell Diary, 88886/4/09.
7. Patrick Campbell: *Siegfried Sassoon: A Study of the War Poetry*, 93-94.
8. WOY, 77; JMW, 128.
9. Hansard, 65: 1874; Duncan Marlor, *Fatal Fortnight: Arthur Ponsonby and the Fight for British Neutrality in 1914*, 112-113; *Northampton Daily Echo*, 7 August 1914; Robert Harris, *Precipice*, 150.
10. Francis Meynell, *My Lives*, 84.
11. OC: 188-190; NA: WO 339/51440; George Parfitt, *English Poetry of the First World War*, 13-15; WOY, 268-278; NA: WO 339/51440 (4 August 1914).
12. CUL: Sassoon to his mother, 9724/3.
13. CUL: Sassoon Journals, 9852/1/4/6 (28 November 1915); 9852/1/4/ 7 (2 December 1915); GTAT, 146.
14. GTAT, 102-150.
15. SJ, 17; CP, 10.
16. CP, 14-15; Campbell, 89-91.
17. CP, 14-15; Campbell, 89-91.
18. BL: Sassoon to Gosse, Ashley 5739/342.
19. CUL: Theresa Sassoon to Siegfried Sassoon, 9877/1/1/4.
20. CP, 10.
21. 'Peace', in *Collected Poems of Rupert Brooke* (Sidgwick and Jackson), 144.
22. CUL: Sassoon Journals, 9852/1/4/12.
23. CUL: Sassoon Journals, 9852/1/4/18-19.

**Chapter 2**

1. OG, 260.
2. CUL: Sassoon Journals, 9852/1/5/30-31. It should be noted that there is an error of transcription from the Sassoon notebook in the edition *Siegfried Sassoon Diaries 1915-1918* by Rupert Hart-Davis, which has (pp. 44-45): 'He [Lieutenant David Thomas] had his notebook in his hand, reading my last poem.' The original reads: '[Thomas] had *this* notebook [my italics] in his hand.'
3. SJ, 18; Campbell, 94-95; JMW, 140-141.
4. JMW, 119-120; SJ, 6; 29.
5. CUL: Sassoon Journals, 9852/1/8/4-5 (24 December 1916).

6. *Daily Chronicle*, 30 July 1915.
7. MIO, 11-12.
8. CUL: Sassoon Journals, 9852/1/5/30-31; JMW, 114-15; 143-144.
9. CUL: Sassoon Journals, 9852/1/5/23.
10. CUL: Sassoon Journals, 9852/1/5/21.
11. CUL: Sassoon Journals, 9852/1/5/17.
12. Sassoon Journals, 9852/1/5/6: Sassoon writes: '*vide* 'Stand-to Good Friday Morning', versified from this at the time; Campbell, 100-101.
13. SJ, 17-18.
14. CUL: Sassoon Journals, 9852/1/5/10-11.
15. CP, 15-16.
16. JMW, 152-154; Campbell, 101-104 (citing Jon Silkin, *Out of Battle: The Poetry of the Great War*, 137); GTAT, 226.
17. MIO, 26-32; Donald C. Richter (Ed.), *Lionel Sotheby's Diaries and Letters from the Western Front*, 141-142.
18. MOI, 33, JMW, 156-159.
19. MIO, 32-36.
20. RR, 186.
21. Paul Fussell, *Sassoon's Long Journey*, 74-76; Philip Zelicow, *The Road Less Traveled*, 108; David French, 'The Meaning of Attrition, 1914-1916', *English Historical Review*, Vol. 103, No. 407 (April 1988), 397-399.
22. MIO, 74-84; Michael Palin, *Great Uncle Harry*, 271-272.
23. MIO, 68-69; 86.
24. CUL: Sassoon Journals, 9852/1/7/18 (4 July 1916).
25. *Regimental Records*, 200-202; GTAT, 174; MOI, 87-93.
26. On the various function of a trench fire-step, see David Jones, *In Parenthesis*, 198.
27. Christopher Hassall, *Edward Marsh*, 398.
28. MIO, 94.
29. BL: Sassoon to Gosse, Ashley 5739/348.
30. GTAT, 175; Martin Gilbert, *The First World War*, 264-265.
31. Campbell, 110-111.

**Chapter 3**

1. CP, 28.
2. Campbell, 111-112; SJ, 19; JMW, 170-171.
3. CUL: Sassoon Journals, 9852/1/7/39 (21 July 1916).
4. CUL: Sassoon Journals, 9852/1/7/38.
5. CUL: Sassoon Journals, 9852/1/7.
6. CUL: Sassoon Journals, 9852/1/7/40.
7. CUL: Sassoon Journals, 9852/1/7/40.
8. CUL: Sassoon Journals, 9852/1/7/3.
9. CUL: Sassoon Journals, 9852/1/7/41.
10. CUL: Sassoon Journals, 9852/1/7/37.
11. BL: 56099/5.
12. TWP, 48.
13. SJ, 19; JMW, 171; Campbell, 116-117.
14. SJ, 19; JMW, 175-176.
15. CP, 29-30.

16. SJ, 7.
17. John Rae, *Conscience and Politics: The British Government and the Conscientious Objector to Military Service, 1916 – 1919*. There is no account (to date) of the anti-conscription group in Parliament, but one of the MPs, Richard Lambert, compiled: *The Parliamentary History of Conscription in Great Britain: A Summary of the Parliamentary Debates*.
18. BL: Lady Ottoline Morrell Diary, 88886/4/09.
19. OG, 121.
20. SJ, 8-11.
21. Kate Roiphe, *Uncommon Arrangements*, 181.
22. OG, 122; Egremont, 110.
23. BL: Ottoline Morrell Diary, 88886/4/09, August 1916.
24. BL: Ottoline Morrell Diary, 88886/4/09, August 1916, undated, 10, 11, 15, 16 October 1916.
25. BL: Ottoline Morrell Diary, 88886/4/09, 16 October 1916; Seymour, 369-370.
26. BL: Sassoon to Hamo Thornycroft, 56099/1; Hansard, 90: 19.
27. SJ, 14-15.
28. SJ, 19-20.
29. MIO, 132-138; JMW, 136-138.
30. MIO, 138-139.
31. BL: 8888/5/2, Lady Ottoline Morrell papers: Visitors' Book for 44 Bedford Square and Garsington Manor, February 1912 - December 1927.
32. SJ, 22-24.
33. OG, 152.
34. Seymour, 370.
35. SJ, 22-23; JMW, 177.
36. SJ, 22.
37. BL: Sassoon to Hamo Thornycroft, 56099/6.
38. SJ, 23-24.

**Chapter 4**

1. SJ, 27-28; NA: WO 339/51440; Samuel Hynes, *A War Imagined*, 12.
2. TWP, 61.
3. *Punch*, 8 December 1915.
4. MIO, 142.
5. MIO, 145-164; SJ, 37.
6. CP, 30-31.
7. *Spectator*, 17 February 1917; JMW, 191-192; Campbell, 136-137.
8. BL: 56099/7, Sassoon to Hamo Thornycroft, 27 February 1917; Paul O'Prey (Ed.), *In Broken Images: Selected Letters of Robert Graves*, 70; Elfrieda Manning, *Marble and Bronze*, 172.
9. WOY, 112.
10. *Spectator*, 24 February 1917.
11. *Punch*, 1 August 1917.
12. *Annual Register*, 1917, 190.
13. MIO, 93.
14. CUL: Sassoon Journals, 9852/1/8/79
15. British Library: 8888/5/2 (Garsington Visitors' Book).

16. CUL: Sassoon Journals, 9852/1/8/74.
17. *Annual Register*, 1917, 55-56.
18. OG, 125; 249; Hansard 103: 161 (13 February 1918)
19. Hansard, 88: 1725 (21 December 1916).
20. CUL: Sassoon Journals, 9852/1/8/3; GTAT, 202.
21. CUL: Sassoon Journals, 9852/1/8/4.
22. Santanu Das (Editor), *The Poetry of the First World War*, 3.
23. E.B. Osborn, *The Muse in Arms*, 149.
24. SJ, 39.
25. CUL: Sassoon Journals, 9852/1/8/10 (27 December 1916); H.G. Wells, *Mr Britling Sees It Through*, 389.
26. SJ, 40-41.
27. David Jones, *In Parenthesis*, xi.
28. CUL: Sassoon Journals, 9852/1/8/18.
29. CUL: Sassoon Journals, 9852/1/8/19.
30. CUL: Sassoon Journals, 9852/1/8/78.
31. D.H. Lawrence, *Women in Love*, 11-12.
32. CUL: Sassoon Journals, 9852/1/8/37.
33. SJ, 41-42; CUL: Sassoon Journals, 9852/1/8/46 (15 January 1917).
34. CUL: Sassoon Journals, 9852/1/8/22.
35. CUL: Sassoon Journals, 9852/1/8/23.
36. CUL: Sassoon Journals, 9852/1/8/24.
37. CUL: Sassoon Journals, 9852/1/8/27.
38. SJ, 46-47.
39. SJ, 46.

**Chapter 5**

1. CUL: Sassoon Journals, 9852/1/9/2-3 (5 February 1917).
2. CUL: Sassoon Journals, 9852/1//9/4.
3. MIO, 169.
4. Julian Putkowski and Julian Sykes, *Shot At Dawn*, 294.
5. CUL: Sassoon Journals, 9852/1/9/4-5.
6. CUL: Sassoon Journals, 9852/1/9/52.
7. BL: Sassoon to Gosse, Ashley 5739/350 (7 January 1917); CUL: Sassoon to his mother, 9454/3/596 (26 May 1917).
8. CUL: Sassoon Journals, 9852/1/9/52.
9. James Scott Duckers, *Handed Over*, 11-33.
10. MIO, 176-177.
11. Hansard, 81: 261 (22 March 1916); Rae, 154-156; John W. Graham, *Conscription and Conscience*, 112-113; 208–209.
12. CUL: Sassoon Journals, 9852/1/9/25.
13. Martin Sixsmith, *Russia*, 194; *Labour Leader*, 29 March 1917; *Forward*, 14 April 1917.
14. MIO, 199.
15. CUL: Sassoon to his mother, 9724/3/1 (2 April 1917).
16. BL: 56099/8, Sassoon to Hamo Thornycroft.
17. CUL: Sassoon Journals, 9852/1/9/39-40.
18. RR, 275.

19. J.E. Dunn (ed.) *The War the Infantry Knew 1914-1919: A Chronicle of Service in France and Belgium with the Second Battalion, the Royal Welch Fusiliers*, 329; OC, 199.
20. Sassoon (Dunn collection), 309.
21. MIO, 210.
22. Sassoon (Dunn collection), 313.
23. Sassoon (Dunn collection), 313.
24. Matthew Hollis, Editor, *Edward Thomas: Selected Poems*, xiii; 67; Santanu Das, 'Reframing First World War Poetry', in *The Cambridge Companion to the Poetry of the First World War*, 21; Judy Kendall, Editor, *Poet to Poet: Edward Thomas's Letters to Walter de la Mare*, 220-221.
25. CUL: Sassoon Journals, 9852/1/10/2-10.
26. Sassoon (Dunn Collection), 318.
27. *Counter-Attack*, 21.
28. Jones, xvii; Hansard, 77: 1055.
29. RR, 281.
30. CUL: Sassoon Journals, 9852/1/10/2-10.
31. RR, 275-285.
32. RR, 282-283.
33. RR, 283-284.
34. MIO, 237.
35. CUL: Sassoon Journals, 9852/1/10/2-10; RR, 284-285.
36. Frank Richards, *Old Soldiers Never Die*, 173-174.
37. CUL: Sassoon Journals, 9852/1/10/ 2.

**Chapter 6**

1. CUL: Sassoon Journals, 9852/1/10/ 17-18.
2. British Library: Sassoon to Hamo Thornycroft, 56099/9.
3. Paul O'Prey, Editor, *In Broken Images: Selected Letters of Robert Graves*, 68.
4. O' Prey, 70.
5. CUL: Sassoon Journals, 9852/1/10/ 22-24.
6. Harry Patch, *The Last Fighting Tommy*, 206.
7. Carbondale: Sassoon to Graves, 30 April 1917.
8. Cinema-viewing on the Western Front: ITV, 6 November 2018.
9. CUL: Sassoon Journals, 9852/1/10/16-17 (the original draft of 'To the Warmongers'); TWP, 77; Sir Edward Troup, *The Home Office*, 260.
10. Sir Edward Troup, *The Home Office*, 260.
11. CP, 75; MIO, 20.
12. SJ, 29; GTAT, 151.
13. HRHRC: Ottoline Morrell Collection, Box 28.3; *The Autobiography of Bertrand Russell*, Volume Two, 42-43;
14. Bertrand Russell, *Justice in War-Time*, 131.
15. Russell, 201-202; Ronald W. Clark, *The Life of Bertrand Russell*, 311-312.
16. HRHRC: Ottoline Morrell Collection, 28.3
17. CUL: Sassoon Journals, 9852/1/15-16; CP, 69-70; BL: Ottoline Morrell Diary, 88886/4/09 (20 February 1917).
18. *Nation*, 3 March 1917; GTAT, 210.
19. SJ, 29-30; TOH, 35; CP, 21; Campbell, 124-126.
20. TOH, 45.

21. *Punch*, 25 April 1917; Hansard, 93: 27-29.
22. O'Prey, 70.
23. Carbondale: Sassoon to Graves, 30 April 1917; Osborn, 293-294.
24. CUL: Sassoon Journals, 9852/1/10/31-32; BL: Sassoon to Hamo Thornycroft, 56099/11 (26 May 1917).
25. Bodleian: Sir Richard Denman Papers, 26-29 and newspaper cutting dated 23 April 1916 in Denman MSS, Cuttings, Box 1; MIO; 251-252; Charles Glass, *Soldiers Don't Go Mad*, 97.
26. MIO, 251.
27. TWP, 101 (originally published in the *Cambridge Magazine*, 8 December 1917).
28. MIO, 250-251.

**Chapter 7**

1. NA: WO 339/51440, May 1917; MIO, 255-257; CUL: 9724/3/12.
2. HRHRC: Ottoline Morrell, Box 28.3.
3. Annette Campbell-White, *Beyond Market Value: A Memoir of Book Collecting and the World of Venture Capital*, 193.
4. CUL: Sassoon to his mother, 9724/3/11 and 12; MIO 260.
5. CUL: Sassoon Journals, 9852/1/10/31.
6. Egremont, 136; Newcastle: CPT 77: 6; *The Memoirs of Prince Max of Baden*, Volume 1, 45.
7. CUL: Sassoon Journals, 9852/1/10/38.
8. MIO, 267.
9. A well-researched debunking of some of the German atrocity mythology is the 1928 book *Falsehood in Wartime* by Arthur Ponsonby; on real German atrocities, see John Horne and Alan Kramer, *German Atrocities, 1914: A Century of Denial.*
10. CUL: Sassoon Journals, 9852/1/10/39-40.
11. Osborn, xvii-xviii; SJ, 12.
12. MIO, 257-265; Egremont, 138; TOH, 34.
13. CUL: Sassoon Journals, 9852/1/8/32.
14. IWM: Special Miscellaneous U4 (Sassoon to Bain, 12 May 1917); Peter Parker, *The Old Lie: The Great War and the Public School Ethos*, 216-217.
15. CUL: Sassoon Journals, 9852/1/10/48.
16. CUL: Sassoon to Festing Jones, 8484.
17. HRHRC: Sassoon to Roderick Meiklejohn, 'Saturday' [c. May 1917].
18. IWM: Documents, 1910, Sassoon to Bain, 12 May 1917.

**Chapter 8**

1. CUL: Sassoon to his mother, 26 May 1917, 9724/3/14.
2. CUL: Sassoon Journals, 9852/1/10/43.
3. BL: Sassoon to Gosse, Ashley 5739/351.
4. BL: Sassoon to Hamo Thornycroft, 56099/11.
5. Egremont, 138-139; JMW, 224-225.
6. *Nation*, 16 June 1917, 225; Alfred F. Havighurst, *Radical Journalist: H.W. Massingham*, 261-262.
7. Gilbert, 336-337.
8. Marvin Swartz, *The Union of Democratic Control in British Politics During the First World War*, 107-108; Marlor, 180-182.
9. Dominic Hibberd, *Wilfred Owen*, 376.

10. *New Witness*, 28 June 1917.
11. Mark Rawlinson, 'Later Poets of the First Word War' in Das, 81, citing Robert Graves in *The Common Asphodel: Collected Essays on Poetry 1922-1949*.
12. CUL: Sassoon Journals, 9852/1/10/43.
13. Carbondale: Sassoon to Graves, 30 April 1917.
14. *The Penguin Book of First World War Poetry*, 101-102.
15. Collins, 34.
16. Jones, 54–55.
17. Osborn, xv; 25.
18. Osborn, 293-294.
19. Hynes, 167.
20. SJ, 46; JMW, 226.
21. CUL: Sassoon to his mother, 9724/3/14.

**Chapter 9**

1. BL: Sassoon to Hamo Thornycroft, 56099/12
2. *Counter-Attack*, 25; *Herald*, 26 May 1917; D1, 140.
3. SJ, 48.
4. TWP, 80.
5. CUL: Sassoon to E.J. Dent, 7973/S40.
6. *Cambridge Magazine*, 9 June 1917.
7. JMW, 142.
8. MIO, 273-292.
9. Havighurst, 250-257.
10. Raymond A. Jones, Arthur Ponsonby, 75; Hansard, 63: 2017; Marlor, 43.
11. *Bradford Pioneer*, 13 April 1917.
12. SJ, 51-52.
13. Arnold Bennett, *The Journals*, 411.
14. SJ, 105.
15. BL: Ottoline Morrell Diary, 88886/4/10.
16. OG, 181-183.
17. D1 (Ross letter, 19 July 1917); CUL: Sassoon to Dent, 7973/S42.
18. BL: Ottoline Morrell Diary, 88886/4/10; NA: WO 339/51440.
19. BL: Ottoline Morrell Diary, 88886/4/10.
20. BL: Ottoline Morrell Diary, 88886/4/10.
21. SJ, 51-52.
22. Roiphe, 181-195.
23. BL: 8888/5/2 (Garsington Visitors' Book). I am grateful to Adrian Goodman for his help regarding the Garsington Manor Visitors' Book.
24. BL: Ottoline Morrell Diary, 88886/4/10.
25. John Middleton Murry, *Between Two Worlds*, 83-95; 426-429
26. Murry, 428; OG, 148-150, 181-182; Cherry A. Hankin, *Letters between Katherine Mansfield and John Middleton Murry*.
27. BL: 88886/4/10 (21 June 1917); Sandra Jobson Darroch, *Garsington Revisited*, 279.
28. Murry, 426-427
29. BL: Ottoline Morrell Diary, 88886/4/10.
30. OG, 182.
31. OG, 183.

32. MIO, 292.
33. KCL: Diary of Edward Joseph Dent, EJD/3/1/13.
34. MIO, 292-295.
35. IWM: Colonel Jones-Williams to Siegfried Sassoon, 16 June 1917.
36. IWM: Sassoon Papers, Kearsley to Sassoon, June 1917.
37. NAM: Study Collection, 1955-08-11-4.
38. MIO, 283-285; OG, 181-182.
39. NAM: Study Collection, 1955-08-11-4.
40. SJ, 52.
41. MIO, 283- 285; Egremont, 146-147, citing Siegfried Sassoon's diary of 18 January 1948 and acknowledging Siegfried's son George Sassoon (1936-2006); Hansard, 81: 261 (22 March 1916).
42. OG, 111.
43. CUL: Sassoon Journals, 9852/1/11/24-25.
44. The longer version, as it was when typed, is in the War Office file WO 339/51440 at the National Archives. Rupert Hart-Davis's book of Siegfried Sassoon's 1915-1918 diaries includes it (but not the shorter one as in Sassoon's notebook): D1, 173-174. Hart-Davis gives the erroneous impression that the longer statement appears on 15 June in Sassoon's diary and is dated.
45. CUL: Sassoon Journals, 9852/1/9/43.
46. TWP, 82-83.
47. Tulsa: Ottoline Morrell to Siegfried Sassoon, 20 June 1917.
48. CUL: 9852/1/11/5-10.
49. GTAT, 202.
50. CUL: 9852/1/11/5-10.
51. The review is in the *Times Literary Supplement* of 21 June 1917. It is entitled 'A Talent Not Buried'. The book is *Your Unprofitable Servant* ('by the author of "An Old Farmhouse"').
52. Egremont, 145-146.
53. CUL: Sassoon Journals, 9852/1/11/10-11.
54. JMW, citing Christie, Manson &Wood's sale catalogue of 4 June 1975.
55. Miranda Seymour, *Robert Graves: Life on the Edge*, 63-65; Carbondale: Sassoon to Graves, 24 June 1917.
56. Carbondale: Sassoon to Graves, 24 June 1917.
57. IWM: Sassoon Papers, SS1, J. Cottrill to Sassoon, 29 June 1917; CUL: Sassoon Journals, 9852/1/7/39-40.
58. Sylvia Pankhurst, *Home Front*, 337-338.
59. O' Prey, 71-72.
60. Carbondale: no date but 'Monday' may be taken from the content of the letter to be 2 July 1917.
61. O'Prey, 71-75.
62. JMW, 237; Egremont, 150; OC, 199.
63. 4 July 1917 telegram: McMaster; Siegfried Sassoon to Bertrand Russell, 'Wednesday' [4 July]: McMaster; Sassoon's promotion: NA: WO 339/51440.
64. CUL: Sassoon Journals, 9852/1/11/21 (copy of letter to commanding officer).
65. HRHRC: Bertrand Russell to Lady Ottoline Morrell, 'Saturday', by inference 7 July 1917.
66. Carlisle: Catherine Marshall Papers, D/Mar/4/7; HRHRC: Russell to Ottoline Morrell, 'Friday' (by inference 13 July 1917).
67. HRHRC: Russell to Ottoline Morrell, 'Friday' (by inference 13 July 1917).
68. Meynell, 103.

69. Carlisle: Catherine Marshall Papers, D/Mar/4/7.
70. CUL: Sassoon Journals, 9852/1/11/26.
71. JMW, 86-88; Sheffield: Carpenter, 386/181 (2 August 1911).
72. JMW, 226.
73. BL: 56099/14, Sassoon to Cox, 7 July 1917.
74. Glass, 119.
75. D1, 179.
76. Tulsa: Lees-Smith to Sassoon, 9 July 1917.
77. Tulsa: Murry to Sassoon, 9 July 1917.
78. D1, 180.
79. BL: 56099/15, Sassoon to Cox, 11 July 1917.
80. Tulsa: Cox to Sassoon, 17 July 1917.
81. D1, 179.
82. JMW (*Robert Graves*), 200.
83. D1, 178.
84. Tulsa: Bennett to Sassoon, 11 July 1917; D1, 180-181: Bennett to Sassoon, 20 July 1917.
85. Duncan Wilson, *Gilbert Murray*, 236.
86. John Plowright (editor), *Repton to the End*, 161; Hynes, 148-152; OG, 147.
87. Hansard, 86: 1531.
88. Meynell, 103; O'Prey, 355.
89. Glass, 141; Clark, 403.
90. McMaster: Sassoon to Bertrand Russell, 11 July 1917.
91. CUL: Sassoon Journals, 9852/1/11/ 1. (The telegram is preserved in Sassoon's diary notebook.)
92. IWM: Sassoon Papers, SS1, J. Cottrill to Sassoon, 11 July 1917.
93. Sheffield City Archives: 386/293.
94. CUL 9852/1/11/2 (the telegram in Sassoon's notebook).
95. O 'Prey, 77. JMW (*Robert Graves*), 200; GTAT, 212-213.
96. HRHRC, Bertrand Russell to Ottoline Morrell 'Friday' (by inference 13 July 1917); BL: Ashley 5739 (Robert Ross to Edmund Gosse, 19 July 1917).

**Chapter 10**

1. MIO, 317.
2. MIO, 318.
3. McMaster: Sassoon to Russell, 'Friday', from which 13 July 1917 may be inferred.
4. MIO, 320-321; SJ, 55; GTAT, 215.
5. MIO, 321.
6. Hans W. Gatzke, *Germany's Drive to the West*, 184-194; Holger Afflerbach, 'War Aims and the Chances for a Compromise Peace during the First World War' in *The Purpose of the First World War: War Aims and Military Strategies (Schriften des Historischen Kollegs*: 91), 252-254; Douglas Newton, *British Policy and the Weimar Republic, 1918-1919*, 101-102.
7. MIO, 245; 322-326.
8. HRHRC, Ottoline Morrell Collection, 17 July 1917.
9. BL: Ottoline Morrell Diary, 88886/4/10.
10. Manning, 17.
11. BL: Ashley 5739, Robert Ross to Edmund Gosse, 19 July 1917.
12. GTAT, 215; BL: Ashley MS 5739.
13. IWM: Wells to Sassoon, 18 July 1917.
14. MIO, 326-331.

15. McMaster: Graves to Russell, 19 July 1917.
16. GTAT, 216.
17. MIO, 332.
18. MIO, 333;NA: WO 339/51440.
19. NA: WO 339/51440.
20. CUL: Sassoon to Dent, 7973/5/43; Sheffield: Carpenter Collection, Sassoon to Carpenter, no date.
21. MIO, 333.
22. IWM: Willis to Sassoon, 20 July 1917.
23. McMaster: Russell to Mrs Swanwick, 20 July 1917.
24. HRHRC: Bertrand Russell to Ottoline Morrell, 21 July 1917.
25. Seymour (*Robert Graves*), 62; HRHRC: Bertrand Russell to Ottoline Morrell, 21 July 1917.
26. GTAT, 214-215.
27. Shrewsbury: Diary of W.C. Bridgeman, 4629/1/2/1, April 1916 and 23 June 1916.
28. Clark, 402-403.
29. Clark, 401.
30. Egremont, 155.
31. Egremont, 157 and note; Marlor, *Churchill the Liberal Reformer: The Struggle for a Modern Home Office.*
32. Catherine Cline, *E.D. Morel*, 111-113; Newcastle: CPT Ex. 111 (2).
33. Jo Vellacott, *Bertrand Russell and the Pacifists in the First World War*, 231-232; Cline, 111-113; Swartz, 178-179; Adam Hochschild, *To End All Wars*, 295-297; Geoffrey Howse, *A History of London's Prisons*, 107-116; Marlor (*Churchill the Liberal Reformer*), 230.
34. Hansard, 98: 1570. On 28 September 1916 Lloyd George, as War Minister, gave an interview to an American journalist which generated the defining phrase of his war, including as Prime Minister He declared that: 'The fight must be to a finish...a knock-out. Peace now or at any time before the final and complete elimination of this [German] menace is unthinkable.' The gung-ho language (and the British dead as an investment) caused disgust in dissenter circles and beyond. *Times*, 29 September 1916; *UDC*, October 1916.
35. CUL: Sassoon to Dent, 7973/S45.
36. HRHRC: Sassoon to Meiklejohn, 1 August 1917.
37. SP, 7.
38. BL: Herbert Farjeon to his mother (in Sassoon to Hamo Thornycroft papers), 56099/20-33.
39. IWM: 9059, W.H.R. Rivers report on Siegfried Sassoon, c. August 1917.
40. SP, 10.

**Chapter 11**

1. Peace-by-negotiation debate: Hansard, 82: 2179-2252 (23 May 1916).
2. Hansard; 96: 1802
3. Hansard, 96: 1582 (26 July 1917)
4. Newcastle: CPT 77 (16 November 1916).
5. *Daily Chronicle*, 27 July 1917.
6. *Bradford Pioneer*, 27 July 1917.
7. GTAT, 213-214.
8. Rachel Holmes, Sylvia Pankhurst, 487-488.
9. *Herald*, 9 June 1917; Carsten, F. L., *War Against War*, 106–107; E.S. Turner, *Dear Old Blighty*, 192-195; Martin Crick, *The History of the Social Democratic Federation*, 278-279;

Millman, Brock: *Managing Domestic Dissent in First World War Britain*, 206–211; Gerard J. DeGroot, *Blighty: British Society in the Era of the Great War*, 149-153; Hochschild, *To End All Wars*, 274; Richard Taylor and Nigel Young, *Campaigns for Peace*, 57-60.

10. Russell, 31-32; Hochschild, 274; *Times*, 30 July 1917; Turner,197.
11. Shulbrede: Arthur Ponsonby Diary, 14 June 1917.
12. Pankhurst, 271-272.
13. Hochschild, 280.
14. Hansard, 96: 1784
15. *Daily News*, 31 July 1917; Roy Jenkins, *Asquith*, 511; Russell, 32.
16. Hansard 96: 1804.
17. *Stockton and Thornaby Herald*, 17 March 1917.
18. Shulbrede: Arthur Ponsonby Diary, 27 November 1915.
19. Hansard, 96: 1799.
20. Hansard, 96: 1804-1805.
21. Hansard, 96: 1805.
22. O 'Prey, 80.
23. CUL: 9375, Dr James Dunn to Siegfried Sassoon, 26 July 1927.
24. Dunn collection, 372.
25. Simon Webb, *1919: Britain's Year of Revolution*.
26. *Times*, 31 July 1917.
27. Brotherton: Edmund Gosse to Hamo Thornycroft, 31 July 1917.
28. IWM: Sassoon Papers, 3 July 1917.
29. Harry Patch, '*The Last Fighting Tommy*', 201.
30. Sheffield City Archives: Carpenter MSS, 386/293; *Daily Mail*, 31 July 1917.
31. *Daily News*, 5 August 1914; 31 July 1917.
32. IWM: Robertson and Seward to Sassoon, 18 August 1917.
33. *Manchester Guardian*, 31 July 1917.
34. *Daily Chronicle*, 31 July 1917; *Liverpool Daily Post*, 31 July 1917; *Birmingham Daily Post*, 31 July 1917; *Birmingham Gazette*, 31 July 1917; *Aberdeen Evening Gazette*, 2 August 1917; *Southampton Echo*, 3 August 1917; *Dundee Advertiser*, 2 August 1917; *Burton Evening Gazette*, 2 August 1917.
35. *Labour Leader*, 2 August 1917.
36. SP, 7-9; Glass, 128-129.
37. IWM, Sassoon to Robert Ross, 26 July 1917.
38. BL: 56099/19, Siegfried Sassoon to Hamo Thornycroft, c. August 1917.
39. HRHRC: Sassoon to Meiklejohn, 1 August 1917.
40. Douglas Newton, *Private Ryan and the Lost Peace*, 119; 297-298.
41. Newton, Appendix 2.
42. Newton, 303.
43. HRHRC, Sassoon to Meiklejohn, 14 August 1917.
44. Osborn, xviii.
45. Robert Nichols, *Ardours and Endurances*, 41; JMW, 269.
46. Nichols, 66.
47. Caroline E. Playne, *Britain Holds On: 1917-1918*.

**Chapter 12**

1. Carbondale: Sassoon to Graves, 10 August 1917.
2. Egremont, 169.
3. Robert Graves, *Selected Poems*, 8.

4. O' Prey, 80 (Graves to Sassoon, 31 July 1917).
5. Carbondale: Sassoon to Graves, 'Saturday' [probably 6 October 1917]; 19 October 1917.
6. O'Prey, 82-88.
7. IWM: SS1, Cottrill to Sassoon, 16 October1917; CUL: Sassoon to Dent, 7973/5/45.
8. I am grateful to Annette Campbell-White, owner of the manuscripts of the 12 November 1917 letter of Siegfried Sassoon to C.K. Ogden and the accompanying original draft of the poem 'Atrocities' for letting me have sight of these. They were unknown until 2013 when they appeared in a Bonhams auction sale in London. The discovery is mentioned in an article in the *Observer* of 3 February 2013.
9. TWP, 145.
10. Patch, 201.
11. GTAT, 153-154; Niall Ferguson, *The Pity of War*, 367–394.
12. HRHRC: Sassoon to Meiklejohn, 29 December 1917.
13. HRHRC: Ottoline Morrell Box 28.3, Sassoon to Ottoline Morrell, 4 December 1917; Lord Newton Diary, 31 December 1917, Lord Newton Papers, Lewes.
14. HRHRC, Sassoon to Meiklejohn, 29 December 1917.
15. NA: WO 339/51440 (18–23 January 1918).
16. David Reynolds, *The Long Shadow, 98-100; First World War* dragon's teeth: David Stevenson, *1914-1918 The History of the First World War,* 587-588;
17. Ibn Saud and the December 1915 agreement with Britain: Bernard Lewis, *The Crisis of Islam*, 95; D1, 222 (13 March 1918); 229 (5 April 1918).
18. *The Tribunal*, 13 June 1918.
19. Max Plowman Letters, *Bridge into the Future.*
20. CUL: Sassoon Journals, 9852/1/13/3 (15 May 1918).
21. CUL: Sassoon Journals, 9852/1/13/16 (4 June 1918).
22. CUL: Sassoon Journals, 9852/1/13/26 (no date).
23. *UDC* magazine, July 1918.
24. CUL: Sassoon Journals, 9852/1/13/21 (12 June 1918).
25. CUL: Sassoon Journals, 9852/1/13/27 (18 June 1918).
26. JMW, 310-311; SP, 177-163.
27. *Nation*, 13 July 1918.
28. *Counter-Attack*, 31.
29. Darroch, 312; *Labour Leader*, 25 July 1918.
30. *Counter-Attack*, 12-13.
31. Carbondale, Sassoon to Graves 24 July 1918.
32. 'Pacifists in Parliament', by a Journalist Observer, *UDC*, September 1918.
33. Hansard, 109: 1597.
34. Hansard, 109: 1697; *Times*, 9 August 1918.
35. Hansard, 109: 1412, 1428 and 1624; *Labour Leader*, 15 August 1917.
36. Michael Korda, *Muse of Fire: World War I as Seen Through the Lives of the Soldier Poets*, 271; Hansard, 84: 986.
37. Michael Howard, The First World War, 129–131.
38. CUL: Sassoon Journals, 9852/1/13/28; SJ, 77-81; Sheffield: Carpenter, 386/295.
39. SJ, 77-81.

**Chapter 13**

1. Douglas Haig, *War Diaries and Letters*, edited by Gary Sheffield and John Bourne, 384; D1 (letter to Vivian. de Sola Pinto, poet, academic, fellow member of Sassoon's company and admirer of his work), 277-278 (4 August 1918).

2. *Labour Leader*, 4 July 1918.
3. CUL: Sassoon Journals, 9852/1/13/31-32 (11 November 1918). Changing of the end of hostilities hour: Wemyss family/BBC Television Armistice Day 2000 programme.
4. CUL: Sassoon Journals, 9852/1/13/31 (11 November 1918).
5. Patch, 203.
6. CUL: Sassoon Journals, 9852/1/13/51.
7. *Labour Leader*, 21 November 1918.
8. HRHRC: Ottoline Morrell Box 28.4, Sassoon to Ottoline Morrell, 27 September 1918.
9. Sheffield: Carpenter, 386/313; 386/315.
10. NA: WO 339/51440; Hansard, 90: 14 (7 February 1917).
11. Hansard, 108: 486.
12. Barbara Stoney, *Twentieth Century Maverick: The Life of Noel Pemberton Billing*, 112; 138-9; *Forward*, 8 June 1918.
13. HRHRC: Ottoline Morrell Box 28.4, Sassoon to Ottoline Morrell, 27 September 1918.
14. Egremont, 217-18; *Cambridge Magazine*, 14 September 1918.
15. *U.D.C.* magazine: 'Pacifists in Parliament' by 'A Journalist Observer', September 1918.
16. IWM: Max Plowman to Sassoon, 22 November 1918; SJ, 110-112.
17. IWM: Plowman to Sassoon, 27 November 1918; Philip Snowden to Sassoon, 27 November 1918; SJ, 111.
18. Hansard, 103: 196 (13 February 1918).
19. HRHRC: Ottoline Morrell Box 28.4.
20. CUL: Sassoon Journals, 9852/1/13/ first enclosure page in the front cover of the notebook.
21. CUL: Sassoon Journals, 9852/1/13/ front-cover first enclosure page.
22. CUL: Sassoon Journals, 9852/1/13/ front-cover second enclosure page.
23. CUL: Sassoon Journals, 9852/1/13/ front-cover second enclosure page.
24. CUL: Sassoon Journals, 9582/1/13/3.
25. IWM: Snowden to Sassoon, 30 November 1918.
26. SJ, 115; Snowden in the House of Commons: U.D.C. magazine 'Pacifists in Parliament', by 'A Journalist Observer', September 1918.
27. Snowden at Blackburn (10-14 December 1918): CUL: Sassoon Journals, 9852/1/13/ 35-38.
28. *Daily Dispatch*, 11 December 1918.
29. *Daily Dispatch*, 11 December 1918 (adjusted to direct speech).
30. Irene Cooper Willis, *England's Holy War*, 331.
31. CUL: Sassoon Journals, 9852/1/13/37; Egremont, 228-229; JMW, 346-347.
32. SJ, 114.
33. SJ, 114.
34. CUL: Sassoon Journals, 9852/1/13/37.
35. CUL: Sassoon Journals, 9852/1/13/38.
36. CUL: Sassoon Journals, 9852/1/13/38-39.
37. HRHRC: Ottoline Morrell Box 28.4, Sassoon to Ottoline Morrell, 14 December 1918.
38. *Daily Dispatch*, 12 December 1918.
39. SJ, 114.
40. *Observer*, 15 December 1918.
41. F.W.S. Craig, *British Parliamentary Election Results 1918-1949.*
42. *Sheffield Independent*, 13 December 1918.
43. F.W.S. Craig, *British Parliamentary Election Results* 1918-1949.
44. Snowden, *An Autobiography*, 502; IWM: Snowden to Sassoon, '11 January' no year.
45. Colin Cross, *Philip Snowden*, 227.

46. Webb, 53-61; SJ, 130-134; Egremont, 231.
47. JMW, 347; SJ, 128.
48. SJ, 134.
49. NA: WO 339/51440; CP, 118-119.
50. Shulbrede: Arthur Ponsonby Diary, 10 May 1919.
51. *Daily Herald*, 17 May 1919.

**Chapter 14**

1. Ferguson, 448.
2. Gary Sheffield, *Forgotten Victory: The First World War: Myths and Realities*, 18-20; 189.
3. SJ, 57.
4. Nigel Biggar, *In Defence of War*, 143.
5. Hochschild, 294.
6. I am indebted regarding consideration of the results of the end of the First World War to BBC Radio 4's 28 September 2023 'In Our Time' discussion on John Maynard Keynes's *The Economic Consequences of the Peace*, with Patricia Clavin of the University of Oxford, Michael Cox of the LSE, and Margaret MacMillan of the University of Oxford, chaired by Melvyn Bragg.
7. Afflerbach, 238.

# Index

*Aberdeen Gazette*, 149
Allenby, General, 159
'American Note, The', 39
Anderson, William, 140
*Annual Register*, 39, 40
'Asbestos Bill', 18, 32
Asquith, H.H, 4, 39, 49, 52, 130, 143,146, 172

Bain, John, 78–9
Balfour, Arthur, 157, 159
Balfour Declaration, 159
Battle of Arras, 53–61, 66, 74, 83, 88
Battle of Festubert, 5
Battle of the Marne, 89
Battle of Messines, 82
Battle of the Somme, 11, 17, 18, 21, 25, 31, 41, 44–5, 53, 64, 72, 86, 151, 164, 191–2
Battle of Passchendaele, 147, 154, 156, 157, 191
Battle of Vimy Ridge, 64
Baldwin, Sergeant, 60
Barbusse, Henri, 105, 163, 164, 192
Beamish, Henry Hamilton, 175
'Belgian Grey Book', 168
Bell, Clive, 2, 93
Bell, Vanessa, 2
Belloc, Hilaire, 104
Bennett, Arnold, 71, 91, 110, 111, 115
Bentinck, Lord Henry, 111
Bethmann-Hollweg, Theobald von, 39
*Birmingham Daily Post*, 149
*Birmingham Gazette*, 149
Birrell, Augustine, 40
Bloomsbury Group, 2, 28,29, 81,93, 94, 111, 163
'Bomb Shop, The', 115, 128, 129
Bondfield, Margaret, 182
*Bradford Pioneer*, 89, 90, 139, 185
Brassey, Thomas, Earl of, 73–6, 110, 111, 168
Brassey Lady Sybil, 73–5, 77–8, 153
Brett, Dorothy, 27–28
Bridges, Robert, 86
Bridgeman, William, 129
Brooke, Rupert, 8, 13, 30
Bryce, Annan, 4
Burton, Nellie, 88
*Burton Evening Gazette*, 149
Butcher, John, 174

*Cambridge Magazine, The*, 7, 15, 35, 87, 88, 96, 111, 115, 143, 157, 176
Campbell, Colonel R. B. (bayonet lecturer), 14–15, 157, 160
Carden, Colonel R.J.W, 21
Carpenter, Edward, 111, 113, 117, 127, 147, 168, 173
Carson, Sir Edward, 49, 104
Casson, 2nd Lt, 55–57
Cave, Sir George, 142, 174
Cecil, Lord Robert, 168
Cenotaph, The, 65
Chamberlain, Neville, 50
Chancellor, Henry, 141
Chesterton, Cecil, 82
Churchill, Winston, 3, 17, 18, 41, 75, 114, 123, 124, 130, 132, 168–9, 182, 187, 188
Churchill, Clementine, 168
Civil Liberties Group in the House of Commons, 109
*Clarion, The*, 170
Clemenceau, Georges, 190
'Conciliation Bill', 187
Conscription, 5, 26, 37, 41, 50–2, 58, 66, 94–5, 101, 109, 116, 129, 137, 140–1, 151, 178, 184, 185
Conscientious objectors, 5, 10, 26, 27, 33, 41, 51, 52–3, 93, 99, 109, 124, 133, 160, 185
Cottrill, Quartermaster 'Joe', 31, 32, 105–6, 117, 146, 155–6, 182, 186
Courtney, Lord Leonard, 36
Cox, Harold, 111
Craiglockhart War Hospital, 127, 131–4, 149, 150, 153–6, 159, 177

*Daily Chronicle*, 12, 139, 148, 166
*Daily Dispatch*, 181, 184, 185
*Daily Express*, 83, 141
*Daily Mail*, 49, 78, 147, 164
*Daily News*, 148

*Daily Sketch*, 83
*Daily Telegraph*, 158
Davidson, Randall, Archbishop of Canterbury, 72
Defence of the Realm Act, 44, 66, 83, 101, 109, 131, 149
De la Mare, Walter, 57
Dadd, Julian, 20, 71–2, 130
Dean, Percy, 176, 178, 181, 185
Delville Wood, 72
Denman, Richard, 71
Dent, Edward J, 88, 91–2, 96–7, 126, 132, 155
Desborough, Lady Ethel Ann Priscilla ('Ettie'), 84
Dobell, Lieutenant Colin, 162
Doughty, Charles Montagu, 159
Duckers, James Scott, 51–2
*Dundee Advertiser*, 149
Dunn, Dr James, 54–6, 145

Edinburgh Review, 146
Edward VII, King, 175
Edwards, Colonel H.J, 91–2, 97
Edwards, Ebenezer, 161
*Eiffel Tower* (restaurant), 95
Elliot T.S, 45
Eton College, 16
Evans, 2nd Lt, 55–6
Evans, Ellis (Hedd Wynn), 147
*Evening Standard*, 83

Farjeon, Herbert, 133–4
Fellowship of Reconciliation, 109
*Fight for Right*, 115
Fisher, Admiral Lord John (Jacky), 169
*Forward*, 175

Garsington Manor, 1, 10, 11, 26–8, 31–3, 37, 39–41, 50, 67, 71, 74, 81–2, 88–94, 101, 111, 128, 130, 132, 140, 146, 170, 182, 189
General Election of 1900, 172
General Election of 1906, 10
General Election of January 1910, 10
General Election of December 1910, 10, 41
General Election of 1918, 172–8, 186, 187
German Peace Note, The, 39–42
Gibbs, Philip, 12, 157
*Globe, The,* 141
Goodall, Marcus, 14, 23
Gosse, Edmund,
Grant, Duncan, 2
Graves, Robert, 6, 11–13, 15, 19, 21, 32, 37–8, 42, 53, 64–5, 68–70, 74, 82–5, 96, 103–7, 114, 118, 120, 123–130, 132, 134, 139, 145–6, 152–5, 157, 165, 172
  first acquaintance with Siegfried Sassoon, 5
  mistakenly reported to have died of wounds, 19
  becomes a trainer of cadets at Oxford, 53
  at Siegfried Sassoon's medical board 125–6
Greaves, Ralph, 56, 59
Grenfell, Gerald William ('Billy'), 84
Grenfell, Julian, 84–5
Greenwood, Sir Hamar, 58
Grey, Sir Edward, 4

Haig, Sir Douglas, 18, 52, 64–5, 148, 170
Hanmer, Robert, 65–6, 105, 114, 160
Hardy, Thomas, 48, 68, 80, 105, 110, 115, 178, 182
Harris, Robert, 4
Harvey, Edmund, 52
Heinemann, William, 35, 48, 51, 58, 73, 84
Henderson, Francis, 115–18, 129
*Herald / Daily Herald*, 87, 159, 179, 188, 190
Herbert, Aubrey, 41
High Wood, 23
Hindenburg, Paul von, 39
Hindenburg Line, 53, 59, 74, 110, 165
Hogge, James, 167
Hope, James Fitzalan, 110. 111, 129
Housman, A.E, 169
Hunter-Weston, Sir Aylmer, 170
Hutchinson, Horace, 111, 112
Huxley, Aldous, 94

*John Bull*, 83
Jones, David, 21, 44, 58
Jones, Harry, 166
Jones, Henry Festing, 79
Jones, L.E, 85
Jones-Williams, Colonel H.R, 97, 110, 120, 158
Jowett, Fred, 89–90, 185

Kearsley, Major Edward Reginald, 97–8
Kerensky, Alexander, 53, 114, 137
King, Joseph, 174

*Labour Leader*, 149, 164, 167, 170
Lambert, Richard, 41, 138, 182
*Land and Water*, 104
Lane, Miriam, 130
Langdon-Davies, John, 188
Lansbury, George, 87
Lansdowne, Fifth Marquess of, 158
Lauder, Harry, 175
Law, Andrew Bonar, 39, 166
Lawrence, D.H, 45–6

Lawrence, Frieda, 46
League of Nations, 42, 167
Ledwidge, Francis, 147
Leeds Convention, 140, 143, 193
Lees-Smith, Hastings Bertrand (Bertie), 42–3, 109–10, 112–3, 121–2, 125, 128–9, 133–4, 137–140, 142–4, 146, 148, 166, 173
  puts down a question in Parliament on Siegfried Sassoon, 128
  reads out Sassoon's statement in the House of Commons, 142
  at the 1918 General Election, 185–7
Liebknecht, Karl, 189
*Liverpool Daily Post*, 149
Liverpool Repertory Theatre, 147
*Llandovery Castle*, 173
Lloyd, Frank, 64–5
Lloyd George, David, 18, 34, 39–41, 48, 95, 104, 107, 121, 124, 130, 132, 148, 167, 170, 172, 182, 185, 190
Loder, Norman, 34
Lodge, Oliver, 77
Ludendorff, Erich, 39, 161, 165–6
Lutyens, Sir Edwin, 65
Luxemburg, Rosa, 189

MacDonald, J. Ramsay, 10, 41, 137, 151, 187
Macpherson, Ian, 137, 144–5
Magna Carta, 10, 109
Malleson, Miles, 116
Mametz Wood, 18–21, 162, 189
Mansfield, Katherine, 2, 94, 99
Marlborough School, 3, 5, 14, 25, 43, 78
Marsh, Edward (Eddie), 3, 20, 35, 38, 82, 84, 107, 111–12, 114, 118, 123, 131, 168, 189
Marshall, Catherine, 109–110, 127, 187
Marx, Karl, 188
Masefield, John, 3, 107
Macartney-Filgate, Major A.R.P, 120
Manchester Guardian, 67, 148
Mason, David, 136–7
Massingham, H.W, 81, 89, 107, 110, 111, 188
Masterman, Charles, 86
Max von Baden, 75, 160, 168
McCurdy, Charles, 173, 182
McKenna, Reginald, 75
McRae, John, 36
Meiklejohn, Roderick, 79, 132, 150, 152, 157, 158
Meynell, Francis, 5, 28, 110
Michaelis, George, 121
Milner, Lord, 49, 104
Moncrieff, C.K. Scott, 83
Morgan, Evan, 129
*Morning Post*, 83, 84, 158
Morel, Edmund Dene, 131–2, 167
Morrell, Julian, 32, 102, 123
Morrell, Lady Ottoline, 2, 10–11, 26–33, 38–41, 45–6, 48, 66–7, 74, 81, 88, 90–96, 98–9, 102, 109, 110, 118, 122–3, 128, 130, 133, 156, 158, 163–4, 172, 175, 177–8, 184, 189, 191
  sees a poem of SS in *The Times*, 1
  first meeting with SS, 22–23
  recognises that her feelings for SS are not reciprocated, 92
  hurt by SS's treatment of her, 95
Morrell, Philip, 1, 10–11, 29, 33, 46, 49, 50, 67, 89, 104, 109, 116, 138, 164, 167, 178
  brought back into politics by the conscription controversy, 26
  joins the peace by negotiation group in the House of Commons, 41
  declines to help SS publicly in his protest against the war, 93
Murray, Gilbert, 115
Murry, John Middleton, 94–5, 98, 99, 113, 116, 133, 163–4

*Nation, The*, 68, 81, 82, 89, 142, 163–4, 177, 188
Newton, Lord Thomas, 158
*New Witness* 82–3
Nichols, Robert, 107, 152–3
Nivelle, General Robert, 41
No Conscription Fellowship, 116
Norman, Sir Henry, 178, 181, 185
Northcliffe, Lord, 49, 104, 147

*Observer, The*, 185
Official Secrets Act, 101
Ogden, Charles K, 110–112, 115, 156, 157
Oh! What a Lovely War, 192
Orlando, Vittorio Emanuele, 190
Osborn, E.B, 83–6, 152
Outhwaite, Cedric, 176
Outhwaite, Robert Leonard, 70, 137–8, 146, 151, 166–8, 176
Owen, Wilfred, 153, 155, 177, 191

Page-Croft, General Henry, 174
Palin, Michael, 18
Pankhurst, Sylvia, 106, 139, 141, 187
Patch, Harry, 64, 157, 171–2
Pentonville Prison, 131, 169
Persia and oil, 89
Pethick-Lawrence, Emmeline, 177
Petition of Right, 10, 109
Plowman, Max, 159, 160, 164, 176–7
Polygon Wood, 155
Ponsonby Arthur, 36, 75, 109, 136, 138, 140, 143, 166–7, 190

Ponsonby, John, 141
Profiteers, 32, 106, 117, 146, 181, 186, 194
*Punch*, 8, 36, 38, 70

Rawlinson, General Henry, 85
Repton School, 115–6
Richards, Frank, 61
Rivers, Dr W.H.R, 132–4, 150, 153, 154, 159
Robertson, Cecile Walton, 148
Romanov, Tsar Nicholas, 53
Ross, Robert, 11–12, 26–8, 31, 36, 69, 71, 79, 82, 86, 91, 101, 112, 118, 123, 133–4, 137, 150
Rothschild, Lord, 159
Russell, Bertrand, 29, 89, 94–5, 99–100, 104, 108–9, 112, 115–6, 118–9, 122, 125, 127–133, 140, 142, 164, 191
  influence on Siegfried Sassoon of his book *Justice in Wartime*, 51, 66–7, 71
  helps Sassoon to compose his statement about the war, 98–9
  physically attacked at a meeting, 140
  imprisoned, 131
Ryan, Private Edward James, 151–2

Samuel, Herbert, 52
Sassoon, Alfred Ezra (SS's father), 3
Sassoon, Hamo (SS's brother), 7, 13, 78
Sassoon, Sir Philip (SS's cousin), 3, 16, 152
Sassoon, Siegfried Loraine
  MILITARY CAREER
  joins the Army, 3–4
  is commissioned as a second lieutenant in the Royal Welch Fusiliers, 5
  awarded Military Cross, 17
  drives Germans from a trench, 19–21
  sent back to Britain to recover from dysentery, 23–5
  returns to France, 49
  wounded by a gunshot in the shoulder, 60
  hospitalised in London, 62–72
  promoted to lieutenant, 108
  recommended for a DSO, 73, 79, 110, 145
  composes a declaration of protest against the war and refuses to do further military service, 98–101
  back on the Western Front, 161
  promoted to acting captain, 161
  suffers a gunshot wound in the head and is returned to Britain, 162–3

  PERSONAL INTERESTS AND CHARACTERISICS
  introverted and self-conscious, 6, 152, 177
  childhood memories, 7
  fox-hunting 3, 31, 33
  effect of the loss of his brother, 8
  empathy with his men and care for his platoon, 6, 12, 20
  conversation and correspondence varying inconsistently, depending on the other person, 34, 54–5, 90–91
  self-centeredness and vanity, 92, 96, 147
  an intermittent diary keeper, 27
  changing tone of his poetry regarding the war, 11, 14, 23, 25–6, 37–8
  fluctuating and shifting feelings regarding the war, 7, 8–9, 13–14, 16, 21–2, 33, 43, 44, 46, 48, 49, 54, 66
  starts to think politically, 33
  attitude to idealisation of English countryside in warrior sentiment, 30–1
  battlefield bravery, 17, 21, 97, 129, 130, 163, 171
  scornful of séances, 77–8
  legal hazards regarding his being homosexual, 12
  lack of women in his poetry, 12
  revenge lust on the battlefield regarding dead comrades, 12, 36, 60
  snobbish tendency, 55–6
  development of an epigrammatical style of poetry, 11, 26, 69–70, 80–81
  development of poetic metaphor, 38
  influenced by the poetry of Charles Sorley, 43–4
  influenced by the writing of H.G. Wells, 44
  admiration of Philip Snowden, 177, 178, 180
  realisation of his talent for humour, 183
  change in his social attitude as a result of his election campaigning, 183

  POETRY WORKS
  The Daffodil Murderer, 3
  The Old Huntsman, 35, 46, 65, 68–70, 73, 80–84, 112, 152
  Counter-Attack, 58, 157, 163–165, 169, 170

  INDIVIDUAL POEMS
  'Absolution', 6–8, 68, 85
  'Aftermath', 189–190
  'Arms and the Man', 36
  'Atrocities', 156–7
  'Base Details', 87–8, 163
  'Blighters', 48, 69, 81
  'Brothers', 68
  'Colin', 162
  'Conscripts', 37–8, 81
  'Counter-Attack', 164–5

'Died of Wounds', 23, 68, 70, 84, 166
'The Dragon and The Undying', 68
'Editorial Impressions', 88, 163
'The Effect, 57–8, 163
'France', 68
'The General', 66, 157, 163
'Golgotha', 68
'I Stood with the Dead', 131
'In the Pink', 11, 69, 81
'In an Underground Dressing Station', 88
'The Kiss', 15, 69
'A Letter Home', 69
'A Mystic as Soldier', 68–9
'The Old Huntsman', 6, 68
'The One Legged Man,' 25–6, 69, 81
'The Patriot', 171–2
'The Poet as Hero', 35–6
'The Rear-Guard', 67, 85, 163
'Reconciliation', 179–180
'The Redeemer', 7
'Stand-to: Good Friday Morning', 14
'Stretcher Case', 26
'Suicide in the Trenches', 163
'Their Frailty', 72
'They', 69
'To Any Dead Officer', 101, 106, 115, 163
'To Victory', 1–2, 6, 8, 11, 68
'To the Warmongers', 65
'The Tombstone-Maker', 70, 81
'Trade Boycott', 176
'Two Hundred Years After', 69, 77
Sassoon, Theresa, née Thornycroft (SS's mother), 3, 6–7, 16, 31, 35, 50, 54, 73–4, 78, 80, 86, 88, 101, 105, 118
Scott, C.P, 149
Seward, Dorothy, 148
Shaw, George Bernard, 172
Sheikh Ibn Saud, 159
Shulbrede Priory, 158
Simon, Sir John, 107, 129
Snowden, Ethel, 180, 184, 187–8
Snowden, Philip, 41, 52, 99, 138, 144, 166, 176–189
Society of Friends, 109
Sorley, Charles, 43–4
*Southampton Echo*, 149
Southeby, Lionel, 16
*Spectator, The*, 37–8, 162
Spender, J. A, 111, 112
Stockwell, Colonel C. I, 14, 16–17, 19–20, 110
Strachey, Lytton, 2, 28, 32, 93, 111
Straker, William, 161
Swanwick, Helena, 127, 141, 174
Sykes-Picot agreement, 98
Syme, ex-Inspector, 87

Thomas, David, 12–13
Thomas, Edward, 56–7
Thompson, Basil, 141
Thornycroft, Hamo (SS's uncle), 25, 30, 31, 34, 38, 54, 62–3, 71, 78, 87, 112, 123, 133, 147, 150
*Times, The*, 1–3, 42, 49, 140, 146–7, 162, 166
*Times Literary Supplement*, 80–1, 103
Trevelyan, Charles, 75, 131, 138, 161
*The Tribunal*, 160
Troup, Sir Edward, 65

Union of Democratic Control, 41, 82, 131, 161, 166

Vorticists, The, 95

Wardle, George, 40
Waugh, Alec, 154
Wedgwood, Commander Josiah, 132
Wells, H.G, 44, 71, 111, 112, 124
Wemyss, Admiral, 170–171
*Westminster Gazette*, 11
Whitman, Walter (Walt), 182
Wickham, Sergeant, 163
Wilde, Oscar, 11–12, 113
Wilhelm II, Kaiser, 43, 70, 134–5, 168, 175
Willis, Irene Cooper, 127, 182, 187
Wilson, Philip, 148
Wilson, Woodrow, 39, 40, 90, 168
Women's International League, 127, 174, 180, 187
Woolf, Virginia, 45, 80, 81
*Workers' Dreadnought*, 139